KB054836

주한미군지위협정(SOFA)

서명 및 발효 2

주한미군지위협정(SOFA)

서명 및 발효 2

| 머리말

미국은 오래전부터 우리나라 외교에 있어서 가장 긴밀하고 실질적인 우호·협력관계를 맺어 온 나라다. 6·25전쟁 정전 협정이 체결된 후 북한의 재침을 막기 위한 대책으로서 1953년 11월 한미 상호방위조약이 체결되었다. 이는 미군이 한국에 주둔하는 법적 근거였고, 그렇게 주둔하게 된 미군의 시설, 구역, 사업, 용역, 출입국, 통관과 관세, 재판권 등 포괄적인 법적 지위를 규정하는 것이 바로 주한미군지위협정(SOFA)이다. 그러나 이와 관련한 협상은 계속된 난항을 겪으며 한미 상호방위조약이 체결로부터 10년이 훌쩍 넘은 1967년이 돼서야 정식 발효에 이를 수 있었다. 그럼에도 당시 미군 범죄에 대한 한국의 재판권은 심한 제약을 받았으며, 1980년대 후반 민주화 운동과 함께 미군 범죄 문제가 사회적 이슈로 떠오르자 협정을 개정해야 한다는 목소리가 커지게 되었다. 이에 1991년 2월 주한미군지위협정 1차 개정이 진행되었고, 이후에도 여러 사건이 발생하며 2001년 4월 2차 개정이 진행되어 현재에 이르고 있다.

본 총서는 외교부에서 작성하여 최근 공개한 주한미군지위협정(SOFA) 관련 자료를 담고 있다. 1953년 한미 상호방위조약 체결 이후부터 1967년 발효가 이뤄지기까지의 자료와 더불어, 이후 한미 합동위원회를 비롯해 민·형사재판권, 시설, 노무, 교통 등 각 분과위원회의 회의록과 운영 자료, 한국인 고용인 문제와 관련한 자료, 기타 관련 분쟁 자료 등을 포함해 총 42권으로 구성되었다. 전체 분량은 약 2만 2천여 쪽에 이른다.

2024년 3월

한국학술정보(주)

| 일러두기

· 본 총서에 실린 자료는 2022년 4월과 2023년 4월에 각각 공개한 외교문서 4,827권, 76만 여 쪽 가운데 일부를 발췌한 것이다.

· 각 권의 제목과 순서는 공개된 원본을 최대한 반영하였으나, 주제에 따라 일부는 적절히 변경하였다.

· 원본 자료는 A4 판형에 맞게 축소하거나 원본 비율을 유지한 채 A4 페이지 안에 삽입하였다. 또한 현재 시점에선 공개되지 않아 '공란'이란 표기만 있는 페이지 역시 그대로 실었다.

· 외교부가 공개한 문서 각 권의 첫 페이지에는 '정리 보존 문서 목록'이란 이름으로 기록물 종류, 일자, 명칭, 간단한 내용 등의 정보가 수록되어 있으며, 이를 기준으로 0001번부터 번호가 매겨져 있다. 이는 삭제하지 않고 총서에 그대로 수록하였다.

· 보고서 내용에 관한 더 자세한 정보가 필요하다면, 외교부가 온라인상에 제공하는 『대한민국 외교사료요약집』 1991년과 1992년 자료를 참조할 수 있다.

| 차례

기록물종류	문서-일반공문서철	등록번호	903 9576	등록일자	2006-07-27
분류번호	741.12	국가코드	US	주제	
문서철명	한.미국 간의 상호방위조약 제4조에 의한 시설과 구역 및 한국에서의 미국군대의 지위에 관한 협정 (SOFA) 전59권. 1966.7.9 서울에서 서명 : 1967.2.9 발효 (조약 232호) *원본				
생산과	미주과/조약과	생산년도	1952 - 1967	보존기간	영구
담당과(그룹)	조약	조약		서가번호	--
참조분류					
권차명	V.5 체결 교섭, 1959				

내용목차	
	★ 일지 :
	1953.8.7 이승만 대통령-Dulles 미국 국무장관 공동성명
	― 상호방위조약 발효 후 군대지위협정 교섭 약속
	1954.12.2 정부, 주한 UN군의 관세업무협정 체결 제의
	1955.1월, 5월 미국, 제의 거절
	1955.4.28 정부, 군대지위협정 제의 (한국측 초안 제시)
	1957.9.10 Hurter 미국 국무차관 방한 시 각서 수교 (한국측 제의 수락 요구)
	1957.11.13, 26 정부, 개별 협정의 단계적 체결 제의
	1958.9.18 Dawling 주한미국대사, 형사재판관할권 협정 제외 조건으로 행정협정 체결 의사 전달
	1960.3.10 정부, 토지, 시설협정의 우선적 체결 강력 요구
	1961.4.10 장면 국무총리-McConaughy 주한미국대사 공동성명으로 교섭 개시 합의
	1961.4.15, 4.25 제1, 2차 한.미국 교섭회의 (서울)
	1962.3.12 정부, 교섭 재개 촉구 공한 송부
	1962.5.14 Burger 주한미국대사, 최규하 장관 면담 시 형사재판관할권 문제 제기 않는 조건으로 교섭 재개 통고
	1962.9.6 한.미국 간 공동성명 발표 (9월 중 교섭 재개 합의)
	1962.9.20~ 제1-81차 실무 교섭회의 (서울)
	1965.6.7
	1966.7.8 제82차 실무 교섭회의 (서울)
	1966.7.9 서명
	1967.2.9 발효 (조약 232호)

마/이/크/로/필/름/사/항

촬영연도	*롤 번호	화일 번호	후레임 번호	보관함 번호
2006-11-21	I-06-0066	13	1-300	

0001

한·미국 간의 상호방위조약 제4조에 의한 시설과 구역 및 한국에서의 미국군대의 지위에 관한 협정(SOFA) 전59권. 1966.7.9 서울에서 서명 : 1967.2.9 발효(조약 232호) (V.5 체결 교섭, 1959)

7

조약 과장 귀하

미균이 사용중인 토지, 건물 및 시설 협정에 관한
연구 자료에 대한 당과 의견.

1. 종래 한미간 재산 관계 제 협정 (한미간 재산 및 재정에
   관한 최초 협정, 군사 원조에 관한 협정, 방위 동맹조약,
   "마이야" 협정 등) 과 본 협정과의 관계는 어떤 것이며,
   종래의 그런 협정과 본 협정간에 서로 모순된 점은 없는가
   를 밝혀 줄것이 요망됨.

2. 종래 미균이 사용하여온 재산들에 관한 보상 청구 가능성의
   여부를 규명할것이 역시 요망됨.

3. 보상 문제가 제기 되었을때 이를 상대방과의 합의 기관에
   의하여 결정할것이되 그 재산 사용에 있어 사용 목적 수행
   기능상의 손해 또는 기능과는 관계없는 손해의 경우들을
   구별하여 그 범위를 미리 명확히하고 보상액 결정에 있어서는
   한미간 부담액의 율을 규정짓고 원측적으로 한미간 쌍방 공동
   부담으로 합의 합리적인 것으로 사료됨. 일방적으로 미균측에만
   어떤 보상이면지 전적으로 부담시킴은 무리가 있는 것으로
   생각되고 교섭에 있어 미측이 난점을 보일것으로 예상됨.

4. 미균에 제공하는 재산에 있어 재산 종류에 따라서는 유상 내지는
   임대차를 원측으로 하는 규정도 설정함이 가하다고 사료됨.

5. 이러한 재산권 행사에 있어 제 3자와의 분쟁 내지 청구 문제
   해결에 관한 규정도 설정함이 가하다고 사료됨.

0002

6. 전쟁 발발시 당연히 변경될 이런 재산 사용권 내용도 미리 규정 지음이 상호간에 유의한 일이락고 사료됨.

7. 가능한 과세 규정도 검토함이 가하다고 사료됨

8. 이런 미군 사용중의 군사 시설 기지 등에 대한 한국 정부의 보안상의 의무 내지는 보안상 한미 양국이 협조를 하는데에 있어서의 의무의 한계등도 명시적으로 규정함으로서 우리 주권 행사에 침범이 없도록 함이 적당하다고 사료됨.

한·미국 간의 상호방위조약 제4조에 의한 시설과 구역 및 한국에서의 미국군대의 지위에 관한 협정(SOFA)
전59권. 1966.7.9 서울에서 서명 : 1967.2.9 발효(조약 232호) (V.5 체결 교섭, 1959)

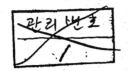

急友로 飜文을 再檢討

주한 미국군이 사용중의 토지, 건물 및
시설에 관한 한미간의 협정안의 기초자료

외　무　부

편　집

0004

주한 미국군이 사용중인 토지, ~~구역~~ 및
시설에 관한 한미간의 협정안의 기초자료

목   차

미국주둔군의

1. ~~미국군주둔~~ 지위에 관한 한미간의 협정 체결을
   위한 고섭 경위.

2. 토지, ~~구역~~ 및 시설에 관한 협정 체결의 필요성과
   법적 ~~해석~~ (대한민국 토지수용령이 요구하는 비상사태의
   검토 및 협정 체결의 긴요성)

3. 협정안의 기초에 있어서 고력하여야 할 문제 및 관계
   국제~~협정과 법례~~ 협정과의 비교.

4. 관계부처의 조사자료.

5. 1955년에 우리정부가 미국측에 정식으로 제안한
   주둔군의 지위에 관한 협정안 ~~반혀~~중 관계조항의 발취.

6. ~~외국주둔군~~ 관계 조항의 발취.
   국제협정에 있어서의

   1. Relevant Articles Excerpted from the Draft Administrative Agreement to the Facilities and Areas to be used by the ~~the~~ U.S. forces in Korea
   2. Administrative Agreement between U.S. and Japan.
   3. Military Bases Agreement between US and the Philippine
   4. Dhahran Air Base Agt. between United Kingdom and U.S.
   5. US. Belgium

한·미국 간의 상호방위조약 제4조에 의한 시설과 구역 및 한국에서의 미국군대의 지위에 관한 협정(SOFA)
전59권. 1966.7.9 서울에서 서명 : 1967.2.9 발효(조약 232호) (V.5 체결 교섭, 1959)

1. 주한 미국군의 지위에 관한 한미간의 협정 교섭 경위

1950년 6월 25일, 공산괴뢰의 남침이 발발하자 국제 연합 안전보장이사회는 동년 6월 25일, 6월 27일 및 7월 7일자 결의에 의거하여 통합사령부하에 국제연합군을 한국에 주둔하여 현재에 이르고 있으나, 1953년 7월 27일자로 체결된 휴전협정에 의거하여, 실제 전투는 종결되고 군사작전에 수반되는 긴박상태가 완화되었으므로 국제연합군의 한국내 배치에 수반되는 제 문제에 관하여 우리나라 국민과 국제연합군 인원간의 오해를 최소한으로 감소하고 반대로 상호간의 협조를 최고도로 증진시키는 방법중의 하나로서 우리나라 정부와 통합사령부로서 행동하는 미합중국간에 주한 미국군의 지위에 관한 협정을 체결할 필요를 한미양정부가 공히 인정하고 다음과 같은 교섭을 해왔다.

1) 1953년 8월 7일자로 이 대통령과 "덜레스" 미국무장관은 공동성명을 통하여 " ... 우리 양국정부는 한미 상호방위조약이 발효하게된 이후 미국이 한국에 주둔하고 있게될 군대의 지위 및 우리들의 공동사업을 수행하는데 필요한 한국측 시설과 인원의 사용에 관한 협약을 즉시 상의하고자한다 ..."고 천명하여 주둔군의 법적 지위를 규제하는 협정이 곧 체결될 것을 선언하였다.

2) 1954년 12월 2일에 조정한 외무부장관 서리는 주한 미국대사 앞으로의 각서에서 주둔군의 지위에 관한 협정의 체결전의 잠정적 조치로서 "한국 세관업무에 관한 한미간의 협정"을 체결할 것을 제의하였다. (1955년 1월 27일자로 주한 미국대사는 이에 대한 회한을 보내면서 이 문제를 신중 검토하겠다고 말하였을 뿐 이후 하등 구체적인 진전이 없었다)

— 1 —

0006

3) 1956년 4월 28일 변장관용 주한 미국대리대사 앞으로의 구서에서 주한 미국군의 지위를 전반적으로 규제하는 협정의 체결을 제의하고 우리나라 정부측에서 그간 예의 검토한 협정안을 송부하는 동시에 이에 대한 미국측의 동의를 촉구하였다. (당시의 우리정부측 초안 별첨 5).

4) 우리 정부의 전기 제의에 대하여 미국측은 본국 정부에서 검토중이라는 점을 회보하였을 뿐 하등 반응이 없었다.

5) 1957년 1월 5일자로 조정한 외무부장관은 주한 미국대사 앞으로의 구서에서 교섭개시를 촉구하는 동시에 본 협정을 체결하는 데에 미국의 국제연합 가맹국정부와의 사전교섭에 과도한 시간소비가 된다면 우리정부는 조속한 협정 체결을 위하여 대한민국을 일방으로 하고 미국을 타방으로하는 단독 협정의 체결에 응할 용의가 있다는 것을 통고하였다. (본 구서에 대하여 미국 대사는 본국정부 의 훈령을 대기중이라는 것을 밝혔고, 동 년 6월 29일에 외무 부장관은 미국대사에게 교섭개시를 독촉하였음).

6) 미국정부의 태도가 전기한 바와 같이 미온적임에 정부는 때마침 우리나라를 방문한 허어터 미국무차관에게 "우리정부의 수차의 체의에도 불구하고 미국측은 아직 특별한 이유를 제시하지도 않으면서 교섭개시를 지연시키고 있는 점을 강조하고, 미군사령관 렘니쩌저장군의 1955년 7월 26일자 공한에서 지적한 점 즉, 한미통상항해조약 및 한미투자보장협정이 체결된 후에 교섭을 개시하자는 점, 및 시간 및 사전교섭상의 난점을 피하기위하여 미국만을 당사자로 하는 한미간의 협정 형식으로 하자는 점에 대하여서는 한미통상항해조약은 체결되었고 또한 투자보장협정은 곧 될 것이라는 점과, 미국과의 단독협정 형식을 찬성한다는 점을 제시하고 현안 협정의 조속한 교섭개시를

— 2 —

0007

촉구하였다.(1957년 9월 10일자.

　　　7) 1957년 10월 10일 주한미국대사는 조정환 외무부
장관과의 회담에서 "공위물 청산협정"과 같은 형식으로 주둔군의
지위에 관한 전면적 협정을 지양하고 개별적으로 각 문제에 관하여
협정을 체결하는 것이 좋다는 의견을 개진하였음에 1957년 11월
26일에 조정환 외무부장관은 전기 미국대사의 제의를 환영한다는
전제하에 "주한 미국군의 지위에 관한 협정을 구매, 과세, 관세에
관한 협정, 청구권 청산 협정, 주둔군이 사용하는 시설 및 지역에
관한 협정, 출입국에 관한 협정 , 형사재판관할권에 관한 협정으로
분리하여 체결할 것과 이에 대한 교섭개시를 제의하였다.

　　　8) 전면적협정의 지양과 개별적 협정의 체결을 제의한
우리정부의 전기 각서에 대한 미국측의 태도는 다시 지극히 미온적인
반응으로 환원하였다.

　　　9) 1958년 9월 18일 미국대사는 조정환 외무부장관을
방문하고 미국측의 태도를 구두로 다음과 같이 개진하였다.

　　　　(1) 전투상태는 중지되었으나 아직 완전한 평화상태는
　　　　　　되지않았다는 점을 강조하고 특별히 형사재판권에
　　　　　　관한 대전협정 (1950년 7월 12일 서명)에 수정을 ~~가하지~~
　　　　　　가하지 않는다는 보장을 한국측이 한다면 기타
　　　　　　문제에 관한 개별 협정에는 즉시 응할 용의가있다.

　　　10)1959년 3월 25일, 다우링 미국대사는 조정환 외무부
장관을 방문하고 미국내의 현안 협정 체결에 대한 반응은 지극히
약할 뿐더러, 전면적 협정을 체결하여도 미국 상원의 비준동의를
받기는 거의 불가능하다는 점을 강조하고 "주한 미국의 잉여 물자
처리에 관한 협정"에 있어서와 같이 개별적 협정으로 추진하되

- 3 -

미국 국방성은 아직 이 문제에 관하여 미온적이므로 주한 미군 사령관 덱커장군을 통하여 미국 국방성에 호의적 권고를 하도록 촉구하여, 개별협정으로라도 한 건식 우선 시급한 것부터 처리하고, 이렇게 함으로써 아직 규제되지못한 주둔군의 지위를 법적으로 해결하는 것이 좋을 듯하다는 것을 개진하였고, 우리 정부도 아직 형사재판권에 관한 하등의 언질을 줌이 없이 처리 할 수 있는 것부터 해결하는 것이 좋을 것으로 해석하고 있음.

제기하였다. 이에 우리정부도 전면협정을 지양하고서라도 한가지씩 문제를 좁혀서 결국 주둔군의 법적 지위를 규제하고저 우선 주둔군이 사용중인 토지, 시설이 관한 문제를 법적으로 해결하려 이 협정의 체결을 추비키로 하는 것이다.

— 4 —

0009

한·미국 간의 상호방위조약 제4조에 의한 시설과 구역 및 한국에서의 미국군대의 지위에 관한 협정(SOFA)
전59권. 1966.7.9 서울에서 서명 : 1967.2.9 발효(조약 232호) (V.5 체결 교섭, 1959)   15

2. 토지 및 시설에 관한 협정체결의 필요성과 법적해석

　　(1) 징발에 관한 특별조치령이 말하는 "비상 사태"
　　는 지금도 계속되고 있다고 보는가 ?

　　먼저 결론부터 말하자면 이 "비상사태"는 지금도
계속되고 있다고 보아야 할것이다. 왜냐하면 한국은 현재
전시하에 있으며 휴전하에 있다는 것은 "비상 사태"하에 있
다는 것을 의미하기 때문이다.

　　그러면, 한국이 현재 전시하에 있다는 이유는 무엇인가.
그 이론적 근거로서는 한국 휴전의 성격을 들어야 할것인데
첫째로 : 국제법상, 휴전은 실전(hostility)의 일시적
중단이며 이 휴전기간은 전시로 규정하는 것이 학자들간의
통설이다.　　또한 휴전기간중 국제법상의 제 관계 및 국내법
상의 제 관계는 전시로 규정되며 그 기간은 아무리 길다
하드라도 그 동안의 법적 관계는 전시법의 적용을 받는 것
이다(Oppenheim, International Law, Vol. II, 8th Ed., p.547)
둘째로 : 국제관행은 거의 예외없이 휴전기간을 전시로 규정
하고 있다.　　즉 1944년 11월 3일 "불란서"의 1
재판소(Court of Cassation)은 "휴전이란 적대행위를 일시적
으로 정지시켰을 뿐 그 자체 전쟁상태를 종결시킨 것이
아니다"고 판시(判示)한 후 피고를 사형에 처한 적이
있었고(이 한기, "한국휴전의 제 문제" 국제법학회 론고
제 3호, (1959), 41면) 또한 "이스라엘"과 "에짚
트"간의 휴전협정이 체결된 4년후인 오늘에 있어서도 양국간
에 있어서는 전쟁상태가 종결되지 않았음이 명백하다.(이 한기
전기 론고 제 48면 참조)
셋째로 : 우리나라의 관례는 현 휴전기간을 전시라고 판시
하였다.　　즉, 단기 4289년 1월 11일, "강 문봉
중장 사건"의 재판 관할군을 제정함에 있어서 고등군법회의
는 현 휴전기간을 전시라고 규정하고 그 재판관할권이 군법
회의에 있음을 밝혔다.

5

참고 : 단기 4290년 7월 21일 국방부는 "군
징발조치에 대한 법령조회의 건"(국방 관 재
4260호 단기 4290년 7월 21일자)에 관
하여 이를 법무부에 문의하였던바 법무부의 견해는
"현재 한국은 전시태세로부터 이탈치 못하였으므로
아직 비상사태가 법적으로 계속되고 있어 전기 조치령
은 지금도 그 효력이 있다고 하였다. (법무 제
302호 단기 4291년 1월 23일자, 대 국방
부 장관 공문)

넷째로 : 한국 휴전은 그 체결당사국인 공산주의자가 이를
그들의 재침략을 위한 준비 기간으로 알고 있는 까닭에
실지에 있어서도 이를 전시라고 봄이 타당하다.

즉 북한 괴뢰를 조종하는 "쏘련"은 조약을 정치적
기회주의와 결부시켜

"조약에는 강국이 약국에게 무력 또는 경제압박을
통하여 강제한 것과 당사자 쌍방을 위하여 체결된
것과의 2개가 있다. 전자는 이것을 강제한 강국
의 실력이 존속하는 기간동안만 이행되며 후자는 쌍방
의 이익이 존재하는 동안만 이행된다" (이 한기
전기 론고 제 79면)

라고 규정하고 있고 또한 의 증명으로서 그들은 한국 휴전
협정에 위반한 사례가 많았으므로 이 휴전협정의 기간은
사실상 전시인 것이다. 그들은 이 휴전협정이 그들의
이익과 배치할 때에는 언제나 이 협정을 폐기할 것이니
이는 평화를 가저오기 위한 휴전이 아니었고 단지 전쟁을
위한 휴전이다.

0011

한·미국 간의 상호방위조약 제4조에 의한 시설과 구역 및 한국에서의 미국군대의 지위에 관한 협정(SOFA)
전59권. 1966.7.9 서울에서 서명 : 1967.2.9 발효(조약 232호) (V.5 체결 교섭, 1959)   17

(2) ||유엔|| 군이 사용하고있는 토지 건물에 대한 고찰

아국은 건국 초기에 있어서 쏘련이 조종하는 북한괴뢰의 무력
침공을 받어 일찍이 볼수없는 국난에 봉착하게 된 까닭에
대통령은 ||징발에 관한 특별조치령||을 발포하게 되었고 또한
이력하여 징발된 토지 및 건물등은 그 첨락을 막기위하여 사용
되게 되었다. 따라서 이렇게 징발된 토지 및 건물등은 ||유엔||
군에도 제공할것을 약속하기에 이르렀다. (대한민국과 통일사령
부간의 경제조정에 관한 협정, 제3조 제13항 참조)
그러나, 이러한 근거에서 제공된 ||유엔||군 사용의 과 토지 및
건물중에는 그것이 무단히 사용되고 있는것이 허다할뿐만 아니
라 그들이 사용중인 이러한 재산에 대하여는 단지 추상적인 근본
원칙이 있을뿐 상세한 규정이 결여되어있고 또한 아래와 같은
여러 이유를 고려할때 이 협정의 체결은 시급한 국가적 요청
이 알임수없다.

가. 한국휴전의 장기성 :

한국휴전은 평화를 전제로한 휴전이 아니고, 또한 우려나라에는
북진통일없어 평화가 있을수없는 까닭에 외세(쏘련의 지배)가
잔류하는 한 평화가 올수없으나, 그들은 좀처럼 한국에서 떠날
따는 좀조가 없는 까닭에, 한국휴전은 장기화 될것이 예상된다.
또한 우려나라는 미국과 체결한 || 상호방위조약||에서, ||각당
사국은 각자의 행정관력하에 ... 합법적으로 드러갔다고
인정되는 영호에 있어서|| 무력공격을 받어야 비로서 ||각자의
헌법상의 수속에 따라서|| 상호 무력원조를 한다 (제3조)고 하고,
또한 ||국제연합에 배치되는 ... .무력행세를 삼가할것을
약속한다 (제1조)라고하여 공산 첨략군에 선수를 부여한 것이
니, 사실상 그들이 선공할때까지 상당한 기간이 쇼오될
것이다. 따라서, 한국과 유엔 군은 유엔 군의 사용하고
있는 토지 및 건물에 관한 조약을 체결하여야 한다.

7

0012

나. ||유엔| 군이 사용중인 토지에 관한 협정의 결여는 쌍방

우호관계에 해가 된다.

||유엔군||의 토지 및 건물의 무계약 사용은 쌍방의 보상에 관한

의견 차이로 인하여, 앞으로 분쟁에 이를 가능성이 현저하며,

이는 지금 해결하지 않으면 앞으로 쌍방 우호증진에 큰 해가

될 우려가 있다.

다. ||대한민국과 통일사령부간의 경제조정에 관한 협정|| (일명

||마이야||협정)은 실지 한국의 ||건전한 경제수립||에 위협이 되고있다.

한국으로 부터 ||유엔||군이 대여받고 있는 모든 토지 및 건물은

||마이야||협정 제 3조 제 13항에 의한 것이나, ||유엔||군측은

왕왕 이들 토지 및 건물시설을 무료 제공할것을 주장하고 있는

바 (1956년 6월 18일 ||유엔||군사령부 참모장 하모니장군 어

김현철 재무부장관에게 보내온 공한, 1957년 4월 16일자

극동군 사령관 공한) 전계 무료제공에 관한 규정은 현존치않을

뿐이며, 일제의 착취 및 6. 25동란의 황폐로부터 어머기는

한국은 이를 부담할 능력이 없다. 뿐만 아니라, 앞으로도

||유엔||군이 이것의 무료제공을 고집함으로서 이에 관한 세칙

규정의 설정을 거부한다면, 이는 ||마이야||협정 전문이 지향하는

정신 즉 ||대한민국의 주권을 침략함이 없이...한국민의 고난을

구제하며, 대한민국의 건전한 경제를 수립 유지하기 위하여..

.||에도 배치되는 것이다. 따라서 빈약한 한국경제의 육성을 위

위하여 그들은 이 협약을 체결하여야 한다.

8

주한 미군인 사용하는 토지, 건물 및 시설에
관한 한미간의 협정 초안에 있어서 고려하여야 할
제 사항 및 국제관계

　　　　미국군의 주둔에 관련하여 발생하는 제반문제를 해결하
기 위한 전면적인 한미 협정을 체결하는 것이 소망됨은
물론이나 현 단계로서는 미국측이 주로 형사재판관할권문제로
인하여 이를 거부하는 태도를 위하고 있기때문에 우선 시급한
문제인 주둔군이 사용하는 토지, 건물 및 시설의 사용에 수
수반되는 행정사항을 해결하기 위하여 건명협정을 체결하고자
한다.　　　본 건 협정의 초안을 작성함에 있어서 정부는
미일행정협정, 바하마에 관한 미영협정, 다히란 비행기지에
관한 미 사우디아라비아 협정, 미백 상호원조조약, 미독간의
손실보상에 관한 각서, 주둔군의 지위에 관한 미독협정 및
쎈트 루치아 기지에 관한 미영협정등을 참고로 하되 미비
군사기지 협정 및 미일 행정협정의 예를 따르는 것을 기본
으로 한다.

　　　　이하에 있어서 기술의 편의를 위하여 위에서 말한
제 협정을 순서대로, 미일, 미비, 북 대서양, 바하마,
다히란, 미백, 미독, 미영이라고 부르기로 한다.

1. 본 협정에 포함된 사항

　　　　본 협정은 주둔군의 지위에 관한 사항중 특히
한국의 토지, 건물 및 시설을 사용하는데 관련하여 발생
하는 제문제의 해결에 필요한 사항 즉 적용범위, 대여한게
대여조건을 규정한다.

　　（1）적용범위 ... 한국은 미국군 대에게 계속하여
　　　　　　건물, 토지 및 시설의 사용을 허가하고 협정
　　　　　　성립시까지 사용중이던 것은 원칙적으로 계속 사용
　　　　　　케하나 양당사자중의 일방당사자의 요청이 있으면
　　　　　　이의 반환 또는 추가적 제공에 관하여 합의한다0014

9

사용을 허가하는 개체와 아울러 토지, 건물 및
그 것을 사용함에 있어서 불가결한 정착물 또는
그 것과 같이 사용되는 제반 설비 및 독립하여
존재하는 시설로 하고(미일 제 2조) 이러한 개체
는 우리나라 토지수용령 제 5조에 열거된 것에
한한다. (이것은 미일 부속양해사항)

수용자는 한국정부로 함은 당연한 것이나 미비
제 22조, 다화란 제 4조, 미독 제 1조는
이것을 명시하고 있다.

한국 내에서 다시 적대행위가 발생할 경우에는 양
당사자는 본 협정의 적용에 관하여 필요하다고
사료되는 변경에 관한 합의에 도달하기 위하여
즉시로 협의한다. (미일 제 24조, 북대서양
제 15조)

(2) 적용한계 ... 미국군은 시설 및 토지에서
설정, 사용, 운영 또는 방위에 필요 또는 적절
한 권리 및 권능을 가진다. (미비 제 3조,
미일 제 3조) 그러나 이러한 권리, 권력,
및 권능의 행사에 관하여는 일방 당사자의 요구에
따라서 그 적법 여부를 협의한다. 이것은
협정이 체결된 후에 우리정부의 권리주장에 법적
근거를 주는데 유리할 것이다.

전기 적용한계를 책정함에 있어서는 이를 주로
합동위원회의 협의사항으로 하고 있는것이 국제관례
인바(미일, 독일) 합동위원회의 구성 및 임무가
문제된다. 구성에 있어서는 미일협정에 의하면
양국정부가 인명하는 1명씩의 대표로 구성하게 되어
있고 미독 협정에서는 구성문제는 명시 되어 있지
않다.

10

0015

합동위원회의 임무에 관하여서는 1) 이들 토지
✓ 건물 및 시설에 관한 시설의 변경, 이전, 반환
에 관한 협의 및 경정(미일 제 2 조, 미비
제 2 2 조)과

✓ 2) 본 협정의 목적상 불필요하게 사용되고 있는
지의 여부의 계속적인 검토 및 검토의 결과 불필
요하게 사용되고 있는 토지, 건물 및 시설의
반환문제 (미일 제 2 조 제 3 항, 다하란 제
4 조)

✓ 3) 사격장 및 연습장등의 시설과 토지가 미국
군에 의하여 사용되지 않을 경우에는 한국국민이
이를 임시사용하도록 허가받는 교섭(미일제 4 조
가, 나항) 및 공동사용의 편의제공에 관한 협의
(미비 제 2 조 제 1 항)

✓ 4) 손실보상금 및 분쟁해결에 대한 거중조정등을
임무로하고 있다. (미일 제 2 6 조 제 1 항 및
제 3 항) 집행기관은 국내법령에 의하여 설치
되고 국내법령에 의하여 임무를 수행한다. (미비
제 2 2 조, 미일에 있어서는 일본이 조달청을
설치하고 있다)

(3) 적용조건 ... 건물, 토지 및 시설의 사용료
문제는 원칙적으로 임대료와 손실보상의 두 가지로
분류하여 사용 허가신청을 조달청(우리나라의 국방부
관제과)에 제출하고 합동위원회는 필요성을
검토한 후, 필요하다고 인정하면 정부에 건의
한다. 국제적 통례에 의하면 공유재산에 대하
여서는 임대료 협의 의무를 부과하지 않으며 사유
재산에 대하여는 임대료를 지불하는 나라와 지불
하지 않는 나라로 구분되고 있다.

11

0016

있어서는 원상회복 또는 손실보상이 문제되나 일반적인 국제관례에 의하면 국유재산에 대하여는 이러한 의무를 명시한 나라가 없고(단 이하란 제16조는 단지 사용 가능한 상태로의 회복을 의무로 하고 있다), 사유재산에 대하여서는 원상회복 또는 손실보상의 책임을 규정한 나라가 독일뿐이다. (미독 제1조 ㄱ, ㄴ) 그러나 우리나라의 본 협정의 체결이유 중의 하나가 손실보상인 이상 우리는 이에 대하여 미국측의 호의적인 고려를 요구할 근거가 있다. 반환의 경우에는 그 토지 및 건물, 시설에 가해진 개량 또는 거기에 잔류된 건물, 기타 공작물에 대하여는 보상의 의무가 없는 것으로 되어 있다.(미일 제4조, 미버 제22조)

분쟁의 해결에 관하여서는 이 협정의 실시에 관한 포괄적인 협의기관인 합동위원회 제도를 택한 일본의 예를 보면 합동위원회가 분쟁해결에 관한 일차적인 조치를 취하고 소위원회가 문제를 해결하지 못하는 경우에는 적당한 경로를 통하여 그 문제를 각자의 정부의 고려에 부하게 하고 있다.(미일 제26조) 이에 반하여 미비협정에서는 재정분쟁의 최종적 해결을 비율빈의 법원에 위촉하기로 규정하고 있다.(미비 제22조 제1항) 또한 이들 분쟁을 중재재판에 부탁하기로 규정한 것도 있다(북대서양 제8조 제2항)

12

0017

별첩 : 국제연합군의 사용중인 징발재산목록 및 보상금관계 자료

　　出 처 : 국방부 관재과

7. 국제연합군이 사용중인 징발재산과 보상금 (별표 ④)

　　　토지　111,686,328평　　81,218,068,062환

　　　건물　　63,918평　　　6,277,994,500환

　　　물자　　91,646점　　　　339,639,370환

　　　계　　　　　　　　　87,835,701,932환
　　　　　　　　　　　　(615,713,379弗)

단, 위의 수자와 금액은 개략적인 수자임. 실지조사후 정확한 수자를 산출코자함.

징발 해제수량
　　토지　62,049,387평
　　건물　201,921평 (1530동)
　　계　　62,251,308평

8. 국제연합국이 한국재산을 사용할수있는 법적근거

대한민국과 통일사령부간의 경제조합에관한 협정(4285년 5월 24일 한국정부 대표 백두진, 미국정부대표 마이야가 서명함. 이를 마이야협정 이락 속층함.) 제3조 13항에 의거 한국정부는 징발에관한 특별조치령의 규정한바에의하여 국제연합군에게 징발제공 하여왔음.

마이야협정 제3조 13항

한국국민은 제약한 통일사령부의 개인 또는 기관에대하여 전기 국제연합의 제경의에 의하여 부여되어있거나 또는 차후 쌍방 또는 일방의 관계기구에의하여 공식 또는 비공식으로 협약될 특권, 면제, 편의을 부여한다.

9. 국제연합군에 징발제공한 재산의 보상대책

　가. 국제연합군에게 징발제공된 경위

6.25동란후 국제연합군이 작전상 필요로하는 부동산은 한국 법명 징발에관한 특별조치령을 적용하여 한국 육군 참모총장과 국제 연합군 사령관간의 작전임무수행상 협의에의하여 육군 참모총장이 징발제공 하여왔으며 4287년 7월 15일자로 국제연합군 사용 재산에관한 업무를 육군으로부터 국방부에 의괄되었음.

0018

적 용 범 위

1. 협정의 객체

(가) 국제협정에 규정된 객체

(1) 미일 협정 제2조는 " .... 목적의 수행에 필요한 시설 및 구역의 사용 ... ", "시설 및 구역은 당해 시설 및 구역의 운영에 필요한 현존의 설비, 비품 및 정착물을 포함한다" 라고 규정함으로써,

(the use of facilities and areas necessary to carry out the purposes....", "facilities and areas" include existing furnishings, equipments and fixtures necessary to the operation of such facilities and areas)

적용 한계를 일일히 열거하지 않고 포괄적으로 규정하였음.

(2) 주일 유엔군 지위에 관한 미일협정 제5조1항은

"U.N. force may use such facilities in Japan, inclusive of existing furnishings, equipment and fixtures necessay for the operation of such facilities"

라고 규정함으로서 역시 포괄적으로만 규정하였음.

(3) 이와는 달리 미비 협정은 객체를 일일히 협정 부속문에 열거하였음.

(4) 미영 협정, 미 사우디 아라비아 협정은 미국의 특정기지에 관한 것이므로 객체도 이에 따라서 특정목적으로서 한정되어 있음.

(나) 우리나라 행정협정안에 규정된 객체 제3조 1, 가

(1)은 " .... 사명과 목적을 수행함에 필요한 시설과 구역의 사용 ... " 이라고 규정함으로서 미일 협정과 같이 포괄적으로 규정하였음.

(다) 우리나라가 취할 입장

우리나라에 주둔하는 미국군대는 특정한 군사기지를 유지하기 위한 것이 아니고 공산침략을 격퇴하며 한국을 방위하는 것이 목적이므로 본 협정의 객체는 상황에 따라서 변동되는 것임.

13-1

0019

따라서 미비, 교환영? 어 싸우디 아라비아 협정과 같이
그 객체를 특정할 수 없는 것이므로 뭐일 협정 및 기왕에 작성
한 우리나라 행정협정 초안이 규정하는 바와 같이 토지 건물 및
이들을 사용함에 있어서 불가결한 정착물 또는 이들과 같이 사용
되는 제반 설비 및 독립하여 존재하는 시설로 한다는 포괄적인
규정을 채용함이 가함.

2. 객체의 구분

(가) 귀속상의 구분

　　　우리나라가 제공하는 토지, 건물 및 이에 종속하는
시설에는 (1) 국유재산에 속하는 것 (2) 공공단체의 재산에
속하는 것 및 (3) 사유재산에 속하는 것이 있는바, 이를
일일이 구분하여 규정할 필요는 없을 것이나 객체 제공에 따르는
임대료, 사용료 또는 보상금 지불을 규정함에 있어서는 이를
구분하여야 할것임.

(나) 위치상의 구분

　　　본 협정이 대상으로 하는 객체는 후방지구 뿐만 아니라
작전지구인 일선 지방에도 있을 수 있는 것인바 이러한 지구에
있는 객체에 대하여 본 협정을 동일하게 적용한다면 경우에
따라서는 국 작전을 방해할 염려가 있을 뿐만 아니라 미국군대의
주둔목적에 비추어 볼때 어색한 점도 없지 않으므로 이러한 점도
유의하여야 할것임.　　　단, 이러한 문제는 쌍방의 군사 전문가
의 의견을 들은후에 고려할 문제임.

(다) 사용시기로 본 구분

　　　본 협정의 객체에는 과거로부터 계속하여 사용되어온
것과 앞으로 새로이 사용될 것으로 구분됨.

　　　과거부터 사용되어온 객체는 일정한 형식 (예: 합동위원회
의 확인)을 통하여 이를 원칙적으로 계속 사용케하고 그 조건은
본 협정이 정하는 바에 따르게 할 것이며 특수한 경우에 있어
서는 우리나라가 반환을 요구할 수 있는 권리를 유보하여야 할
것이며 새로운 객체의 사용은 전적으로 본 협정이 정하는 바에

13-2

0020

의하여야 할것임.

　　사용 시기로…본 구분을 보상문제와 관련하여 고찰하면
첫째로, 이 협정의 효력이 발생되는 날자 이후로부터 사용하는
토지 또는 건물등에 관하여는 그 보상문제도 이 협정의 규정에
따르도록 할 것이므로 그 구체적 규정은 "적용조건"에서
하여야 할 것임.

둘째로, 이 협정의 성립이전부터 계속하여 사용하고 있는 건물
또는 토지등에 관하여서 보상을 요구할 객체를 어떻게 구분할
것인가에 관하여는 사용시기를 휴전협정의 성립 이전과 이후로
구분하여 고려하는 것이 가하다고 사료됨.

3. 객체 제공자의 입장에서 본 제한점

　　본 협정에 의하여 제공되는 객체중 국가가 소유하는 것을
제외하고는 이를 일단 국가가 수용하여야 하는바 이러한 수용은
법률에 의하여서만 가능함으로 객체의 범위는 관계 법령 즉
(1) 토지수용령 (2) 징발령에 의하여 수용할 수 있는
것에 한정되어야 할것이다.

　　이에 관하여 미일 협정은 그 양해사항에서 이를 명백히
하였다. 뿐만아니라 본 협정 객체의 사용은 사회, 경제 및
문화생활에 대한 영향을 고려하여야 한다"는 규정이 필요할
것이며 만일 이러한 규정이 너무나 우리나라의 입장만을 위주로
한것이므로 적당하지 않다고 생각될 경우에는 최소한 전문에
"양 당사자는 한국에서 공산 침략에 대비하여 가장 효과적인
군사작전을 가능케하는 것이 중요하다고 인정함과 동시에 한국
국민의 사회, 경제 및 문화생활의 발전을 기하는 것도 또한
중요함을 인정한다" 라는 뜻을 규정함이 필요하다고 인정됨.

한·미국 간의 상호방위조약 제4조에 의한 시설과 구역 및 한국에서의 미국군대의 지위에 관한 협정(SOFA)
전59권. 1966.7.9 서울에서 서명 : 1967.2.9 발효(조약 232호) (V.5 체결 교섭, 1959)　　27

군 의 무 관 계

1. 주둔군이 행사할 수 있는 권리

(가) 국제협정에 규정된 권리

(1) 미일 협정 제 3 조는 "... 미국은 시설 및
구역내에 있어써 그들의 성질, 사용, 운영, 방위 또는 그 관리에
필요한 또는 적당한 권리, 권력 및 권능을 가진다. 미국은
또한 전기의 시설 및 구역에 인접하는 토지, 영수 및 공간 또는
전기의 시설 및 구역의 근방에 있어서 그들의 지지, 방위 및
권리를 위하여 전기의 시설 및 구역에의 출입의 편리를 도모하는
데 필요한 권리, 권력 및 권능을 가진다" 라고 규정함으로써

"The United States shall have the rights, power and

authority within the facilities and area which are necessary,

or appropriate for their establishment, use, operation,

defense or control. The United States shall also have

such rights, power and authority over land, territorial

waters and airspace adjacent to, or in the vicinities of

such facilities and areas, as are necessary to provide

access to such facilities and areas for their support,

defense and control."

시설 및 구역내에서의 권리와 이에의 접근에 관한 권리를 부여
하고 있다.

(2) 주일유엔군의 지위에 관한 협정에 관련하여 1953년
1월에 시설사용료에 관한 일체협정이 성립한 것에 의거하여도
미일 협정과 그 방향을 대체로 같이 하고 있으며,

(3) 미비 협정 제 3 조의 규정도 이 점에 있어서는
미일협정과 등일한 권리를 인정하고 있으며,

(4) 기타 미영 협정 미 사우디 아라비아 협정도
예외없이

13-4

이와같은 시설 및 구역내에서 그들의 선정 운영, 방위 또는
관리에 필요한 또는 적절한 권리, 권력, 권능을 가질 뿐만
아니라, 전기 개체에의 접근에 관련되는 제 권리를 부여하고 있다.

(나) 우리나라 행정협정 제 3 조의 2 (가) 은 "......시설 및
구역내에서 설정, 사용, 운영 또는 방위에 필요한 또는 적합한
권리, 권력 및 권능을 가진다. .... 또한 여사한 시설과 구역에
인접한 또는 그 부근의 토지, 영수 및 공간에 대하여 그 보급
지원과 방위를 위하여 여사한 시설과 구역에의 출입의 편의를
보유하는데 필요한 권리, 권력 및 권능을 가진다. ..." 라고 규정
하므로써, 전기 국제협정의 선례를 따르고 있다.

(다) 우리나라가 취할 입장

위에서 본바와 같이 우리나라의 행정협정안 제 3 조의
규정은 각국의 유사협정과 그 범위를 같이 하고 있는바, 시설 및
구역(토지)를 사용할 권리를 허가함에있어서, 그것에의 접근 및
사용의 불가결한 부수조건까지 허여하여야한다는 것은 오히려
이를 당연한 것이라고 까지 하지 않을 수 없을 것이다.

단지, 이에 관한 제한(과잉 사용 또는 무허가 사용에 관한)
은 별도로 합동위원회에서 교참할 근거만 삼어두면 될줄로
해석한다.

2. 권리 행사에 있어서의 제한

(가) 국제협정에 규정된 제한

(1) 미 일 협정 제3 조는 "......전기 권리, 권력, 권능을
허가된 구역 또는 시설 밖 에서 행사 함에 있어서는 , 필요에
따라서, 합동위원회를 통하여 양국 정부간에서 합의하지 않으면
안된대고 규정하고 있고,

" In the exercise outside the facilities and areas of the
right, power and authority granted in this article, there

0023

13 - 5

한·미국 간의 상호방위조약 제4조에 의한 시설과 구역 및 한국에서의 미국군대의 지위에 관한 협정(SOFA)
전59권. 1966.7.9 서울에서 서명 : 1967.2.9 발효(조약 232호) (V.5 체결 교섭, 1959)

should be, as the occasion requires, consultation between
the two Governments through the Joint Committee."

(2) 미 비 협정 제 3 조의 3의 후단에 있어서도 합동
위원회를 통하여라는 구절이없을뿐 전기 규정과 동일한 제한을
부과하고있으며,

(3) 또한 미 일 협정 제3 조의 제2 항에서는 미국은 전
기 권리, 권력 및 권능의 행사에있어서, 일본국 영역에르의, 영역
으로 부터의 따는 영역내에서의 항해, 항공, 통신 또는 육상
교통을 불필요하게 방해하는 방법으로 행사하여서는 안된다는
점에 합의한다는 규정이 있다.

"The United States agrees that the above-mentioned rights,
power and authority will not be exercised in such a manner
as to interfere unnecessarily with navigation, aviation,
communication or land travel to or from or within the territories of Japan."

(4) 미 비 협정 제3 조의 제3 항 전단에서도 이와 유사한
일반적인 제한 규정을 두고 있다,

"In the exercise of the above-mentioned rights, power and
authority, the United States agrees that the powers granted
to it willnnot be used unreasonably er, unless required
by military necessity determined by two Governments, so as
to interfere with the necessary rights of navigation,
aviation, communication, or land travel within the territories
of the Philipplines."

(나) 우리나라 행정협정안에서도 이와 유사한 규정을 두고
있있는 바, 즉 제 3 조의 2의 (나)에서는 "....전기 권리, 권력,
권능을 한국영역의 출입 또는 한국영역내에서의 항해 항공, 통신
또는 지상교통을 불필요하게 저해하는 방법으로 행사하지 않음에

동의 합대고 규정하고 협피협치에 의한 통신사항에 관한것은
상호약정에 의하여 해결한다고 문서를 붙이고 있는바, 이는 미 일
협정 또는 미 비협정에서도 전적으로 통일한 규정을 두고 있는
점에 비추어 볼때 새로운 것은 아니다. 그러나, 미일 협정이나
미 비 협정의 체결 배경과 한미협정의 체결배경은 다소 상이한
바 있음이 사실이므로, 한국에 있으서는 우선 군사주전에 방해를
주지않는 한도라는 점이 강조되는 것은 재언을 요치 않는다.
그럼에도 불구하고 한미협정에 있어서도 통일한 규정을 두고저
하는 이유는 "권기 권미 행사에 따르는 제한은 양국정부의 합의
에 의거한대고 한것은 한국정부가 군사주전의 우월성을 인정하는
한 그러한 원칙을 규정하고 실제운영에 있어서 한국정부가 이를
상황에따라서 광대하게 해석하는 것을 방해하지 않을 뿐 머러
이것을 규정하므로써, 실제적으로 양국 정부간의 권미상의 침해
행위를 사전에 방지하고 나아가서 협조를 촉진시킨다는 점에서
생구할때, 이 규정도 별수없는 중요성을 가진다고 할것이다.
끝으로 권미 행사에 있어서의 일반적인 규정으로써, 미 일
협정 제 3 조의 온 "미국군대가 사용하는 시설 및 구역에 있어
서의 작업은 공공의 안전에 타당한 고려를 해야 한다고 규정
하고있는바, 우리나라에 있어서도, 이러한 규정은 총체적인 규
정으로써, 전문에서나, 또는 본 권미 의무 관계에서 명시 할
필요성이 충분히 있는 것이다.

3, 합동위원회의 설치
   (가) 규제협정에 규정된 합동위원회
      (1) 미 일 협정 및 미독협정에서는 협정의 효과적인 시
행을 위하여 합동위원회를 두기로 하고 있는 바, 미 일 협정에
서는, 제 26 조에서,

" 1. A Joint Committee shall be established as the means

0025
— 7

한·미국 간의 상호방위조약 제4조에 의한 시설과 구역 및 한국에서의 미국군대의 지위에 관한 협정(SOFA)
전59권. 1966.7.9 서울에서 서명 : 1967.2.9 발효(조약 232호) (V.5 체결 교섭, 1959)

means for consultation between the United States and Japan
on all matters requiring mutual consultation regarding the
implementation of this Agreement. In particular, the
Joint committee shall serve as the means for consultation
in determing the facilities and areas in Japan which are
required for the use of the United States in carrying out
the purposes stated in Article I of the Security Treaty.

2. The Joint Committee shall be composed of a representative of the United States and of Japan, each of whom shall
have one or more deputies and a staff. The Joint Committee
shall determine its own procedures, and arrange for such
auxiliary organs and administrative services as may be
required. The Joint Committee shall be so organized that
it may meet immediately at any time at the request of the
representative of either the United States or Japan.

3. If the Joint Committee is unable to resolve any
matter, it shall refer that matter to the respective Governments for further consideration through appropriate channels."

(2) 미 독 협정에서도 제 17 조 에서

" A Standing Committee shall be established, to be composed
of representatives of the appropriate authorities of the
Three Powers and of representatives of authorities of the
Fedral Republic. The duty of this Commission shall be to guarantee effective coordination between civil and military air
activities."

라고 규정하여 합동 위원회의 구성을 합의 하고 있다.

(3) 기타 협정에서도 합동위원회라는 기관을 별도로
설치하

조...

고 있는지 않으나, 그 대신 예외없이 정부 간의 협의로 해결한다고 규정을 두고 있다.

(나) 우리나라 행정협정 제 16 조에 있어서도 미일협정의 규정과 거의 흡사한 규정을 두었었다.

(다) 우리나라가 취할 입장

전기한 바와 같이 미일협정에 있어서는 합동위원회를 설치하여 협정의 시행에 관한 모든 문제를 포괄적으로 규정하고 있고, 미비협정에서는 각 권리 의무에 관하여 일일히 협의대상인지 아닌지를 규정하고 있는 바, 우리나라에서는 일본이 취한 형식을 취함이 좋을 줄로 안다. 그것은 위에서도 언급한 바와 같이 미비협정이나 미영협정에 있어서는 그 객체를 일일히 부록에 특정하고 있기때문에 정부간의 협의 대상이 되는 것을 일일히 상세히 예측할 수 있으나 우리나라와 같이 미국군의 작전상 필요를 무엇보다도 우선적으로 인정하여야 하는 입장에서는 미비협정이나 미영협정 과 같은 한정적인 규정을 두는 것이 사실상 불가능 하기 때문이다.

따라서 우리가 본 협정에서 합동위원회에 관하여 규정할 한계는 종래 우리가 이미 작성한 행정협정안의 제 16 조 의 선을 따르면 좋을 것이다.

구성, 임무 등에 관하여서는 이를 종래의 협정안에 따르기로 하고 추가해서 구조항에 언급된 양국정부간의 협의대상 까지 포함한 임무를 별도로 조항을 신설함이 일본의 경우보다 좀 더 상세한 방식이 될것이다

13-9

0027

한·미국 간의 상호방위조약 제4조에 의한 시설과 구역 및 한국에서의 미국군대의 지위에 관한 협정(SOFA)
전59권. 1966.7.9 서울에서 서명 : 1967.2.9 발효(조약 232호) (V.5 체결 교섭, 1959)

33

적 용 조 건

적용조건에 관하여는 우선 이를 대역시의 조건과 반환시의 조건으로 대별하고 대역시의 조건으로서는 임대료문제 게체에 대한 개조 문제, 및 기타 대역조건으로 분리하고 반환시의 조건으로서는 원상회복 또는 보상 및 개체가 개축 또는 조축되었을 때의 문제로 분리하여 각국의 조약례를 고찰하면 다음과 같다.

가. 대역조건

✓ (임대료문제) 각국이 체결한 조약중에는 임대료나 사용료를 지불하지 않을 것으로 명시한 것도 있으나 단지 토지나 건물등을 제공하기로 규정할 뿐, 전혀 임대료나 사용료에 관한 규정을 하지 않은 것도 있다. 대체의 경향은 임대료나 사용료를 지불하지 않는 것으로 되어있다.

즉 무료제공을 규정한 것으로서 미국이 센트 루시아와 체결한 협정을 보면

"The Government of Saint Lucia shall have the right to occupy and utilize for any purpose the areas mentioned in Article II hereof without liability for the payment to the United States Government of rental or compensation for the use thereof. This right shall extend to any license of the Government of Saint Lucia without prior consent of the United States Government." (Article 3, Saint Lucia Agreement)

라고 하여 임대료를 받지않기로 하였고 미국이 영국과 체결한 "바하마" 협정 제 23조, 미국이 중국과 체결한 "상호방위원조협정" 제 3조 및 미국과 사우디 아라비아가 체결한 "다하란" 협정 제 4조 등은 모두 임대료나 사용료를 받지 않는다고 규정하였다.

임대료에 광한 규정을 전혀 하지 않은 것으로써는

미국이 이태리와 체결한 "상호방위원조조약"에서

> "It will furnish all of the land, buildings, equipment,
> materials, and services required for the additional
> production facilities, except for the equipment and tech-
> nical advice to be furnished by the Government of the
> United States, ..." (4-c, Mutual Defense Assistance)

라고 하였고

미국이 벨기와 체결한 조약에 의하면

> "The Government of Belgium will continue to contribute
> to the defense of the United States of America and the
> stregthening thereof and will provide such articles,
> services, facilities or information as it may be in a
> position to supply". (Article II, Principles applying
> to mutual aid in the prosecutuion of the war against agr-
> ression)

라고 하여 임대료 및 사용료에 관한 규정을 설정하지 않었다.

(징발시의 손실보상)

센트 루시아 협정에서는 제 3 조 1 항에서 사용에 대한
보상의무가 없다고 명시하였으나 먼일 행정협정, "바하마"
협정, 및 "다하탄" 협정에는 그에 관한 규정이 전혀 없으며
다만 미비 협정에서는 손실보상의 의무가 있다고 명기하고
비교적 상세한 규정을 하고 있는 것이다. 즉,

> "Whenever it is necessary to acquire by condemnation
> or expropriation proceedings real property belonging
> to any private persons, associations or corporations .
> located in bases named in Annex A and Annex B in order
> to carry out the purposes of this Agreement, the
> Philippines will institute and prosecute such con-
> demnation on expropriation proceeding in accordance
> with the laws of the Philippines. The United States
> agrees to reimburse the Philippines for all the reason-
> able expenses, damages and costs thereby incurred,

13-11

0029

including the value of the property as determined
by the Court." (Article XXIII - Agreement between
the United States of America and the Republic of Philip-
ppines concerning Military Bases)

(개체에 대한 개조문제)

개체에 대한 개조에 관하여 사전에 대여자의 동의를
얻을 필요가 있는가에 대하여 명기한 협정은 없는데 이것은
개체의 가치증가가 되는 개량을 방해할 필요가 없는 것이므로
개체에 대한 개량을 당연히 허용하는 것으로 보아야 할것이다.

제협정에서는 개조 또는 신축에 관한 조건만을 규정하고
있는 것인데 즉 미비협정에서는

"It is mutually agreed that the United States shall

have the right to remove or dispose of any or all

removable improvements, equipment or facilities located

at or on any base and paid for with funds of the United

States. No export tax shall be charged on any mater-

ial or equipment so removed from the Philippines."

(Article 17, Item 1)

"A buildings and structures which are erected by

the United States in the bases shall be the property

of the United States and may be removed by it before

the expiration of this Agreement or the earlier relin-

quishment of the base on which the structures are

situated." (Article 17, Item 2)

라고 하였고,

쎄인트 루치아 협정에서는 사용국의 개량권을 명시하고
있으나 반면에 개량의 한계에 대하여도 규정하고 있는 것이다.
즉, 다음과 같다.

13-12

0030

" The Government of Saint Lucia or its licenses shall
have the right-to construct or carry out all needful
improvements to the said areas so long as such
improvements to the said areas will not hinder the
expeditious reoccupation of these areas by the
United States Government for the purpose of the
Bases Agreement."

(Article III (2))

(기하 조건)

(1) 토지는 사용하도록 하나 그 안에 있는 광물등에 대하여
본국의 권한을 명시한 규정도 있는 바, 즉

" All minerals (including oil), and antiquities and
all rights relating thereto and to treasure trove
under, upon, or connected with the land and water
comprised in the bases or otherwise used or occupied
by the United States by virtue of this Agreement,
are reserved to the Government and inhabitants of
the Phillippines ; but no right as reserved shall
be transfered to third parties, or exercised within
the bases without the consent of the United States.

(Article XXIV)

라고 하고 있다.

(2) 토지 및 시설을 제 3 국에 양도할수 없다는 규정을
한것으로는 미비협정에서

한·미국 간의 상호방위조약 제4조에 의한 시설과 구역 및 한국에서의 미국군대의 지위에 관한 협정(SOFA)
전59권. 1966.7.9 서울에서 서명 : 1967.2.9 발효(조약 232호) (V.5 체결 교섭, 1959)

37

" The Phillippines agrees that it shall not grant,
without prior consent of th United States, any
bases or any rights, power, or authority whatsoever,
in or relating to bases, to any third power,

It is further agreed that the United States shall
not, without the consent of he Phillippines, assign,
or underlet, or part with the possession of the
whole or any part of any base, or any right, power
or authority granted by this Agreement, to any third

라고 한것이다.   power." (Article XXV)

나. 반환시의 조건

(원상회복의 의무)

반환시의 원상회복의 의무는 대체로 없다고 규정하는 것
이 보통이며 특수한 협정에서만 별도의 규정을 하고 있는 것이다.

즉 미국이 각국과 체결한 조약중 정상적 입장에서 체결
된 것이라고 볼수있는 미비 협정 및 미일 협정에서는 원상회복의
의무 가 없다고 규정하고 있는바 즉 미비 협정에서는 제 22 조에서

" The United States is not obligated to turn over
the bases to the Phillippines at the expiration of
this Agreement or the earlier relinquishment of any
bases in the condition in which they were at the time
of their occupation, ..."

이라 하였고

미일 협정에서는 제 4 조에서

" The United States is not obliged, when it returns
facilities and areas to Japan on the expiration of
this Agreement or at an earlier dates to restore the
facilities and areas to the condition in which they
were at the time they became available to the United
States armed forces, or to compensate Japan in lieu
라고 하고 있는 것이다.   of such restoration, ..."

0032

13 - 14

그리고 1951년의 미중 상호방위원조 협정에서는 명시적 규정은 안했으나 제 3 조에서 " free of future liability"라고 하였음으로 원상회복의 의무 가 없는 것으로 해석된다.

ⓒ 또한 선후 무시한 협정에서는 원상회복의 의무는 규정하지 안했으나 제 4 조 4 항에서 대체들에 대한 개량에 대하여 미국은 구매권을 가지고 있으며 단지 그 구매를 하지 않을 경우 에는 미국의 요구가 있으면 개량부분을 철거 이전할 의무 가 있다고 규정하였다.   즉

> " In the event that improvements are not purchased (St Lucia)
> by the United States Government, the United States 여4. — 4.
> Government may require the removal of any improve-
> ments constructed during the occupation of the
> Government of Saint Lucia under this Agreements,
> without cost to the United States Government."

라고 하였다.

또한 특수한 규정을 하고 있는 " 다하란 " 협정 제 16 조는 완전히 이용할수 있는 상태로 반환할 것을 규정하였으니   즉

> " Upon the termination of this Agreement, the Mission
> will return to Saudi Arabian Government in sound
> operating condition all fixed, installations, properties
> and equipment of which it makes use in the operations
> and maintenance of Dhahran Airfield. "

라고 한것이다.

결국 원상회복의 의무는 특수한 사정하에서 체결된 몇개의 협정을 재외하면 대체로 없는 것으로 규정하고 있는 것이다.

(개량 증축에 대한 보상문제)

요지나 건공을 일정한 목적을 위하여 사용함에 있어서 그 이용의 효과를 증진시키기 위하여 불가피하게 가하게 되는 객체에 대한 개량이나 증축에 대하여는 그 반환시에 대여국이 개량이나 증축에 대하여 보상할 의무만 없는 가에 대하여 보상할

한·미국 간의 상호방위조약 제4조에 의한 시설과 구역 및 한국에서의 미국군대의 지위에 관한 협정(SOFA)
전59권. 1966.7.9 서울에서 서명 : 1967.2.9 발효(조약 232호) (V.5 체결 교섭, 1959)   39

의무가 있는가에 대하여는 명시적으로 보상의무가 없다고 규정하는 것이 대체의 경향이다.

즉 미비 협청 제 17 조 2 항은

" ......, nor is the Phillippines obliged to make any compensation to the United States for the improvements made in the bases or for the buildings or structures left thereon, all of which shall become the property of the Phillippines upon the termination of the Agreement or the earlier relinquishment by the United States of the bases where the structures have been built".

라고 하였고

또한 미일 협정 제 4 조는

" Japan is not obliged to make any compensation to the United States for any improvements made in the facilities and areas or for the buildings or structures left thereon the expiration of this Agreement or the earlier return of the facilities and areas."

라고 하였다.

그리고 보상의무를 규정한 것으로서는 세트 루시아 협정 제 4 조 3 항 에는

" In the event of reoccupation, the United States Government shall have the right to purchase from the Government of Saint Lucia any improvements constructed by the said Government of Saint Lucia or licenses within areas referred to in Article II hereof. The purchase price shall be mutually agreed upon and in default of agreement the price shall be settled by arbitration under the provisions for arbitration contained in the Civil Code in force in the Colony".

라고 하였으니 결국 보상하여야 개량부분을 취득할 수 있게 한 것이다.

13 - 16   — 0034

다. 우리나라의 입장

이상 제국 제협정의 경향을 고찰하였는바 한국의 토지 및 건물사용에 관한 한미간의 협정을 체결하에 이어서는 대여시의 조건 및 반환시의 조건으로 분리하여 생각함이 편리하다.

대여시의 조건중 임대료에 관하여는 대부분의 국가가 이를 받지 않고 있으므로 우리나라도 임대료를 받지는 곤란할 것이다.

그러나 우리나라와 입장이 유사하다고 볼수있는 미비협정에서는 토지 및 건물의 사용에 의하여 발생하는, 목적물의 가격을 포함하는 모든 손해에 대하여 보상을 할것을 규정하였으므로 우리나라도 이에 따름이 가하다고 생각한다.

객체에 대한 개량은 그것이 우리나라에 불리할것이 없으므로 우리나라에 대한 사전통고를 조건으로 하여 임의로 개량할수 있도록 하여야 할것이다.

사용을 완료하여 반환할 때에는 제국의 압도적인 선례에 따라 원상회복의 의무를 면제하고 그 대신 개량부분이나 신축물은 우리나라에 귀속한다고 하여야 할 것이다.

13 - 17

한·미국 간의 상호방위조약 제4조에 의한 시설과 구역 및 한국에서의 미국군대의 지위에 관한 협정(SOFA)
전59권. 1966.7.9 서울에서 서명 : 1967.2.9 발효(조약 232호) (V.5 체결 교섭, 1959) 41

분 쟁 해 결 방 법

1. 분쟁해결방법에 관한 다른조약의 예

가. 미일 행정협정   본협정의 실시에 관한 포괄적인 협의
기관인 합동 위원회 제도를 두고 이 합동 위원회가 분쟁해결에 관한
1차적인 조치를 취하고 동위원회가 문제를 해결하지 못하는 경우에
는 적당한 계통을 통하여 그 문제를 각자의 정부의 교섭에 부하게
하고있다.

나. 미비 군사 기지협정———— 미국측에게 비국법원이 결정한
수용에 수반하는 모든 상당비용 손해액 재산 가격등을 보상할 의무
를 지우고 있다.

다. 북 대서양 조약기구 가입국간의 협정———— 주둔국의 재산
상의 손해에 관한 ㅂ 배상책임과 배상액은 관계국간에 별로 합의가
없는 한 주둔국 국민이며 고급법관 중에서 관계국이 합의하여 선출한
1인의 종재관이 결정하도록 되여있다. 이결정에는 구속력이 있다.

라. 한미 국제연합 기념묘지협정———— 본협정의 해석과 적용에
관한 복제은 한국측 1인, 국제연합측 1인, 전기 2인이 합의하여
선출한 1인 계 3인으로 구성된 종재재판소에 의하여 해결하도록
되어있다. 이 종재재판소의 결정에는 구속력이 있다.

2. 검토

미일 행정협정과 같이 합동위원회 제도를 설치하여 이로하여금
협정의 실시에 관한 포괄적인 사항을 협의케 한다면 이 합동위원회
가 분쟁해결기관이 될것이나 그 구성을 양측대표 1 명식으로 한다면
(미일협정) 이해가 상반되는 분쟁은 대부분이 분쟁으로 남을 가능
성이 많을 것이다. 미일협정에 의하면 합동위원회가 분쟁을 해결하지
못하는 경우에는 양정부간의 외교방법에 마끼고 있는데 우리나라에서
이 방법을 취하게 되면 약소국가인 우리나라가 미국측의 압력으로
불리하게 될 경우가 많을것이다. 어떤점으로 보아 한미 국제연합기념
묘지협정에서와 같은 방법도 생각할수 있으나 결국은 우리나라의
국제적지위치, 체약가능성 등을 고력하여야 할것이다.

0036

본협정 체결의 주요목적이 손실보상, 손해배상등의 재산상의 배상을 받음에 있는바, 그러한 문제에 관한 분쟁으로서 배상책임의 유무 배상액 등에 관하여 합동위원회에 의한 합의에 도달하지 못할경우에 그 결정기관으로서 법률전문가를 관여케 하는 방법을 생각할 필요가 있다. 이런점으로 보아 가장 우리나라에게 유리한 방법으로는 미비군사기지협정과 같이 우리나라 법원으로 하여금 결정케 하는 방법을 생각할수 있으나 체약가능성을 고려하여야 할 것이고 북대서양조약기구 가입국·간의 협정을 모방하여 합동위원회로 하여금 우리나라의 노련하고 신망이 있는 법관중에서 1 인의 중재관을 선출케 하여 그로 하여금 결정케 하는 방법도 생각할수 있다.

이상 검토한 이외에도 분쟁해결 기관에 의한 결정의 구속력 문제등 중요한 문제가 있으나 해결방법과 관련을 가지고 연구하여야 할것이며 우리나라의 이익, 협약체결의 목적과 우리나라의 위치, 협약체결의 가능성등을 비교 교량하여 연구 하여야 할것이다.

한·미국 간의 상호방위조약 제4조에 의한 시설과 구역 및 한국에서의 미국군대의 지위에 관한 협정(SOFA) 전59권. 1966.7.9 서울에서 서명 : 1967.2.9 발효(조약 232호) (V.5 체결 교섭, 1959)   43

국제연합군의 부동산 사용요청은 계엄령이 해제된 이후에도 계속되므로 합법징발은 하지않고있으나 재산소유자의 동의가 있을 때만 특별한 사용 승인하여 제공하고있음.

나. 대미 절충 경위

(1) 1951.5.17자로 콜터장군이 미대통령에게 보내온 공한에는 "미군을 포함한 국제연합군은 공공용의과 물자 급 시설등의 사용료 청산관계를 후일 한국 정부와의 협의하에 해결하도록 미육군성과 재무성의 지시가 있었다"고 하였음.

(2) 1954.8.5 한국 경제사절단이 도미시 145,322,706,070환 (1954.6.30현재)을 요구절충 하여 미국조야의 여론을 환기시켜 이를 조사하고저 미국정부 관계관이 내한목적으로 일본 동경에 도착한바 때마침 유류소동으로 미측 관계관은 내한을 중지 귀국하였음.

(3) 1955.5.23 손원일장관께서 도미사실시 167,953,529,360환 (1955.5.30현재)을 요구함.

(4) 1955.9.16자로 타자스장군 (국제연합군 참모장)이 김현철 재무부장관에게 보내온 공한에의하면 청산관계를 3단계로 제안하여왔음. 3단계란,

　7. 1단계　　휴전까지의(1953.7.27) 견판가.

　나. 2단계　　휴전기간(1953.7.27)부터 한국정부 관계 부처와 협정을 체결하는 날까지의 기간.

　다. 3단계　　협정 체결일로부터의 기간.

이상 3단계로 나누어서 휴전기간이전의것은 청산불 가능하나, 협정체결일부터의것은 청산 가능하다고 시사하였음.

(5) 1955.12.15 재무부장관실에서 국제연합군이 사용한 전기, 수도, 부동산등의 보상에대하여 한미간 회의를 개최할시 요청함.(미국대표 핫모니장군)

(6) 1956.6.18 하모니장군(국제연합군사령부 참모장)이 김현철 재무 장관에게 보내온 공한에의하면 부동산의 사용료청산을 삭제 할것을 제안하여왔으나 차에대하여,

(7) 1956.8.7자로 김현철장관께서 하모니장군에게 보낸공한 에는 아래와같이 제안하였음.

　7. 휴전기간 이저의 토등 사용료청산은 후일에 협의할것을

0038

전제로 보류

　ㄴ) 부동산 사용료 청산은 후일 협의 키로 보류

(8) 1956.9.9 미8군 사령관에게 앞으로 유엔군이 필요한 재산을 취득 함시는 사용료를 지불하지 않은한 취득할수 없을것이며 현재까지 사용중인 재산의 보상도 부담하여야 한다는 협의 문을 발송한바 미8군사령관 화이트 장군은 1956.9.22일자로 유엔군사령부에서 상세한 회신을 받도록 회신이 있었음.

(9) 1956.11.25 유엔군사령관 렘니저 장군으로부터 회답이 유 한측 교위결정(연합국 참전국 간의 협의 대상)하기 위하여 미육군성에 상신 하였다함.

(10) 1957.1.17 자로 극동군사령관에게 재차 요청하였으며 1957.4.16일자로 불가하다는 회신이 왔음.

(11) 1957.3.15 김용우 장관 도미시 76,843,372,236환 (4288.12.31 현재)을 요구 하였음.

(12) 1958.3.3 백육군참모총장 도미시 87,885,701,932환 (4290.12.31 현재)을 요구 하였음.

다. 대책

(1) 현재까지의 공한 또는 도미사절을 통한 절충방법은 결과적으로 하등의 성과를 보지 못하였으므로 우선 미국정부에 대하여 보상촉구공한을 보내고 반건 유엔군사용징발 재산 보상문제를 전문적으로 효의 절충 하기 위한 관계부처 합동으로 구성된 자문위원회를 설치하여 추진 해결토록 하여야 함.

(2) 전기 추진 방법에 의하여도 별다른 반응이 없을시는 다음 방안에 의거 시행함.

　ㄱ) 유엔군에 징발재산 제공을 제한함.

　ㄴ) 한국 정부예산에 유엔군사용징발재산의 보상금을 계상 신청함.

(3) 피징발자로 하여금 미측에 진정케하여 대상자의 애로사실을 반영케하고 또한 국내 보도에 반영케 한후 대외 통신에 반영케함.

15

0039

UN군가 물자관리 현황표

참고 표 4

Relevant Articles excerpted from the

Draft Administrative Agreement on the

Facilities and Areas to be used by the

United States Forces in Korea proposed

on April 28, 1955)

ARTICLE III

1. (a) (i) Korea agrees to grant to the Unified Command the
use of the facilities and areas necessary to carry out the mission
and purposes of the United Nations forces in Korea.

(ii) Agreements as to facilities and areas to be used
by the United Nations forces in accordance with this
agreement shall be concluded by the two Parties through the
Joint Committee provided for in Article XVII of this Agreement.

(iii) Until such agreements are concluded between the two
Parties the United Nations forces shall continue to use such
facilities and areas as are being used at the time this
Agreement becomes effective.

(b) At the request of either Party, Korea and the
Unified Command shall review such arrangement and may
agree that such facilities and areas shall be returned
to Korea or that additional facilities and areas may be
provided.

(c) The facilities and areas used by the United
Nations forces shall be returned to Korea whenever they
 are no longer needed for purposes of this Agreement, and
the Unified Command agrees to keep the needs for
facilities and areas under continual observation with
a view towar such return.

(d) When facilities and areas such as target

16

0041

ranges and maneuver grounds are temporarily not being used by the United Nations forces, interim use may be made by Korean authorities and nationals in accordance with the decision made by the Joint Committee provided for in Article XVII of this Agreement.

2. (a) The Unified Command shall have the rights, power and authority within the facilities and areas which are necessary or appropriate for their establishment, use, operation, or defense. The Unified Command shall also have such rights, power and authority over land, territorial waters and airspace adjacent to, or in the vicinities of such facilities of such facilities and areas, as are necessary to provide access to such facilities and areas for their support and defense. In the exercise outside the facilities and areas of the rights, power and authority granted in this Article there should be, as the occasion requires, consultation between the two Parties through the Joint Committee.

(b) The Unified Command agrees that the above mentioned rights, power and authority will not be exercised in such a manner as to interfere unecessary with navigation, aviation, communication, or land travel to or from or within the territories of Korea. All questions relating to frequencies, power and like matters used by apparatus employed by the United Nations forces designed to emit electric radiation shall be settled by mutual arragement. Pending such arrangement, the United Nations forces shall be entitled to use, without radiation interference from Korean sources, electronic devices of such power,

17

0042

design, type of emission, and frequencies as are reserved for such forces at the time this Agreement becomes effective.

(c) Operations in the facilities and areas in use by the United Nations forces shall be carried on with due regard for the public safety.

3. (a) The Unified Command is not obliged, when it returns facilities and areas to Korea on the expiration of this Agreement or at an earlier date, to restore the facilities and areas to the condition in which they were at the time they become available to the United Nations forces, or to compensate Korea in lieu of such restoration. In case of private property demolished by such use, the Unified Command shall pay sympathetic consideration to its restoration.

(b) Korea is not obliged to make any compensation to the Unified Command for any improvements made in the facilities and areas or for buildings or structures left thereon on the expiration of this Agreement or the earlier return of the facilities and areas.

4. (a) Vessels and aircraft operated by, for, or under the control of the United Nations forces for official purposes shall be accorded access to any port or airport of Korea free from toll or landing charges. When cargo or passengers not accorded the exemption of this Agreement are carried on such vessels and aircraft, notification shall be given to the appropriate Korean authorities, and such cargo or passengers shall be entered in accordance with the laws and regulations of Korea.

(b) When the vessels mentioned in paragraph 4 (a) enter Korean ports, approapriate notification shall, under normal conditions, be made to the proper Korean authorities. Such

18

0043

vessels shall have freedom from compulsory pilotage, but if
a pilot is taken pilotage shall be paid for at appropriate
rates.

5. (a) All civil and military air traffic control and
communications systems shall be coordinated in accordance
with the decision made by the Joint Committee.

(b) Lights and other aids to navigation of vessels and
aircraft placed or established in the facilities and areas
in use by the United Nations forces and in territorial waters
adjacent thereto or in the vicinity thereof shall conform
to the system in use in Korea. The Korean and the United
Nations forces authorities which have established such
navigation aids shall notify each other of their positions
and characteristics and shall give advance notification before
making any changes in them or establishing additional navigation aids.

6. The United Nations forces may use all public utilities and services belonging to the Government of Korea under
conditions no less favorable than those applicable to the
armed forces of Korea.

7. Korea and the United Nations forces shall cooperate
in meteorological services through exchange of meteorological
observations climatological information and seismographic
data.

19

대한민국과 통합사령부간의 국제연합군의
지위에 관한 행정협정안

(밥체)

제 3 조

1. (ㄱ) (1) 한국은 통합사령부에 대하여 한국에 있어서 국제
연합군의 사명과 목적을 수행함에 필요한 시설과
구역의 사용을 허가함에 동의한다.

(2) 본 협정에 의하여 국제연합군이 사용할 시설 및
구역에 관하여는 본 협정 제 17조에 규정된
합동위원회를 통하여 양당사자간에 합의 결정하
기로 한다.

(3) 양 당사자간에 여사한 합의가 성립되기까지는
국제연합군은 본 협정발효시에 사용중인 시설 및
구역을 계속 사용한다.

(ㄴ) 한국과 통합사령부는 일방당사자의 요청이 있는 경우
에는 여사한 약정을 재검토하여야 하며 그러한 시설과
구역의 한국에의 반환 또는 추가적 제공에 관하여
합의 할수있다.

(ㄷ) 국제연합군에 의하여 사용되고 있는 시설과 구역을
본 협정의 목적상 불필요하게 되는 경우에는 한국에
반환되어야 하며 통합사령부는 여사한 반환을 목적으로
하여 시설과 구역의 필요성을 계속적인 검토하에 두는데
동의한다.

(ㄹ) 사격장 및 연습장등의 시설과 구역이 국제연합군에 의하여
일시적으로 사용되지않을 경우에는 본 협정 제 17조에
규정된 합동위원회의 결정에 의하여 한국당국과 국민이
여를 일시사용할 수 있다.

0045

한·미국 간의 상호방위조약 제4조에 의한 시설과 구역 및 한국에서의 미국군대의 지위에 관한 협정(SOFA)
전59권. 1966.7.9 서울에서 서명 : 1967.2.9 발효(조약 232호) (V.5 체결 교섭, 1959) 51

2. (ㄱ) 통합사령부는 시설 및 구역내에서 설정 사용 운영 또는
방위에 필요 또는 ... 권리 권력 및 권능을 가진다.

통합사령부는 ... 어 사용 ... 시설과 구역에 인접한 또는
그 부근의 토지 영수 및 ... 에 대하여 그 보급지원과
방위를 위하여 여사한 시설과 구역에의 출입의 합의를
보유 받는 ... 필요 ... 시설과 구역에서의
... 행사에 있어서는 필요에 따라서 합동위원회를
통하여 양당사자간의 합의가 있어야 한다.

(ㄴ) 통합사령부는 전기의 권리 권력 및 권능을 한국영역의
... 또는 한국영역내에서의 ... 항해 항공 통신 또는
지상교통을 불필요하게 저해하는 방법으로 행사하지
않음에 동의한다.

국제연합군에 의해서 사용되는 전파 방사의 장치가
있고 있는 주파수 전력 및 용량의 사항에 관한 모든
문제는 상호약정에 의하여 해결되어야 한다.

여사한 약정이 있을 때까지는 국제연합군은 ... 협정
효력 발생시에 확보하고 있는 전파 ... 방사의 힘
및 주파수의 전자점 ... 한국측으로 부터의 방사방해없이
사용할 권력을 갖는다.

(ㄷ) 국제연합군이 사용하고 있는 시설과 구역내에 있어서의
... 공공안전은 적당히 고려하고 행하여져야 한다.

3. (ㄱ) 통합사령부는 본협정의 만료시 또는 그 이전에 시설과 구역을 한국에 반환할 경우 당해시설 및 구역을 국제연합군의 사용에 제공된 당시의 상태로 복구시키거나 또는 그 원상회복 대신에 배상할 의무가 없다. 이유재산이 그 편한 사용으로 말미암아 훼손된 경우에는 통합사령부는 그 원상회복에 호의적인 고려를 하여야 한다.

(ㄴ) 한국은 본 협정 만료시 또는 그 이전에 시설 및 구역이 반환되는 경우에 그 시설과 구역에 가하여진 개량 또는 거기에 잔류된 건물, 기타 공작물에 대하여 통합사령부에 아무런 보상을 할 의무가 없다.

4. (ㄱ) 국제연합군에 의하여 국제연합군을 위하여 또는 국제연합군의 관리하에 공적목적으로 운항되는 선박 및 항공기는 입항료 또는 착륙료를 부과됨이 없이 한국의 어떠한 항구 또는 공항에도 기항할수 있다. 본협정에 의한 면제를 받지않는 화물이나 여객이 여사한 선박이나 항공기에 적재운송된 경우에는 한국의 관계당국에 통고되어야 하며 그러한 화물이나 여객은 한국의 관계 법령에 따라 입국되어야한다.

(ㄴ) 제 4 조 (ㄱ) 에 규정한 선박이 한국항구에 입항할 시에는 통상상태에 있어서는 한국의 관계당국에게 적당한 통고를 하여야 한다. 여사한 선박은 강제적항도를 면제된다. 단 항도를 받는 경우에는 적당한 율의 항도료를 지불하여야 한다.

5. (ㄱ) 모든 비군용 및 군용항공 교통관리와 통신체계는 합동위원회의 결정에 의거하여 조정된다.

(ㄴ) 국제연합군이 사용하는 시설 및 구역내와 그에 인접한 영수 또는 그 부근에 설치 또는 설비된 등화 및 기타선박과 항공기의 항해보조시설은 한국에서 사용되는 제도에 일치하여야 한다. 여사한 항해보조수단을 설비한 한국과 국제연합군당국은 그 위치와 특성을 상호통고하여야 하며 그를 변경하거나 또는 다른 보조시설을 추가설비할때에는 이를 실시하기 전에 사전통고를 하여야 한다.

6. 국제연합군은 한국정부에 소속되는 모든 공익사업과 공공역무를 한국군에게 적용되는 조건보다도 불리하지않은 조건으로 사용할 수 있다.

0047

article XVII

7. 한국과 국제연합군은 기상관측 기후현상의 정보 및 지진관측의 자료의 교환을 통하여 기상업무에 있어서 상호협조한다.

ADMINISTRATIVE AGREEMENT

UNDER ARTICLE III OF THE SECURITY TREATY

BETWEEN THE UNITED STATES OF AMERICA AND JAPAN

ARTICLE II

1. Japan agrees to grant to the United States
the use of the facilities and areas necessary to carry
out the purposes stated in Article I of the Security
Treaty. Agreements as to specific facilities and
areas, not already reached by the two Government by the
effective date of this Agreement, shall be concluded
by the two Governments through the Joint Committee
provided for in Article XXVI of this Agreement.
"Facilities and areas" include existing furnishings,
equipment and fixtures necessary to the operation of
such facilities and areas.

2. At the request of either party, the United
States and Japan shall review such arrangements and
may agree that such facilities and areas shall be
returned to Japan or that additional facilities and
areas may be provided.

3. The facilities and areas used by the United
States armed forces shall be returned to Japan whenever
they are no longer needed for purposes of this Agreement,
and the United States agrees to keep the needs for
facilities and areas under continual observation with
a view toward such return.

4. (a) When facilities and areas such as
target ranges and maneuver grounds are temporarily
not being used by the United States armed forces,
interim use may be made by Japanese authorities and
nationals provided that it is agreed that such use

0048

20

would not be harmful to the purposes for which the facilities and areas are normally used by the United States armed forces.

(b) With respect to such facilities and areas as target ranges and maneuver grounds which are to be used by the United States armed forces for limited periods of time, the Joint Committee shall specify in the agreements covering such facilities and areas the extent to which the provisions of this Agreement shall apply.

ARTICLE IV

1. The United States is not obliged, when it returns facilities and areas to Japan on the expiration of this Agreement or at an earlier date, to restore the facilities and areas to the condition in which they were at the time they became available to the United States armed forces, or to compensate Japan in lieu of such restoration.

2. Japan is not obliged to make any compensation to the United Stats for any improvements made in the facilities and areas or for the buildings or structures left thereon on the expiration of this Agreement or the earlier return of the facilities and areas.

3. The forgoing provisions shall not apply to any construction which the United States may undertake under special arragements with Japan.

0049

한·미국 간의 상호방위조약 제4조에 의한 시설과 구역 및 한국에서의 미국군대의 지위에 관한 협정(SOFA)
전59권. 1966.7.9 서울에서 서명 : 1967.2.9 발효(조약 232호) (V.5 체결 교섭, 1959)   55

공   란

A G R E E M E N T

BETWEEN THE UNITED STATES OF AMERICA AND THE REPUBLIC
OF PHILIPPINES CONCERNING MILITARY BASES.

ARTICLE I

1. The Government of the Republic of the Philippines (hereinafter referred to as the Philippines) grants to the Government of the United States of America (hereinafter referred to as the United States) the right to retain the use of the bases in the Philippines listed in Annex A attached hereto.

2. The Philippines agrees to permit the United States, upon notice to the Philippines, to use such of those bases listed in Annex B as the United States determines to be required by military necessity.

3. The Philippines agrees to enter into negotiation with the United States at the latter's request, to permit the United States to expand such bases, to exchange such bases for other bases, to acquire additional bases, or relinquish rights to bases, as any of such exigencies may be required by military necessity.

4. A narrative description of the boundaries of the bases to which this Agreement relates is given in Annex A and Annex B. An exact description of the bases listed in Annex A, with metes and bounds, in conformity with the narrative descriptions, will agreed upon between the appropriate authorities of the two governments as soon as possible. With respect to any of the bases listed in Annex B and exact description with metes and bounds, in conformity with the narrative description

22

한·미국 간의 상호방위조약 제4조에 의한 시설과 구역 및 한국에서의 미국군대의 지위에 관한 협정(SOFA)
전59권. 1966.7.9 서울에서 서명 : 1967.2.9 발효(조약 232호) (V.5 체결 교섭, 1959)

ARTICLE II

MUTUAL COOPERATION

3. In the interest of international security any bases listed in Annexes A and B may be made available to the Security Council of the United Nations on its call by prior mutual agreement between the United States and the Philippines.

ARTICLE XXII

CONDEMNATION OR EXPROPRIATION

1. Whenever it is necessary to acquire by condemnation or expropriation proceedings real property belonging to any private persons, associations or corporations located in bases named in Annex A and Annex B in order to carry out the purposes of this Agreement, the Philippines will institute and prosecute such condemnation on expropriation proceeding in accordance with the laws of the Philippines. The United States agrees to reimbures the Philippines for all the reasonable expenses, damages and costs thereby incurred, including the value of the property as determined by the Court. In addition, subject to the mutual agreement of the two Governments, the United States will reimburse the Philippines for the reasonable costs of transportation and removal of any occupants displaced or ejected by reason of the condemantion or expropriation.

2. Prior to the completion of such condemnation or expropriation proceedings in cases of military necessity the United States shall have the right to take possession of such property required for military

23

0052

purposes as soon as the legal requisites for obtaining possession have been fulfilled.

3. The properties acquired under this Article shall be turned over to the Philippines upon the expiration of this Agreement, or the earlier relinquishment of such properties, under such terms and conditions as may be agreed upon by the two Governments.

ARTICLE XXIV
MINERAL RESOURCES

All minerals (including oil), and antiquities and all rights relating thereto and to treasure trove under, upon, or connected with the land and water comprised in the bases or otherwise used or occupied by the United States by virtue of this Agreement, are reserved to the Government and inhabitants of the Philippines; but no right so reserved shall be transferred to third parties, or exercised within the bases without the consent of the United States. The United States shall negotiate with the proper Philippines authorities for the quarrying of rock and gravel necessary for construction work on the bases.

ARTICLE XXV
GRANT OF BASES TO A THIRD POWER

1. The Philippines agrees that it shall not grant, without prior consent of the United States, any bases or any rights, power, or authority whatsoever, in or relating to bases, to any third power.

2. It is further agreed that the United States shall not, without the consent of the Philippines, assign, or underlet, or part with the possession of the whole or any part of any base, or of any right, power or authority granted by this Agreement, to any third power.

24

0C53

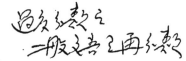

UNITED KINGDOM

THE BAHAMAS LONG RANGE PROVING GROUND

Agreement and exchange of notes signed at Washington,
July 21, 1950; entered into force July 21, 1950.

A G R E E M E N T

BETWEEN THE GOVERNMENT OF THE UNITED STATES OF AMERICA AND THE GOVERNMENT OF THE UNITED KINGDOM OF GREAT BRITAIN AND NORTHERN IRELAND CONCERNING A LONG RANGE PROVING GROUND FOR GUIDED MISSILES TO BE KNOWN AS "THE BAHAMA LONG RANGE PROVING GROUND"

ARTICLE X

The Government of the United States of America
shall have the right to employ and use all utilities,
services and facilities, harbors, roads,. . .belong-
ing to or controlled or regulated by the Government
of the Bahama Islands or the Government of the United
Kingdom on such conditions as shall be agreed between
the Contracting Governments.

ARTICLE XXIII

FREEDOM FROM RENTS AND CHARGES

Except as provided in Articles XVII and XXII
the Sites shall be provided, and the rights of the
Government of the United States of America under this
Agreement shall be made available, free from all rent
and charges to the Government of the United States of
America.

25

0054

SAUDI ARABIA

AIR BASE AT DHAHRAN

AGREEMENT EFFECTED BY EXCHANGE OF NOTES SIGNED AT MECCA AND
AT JIDDA JUNE 18, 1951 ; entered into force June 18, 1951.

4. In accordance with paragraph 23 of the existing Dhahran
Air field Agreement which states that .all fixed installations
and other property used in operation and maintenance of the
Airfield will be returned to the Saudi Arabian Government
upon termination of the Agreement, and in view of the fact
that the said Agreement is being terminated and that such
installations and properties thereby revert to the Saudi
Arabian Government, and, due to the desire of the Saudi
Arabian Government to facilitate the errand of the Mission,
it agrees to place at the disposition of the Mission at
Dhahran Airfield, rent free, certain existing buildings
and installations as specified in the list agreed upon by
the appropriate authorities of the two Governments and
approved by the Saudi Arabian Minister of Defense. This
list will be reviewed from time to time in the light of developing circumstances and requirements.

16. Upon the termination of this Agreement, the Mission
will return to the Saudi Arabian Government in sound operating condition all fixed installations, properties and
equipment of which it makes use in the operation and
maintenance of Dhahran Airfield.

한·미국 간의 상호방위조약 제4조에 의한 시설과 구역 및 한국에서의 미국군대의 지위에 관한 협정(SOFA)
전59권. 1966.7.9 서울에서 서명 : 1967.2.9 발효(조약 232호) (V.5 체결 교섭, 1959)

PRINCIPLES APPLYING TO MUTUAL AID

IN THE PROSECUTION OF THE WAR

AGAINST AGGRESSION

PRELIMINARY AGREEMENT

BETWEEN THE UNITED STATES OF AMERICA

AND BELGIUM

Signed at Washington June 16, 1942

Effective June 16, 1942

ARTICLE II

The Government of Belgium will continue to contribute to the defense of the United States of America and the strengthening thereof and will provide such articles, services, facilities or information as it may be in a position to supply.

27

0056

The Executive Director of the Office of the United States
High Commissioner for Germany to the Minister of Finance
for the Federal Republic of Germany

OFFICE OF THE UNITED STATES HIGH COMMISSIONER FOR GERMANY

Office of the Executive Director

Bad Godesberg

Mehlemer Aue

March 24, 1953

MY DEAR MINISTER SCHAEFFER :

I am writing to you on behalf of Headquarters
USAREUR in order to propose an agreement relative to the
settlement of a certain category of occupation damage
claims commonly known as Pre-1 July 1947 Claims.   The
proposal of USAREUR is as follows :

1.   Headquarters USAREUR hereby authorizes the
competent authorities of the Federal Republic of Germany
to receive, process and pay, in accordance with existing
occupation legislation and without reference to and U.S.
agency, all claims for :

a.   Damage caused as a result of acts or omissions
committed in the territory of the Federal Republic and the
Western Sectors of Berlin during the period from 1 August
1945 to 30 June 1947 inclusive by the United States
Forces and authorities and other persons, agencies and
organizations that acted on their behalf or authority or
for whose acts or omissions the United States assumed
responsibility.

b.   Arrears of rentals accrued for the same period.

c.   Damage caused to personal property not subject
to requisition, in connection with real estate released
during the period from the day following 30 June 1947 up to
and including the day preceding 1 October 1952.

28

0057

2. The criteria to be utilized in the adjudication of the foregoing types of claims are those established by USAREUR Circulars Nos. 37, 57, 75 and 187.

3. Headquarters USAREUR will make available to the competent authorities of the Federal Republic an amount of DM 6,400,000 for payment of the claims referred to under paragraph 1, a, b and c above.

The competent authorities of the Dederal Republic will provide such additional amounts from the Federal Budget, not chargeable as occupation costs, as may be necessary to satisfy the aforementioned claims, and will hold the U.S. authorities and Forces harmless against payment of any amount in excess of the DM 6,400,000 above provided for on account of the said claims. The competent authorities of the Federal Republic agree that the U.S. Forces will have no further responsibility for claims covered by this agreement.

29

0058

CONVENTION ON THE RIGHTS AND OBLIGATIONS OF FOREIGN FORCES AND

THEIR MEMBERS IN THE FEDERAL REPUBLIC OF GERMANY. Bonn, May 26, 1952

(as amended by Schedule II to the Protocol on the Termination
of the Occupation Regime in the Federal Republic of Germany
signed at Paris on October 23, 1954.)

Article 17, (8.)   A Standing Commission shall be established,
to be composed of representatives of the appropriate authorities
of the Three Powers and of representatives of authorities of the
Federal Republic.   The duty of this Commission shall be to
guarantee effective coordination between civil and military
air activities.

Article 20. 1)   Installations and works directly serving
the purpose of defense, as well as safety installations, shall
be erected or adopted by the Federal Republic of Germany in
such amounts, areas and types as are needed for the common
defense.   Where there is a special need for security, the
Forces themselves may erect or adopt such installations or
works, provided that there is prior consultation with the
Federal Government.

30

0053

SAINT LUCIA

LEASED BASES IN SAINT LUCIA

Agreement signed at Castries, Saint Lucia, July 29,
1952; entered into force July 29, 1952

TIAS 2673
July 29, 1952

A G R E E M E N T

concerning the utilization of leased base area

In Saint Lucia

ARTICLE II

Definition of Areas

The areas covered by this Agreement are those described
in paragraph 8 of the lease executed on the 29th March, 1950,
and in the schedules attached thereto.

ARTICLE III

Conditions of Occupation by the Government of Saint Lucia

(1) The Government of Saint Lucia shall have the right
to occupy and utilize for any purpose the areas mentioned in
Article ii hereof without liability for the payment to the
United States Government of rental or compensation for the use
thereof. This right shall extend to any license of the Government
of Saint Lucia without prior consent of the United States Government.

(2) The Government of Saint Lucia or its licensees shall
have the right to construct or carry out all needful
improvements to the said areas so long as such improvements
to the said areas so long as such improvements will not hinder
the expenditious reoccupation of these areas by the United
States Government for the purposes of the Bases Agreement.

31

0060

(3) The occupation by the Government of Saint Lucia or any licensee thereof shall be accomplished in such manner as to cause no obstruction or permanent damage to existing bridges, roadways, runways and approach areas thereto, and drainage work allied thereto. This stipulation shall not impose a responsibility upon the said Government for damage thereto resulting from natural causes.

(4) The areas and the improvements thereto shall be open at all reasonable time for inspection by the military authorities of the United States or by their duly authorized agents.

ARTICLE IV

Reoccupation by the Government of the United States right to reoccupy and activate any portion or the whole of the areas covered hereby on giving thirty days' previous notice to the Government of Saint Lucia; provided that in the event of a war breaking out in which the United States is involved, ˌ ˌ˘ or of any other overriding military necessity asvdetermined by the Government of the United States of America, the United States Government shall have the right to reoccupy and activate immediately any portion or the whole of any of the areas aforesaid on giving 48 hours previous notice in writing to the Government of Saint Lucia.

(2) The United States Government shall not be liable to the Government of Saint Lucia or to any third party for any damage caused solely as a result of such reoccupation.

(3) In the event of reoccupation, the United States Government shall have the right to purchase from the Government of Saint Lucia any improvements constructed by the said Government of Saint Lucia or its licensees within

32

0061

the areas referred to in Article ii hereof. The purchase price shall be mutually agreed upon and in default of agreement the price shall be settled by arbitration under the provisions for arbitration contained in the Civil Code in force in the Colony.

(4) In the event that improvements are not purchased by the United States Government, the United States Government may require the removal of any improvements constructed during the occupation of the Government of Saint Lucia under this Agreement, without cost to the United States Government.

(5) The Government of Saint Lucia or any licensees thereof shall begiven a period of time, consistent with the exigencies of the military situation, for the removal of any such improvements as are not desired for purchase by the United Statees Government.

(6) The Government of Saint Lucia shall hold and save the United States Government free from any cost arising from third party claims as a result of such occupation.

ARTICLE V

Status of Previous Rights

(1) Nothing in this Agreement shall be construed to deprive the Government of the United States of America of any of its rights, privileges, immunities or exemptions under the Bases Agreement or the Civil Aviation Agreement.

(2) Nothing in this Agreement shall be construed to confer upon the Government of Saint Lucia, with respect to the use in place of any of the buildings or improvements enumerated in Contract of Sale Ns. DA(a)   96-505-Eng-114 dated the 94th August, 1949, any rights or privileges not

33

0062

specifically granted by the said Contract of Sale or by separate agreements made in pursuance of the provisions thereof.

Done in duplicate at Casties in the Colony of Saint Lucia of the Wind ward Islands this 29th day of July, 1952.

For the Government of the
Colony of Saint Lucia,
Sindwar Islands.

For the Government of the
United States of America.

CARL BREUER
Consul of the United
States of America

F E DEGAZON
Acting Administrator
(SEAL)

(SEAL)

BEfore me:

Before me:

한·미국 간의 상호방위조약 제4조에 의한 시설과 구역 및 한국에서의 미국군대의 지위에 관한 협정(SOFA)
전59권. 1966.7.9 서울에서 서명 : 1967.2.9 발효(조약 232호) (V.5 체결 교섭, 1959)   69

MUTUAL DEFENSE ASSISTANCE

CONSTRUCTION OF MILITARY INSTALLATIONS AND

FACILITIES

Agreement effected by exchange of Notes signed at
Taipei November 21, 1956, entered into force November
12, 1956.

2. The Government of the Republic of China,
at times appropriate to the orderly and economical
prosecution of the agreed construction work, and
without cost to the United States Government, its
Contractors or sub-contractors, will, on request,
place at the disposal of the Chief, MAAG, areas necessary
for carrying out the construction and related work
contemplated by these understandings. The term
"necessary areas" shall be understood to include, in
addition to the real estate on which construction
will be performed, rights to use of water available,
rights of entry for purposes of survey, and such
borrow areas, spoil areas, quarry sites and aggregate
production sites in streams or elsewhere as may be
necessary, together with rights of ingress and egress
and rights to remove such materials or deposit
excess materials as may be necessary to the agreed
construction work. Such "necessary areas" shall
cease to be at the disposal of the Chief, MAAG, upon
completion of the construction work contemplated by
these understandings.

3. The Government of the Republic of China will
hold the Government of the United States, its
Contractors and their sub-contractors harmless for
such destruction of any buildings, streets, roads,
public utilities and improvements of any kind on real

0064

property placed at the disposal of the Chief, MAAG,
as necessary to the construction work contemplaced by
these understandings. Should any relocation of
facilities be required or resettlement costs be involved,
relocation and resettlement shall be accomplished by
the Government of the Republic of China at its own expense and at such time as not to interfere with the
orderly and economical proseeution of the work.

한·미국 간의 상호방위조약 제4조에 의한 시설과 구역 및 한국에서의 미국군대의 지위에 관한 협정(SOFA)
전59권. 1966.7.9 서울에서 서명 : 1967.2.9 발효(조약 232호) (V.5 체결 교섭, 1959)   71

MUTUAL DEFENSE ASSISTANCE (facilities Assistance)

Agreement between the United States of America and
Italy, entered into force June 24, 1954. 過友 紅葱로 一般之喜로
再 紅喜?

    c. It will furnish all of the land, buildings,
equipment, materials, and services required for the
additional production facilities, except for the
equipment and technical advice to be furnished by the
Government of the United States, and will take whatever
measures are required to accomplish the increase in
production facilities envisaged in the program.

    (5) In carrying out the facilities assistance
program, the two Governments, acting through their
appropriate contracting officers, projects involved,
which will set forth the nature and amounts of the
contributions to be made by the Government of the
United States and the Government of Italy, the description and purpose of the facilities to be established,
and other appropriate details. Such arrangements may
include provisions for the procurement of equipment
to be furnished by the United States Government from
the Government of Italy under the offshore procurement
program, and the transfer of such equipment to the
Government of Italy in accordance with the provisions
of the Mutual Defense Assistance Agreement.

0066

<u>MUTUAL DEFENSE ASSISTANCE</u>

AGREEMENT AMENDING THE AGREEMENT OF JANUARY 30 AND
FEBRUARY 9, 1951. Effected by exchange of notes
signed at Taipei-Cetecer 23 and Nov 1, 1952; entered
to force Nov. 1, 1952.

3. The Government of the Republic of China
agrees to furnish free of charge and without present
or future liability to the Government of the United A.
States or individual members of the MAAG, use of all
lands, buildings, services, personnel, utilities,
communication services, and vehicles which are to be
determined or have been dtermined or have been
determined by mutual agreement to be necessary and
reasonable for the efficient operation of the MAAG,
and which are incident to the official functions of
the MAAG or its member. Without prejudice to the mutual
agreement referred to in the preceding sentence, the
facilities to be extended to MAAG under the present
agreement shall include the use of lands and buildings
 for office space, motor pools and storage areas;
necessary transport facilities to permit the free
ingrese and egress of official aircraft and naval vessels,
and the use without charge of air strips, air fields,
roads, ports and railroads by official aircraft, naval
vessels and or official vehicles, as well as the exemption
from payment of handling and stevedoring charges concerning goods and carges destined for MAAG or for the
members of MAAG; military vehicles necessary to supplement US vehicles for the official use of MAAG personnel;
utilities inclusing heat, light, water and telephones;
personnel such as aborers interpreters and trans-

0067

lators, custodial personnel, drivers and mechanics.

6. Claims for compehsation for damages arising from acts of military members of MAAG shall be settled by agreement between the appropriate authorities of the Government of the Republic of China and the Government of the United States of America. In event that no such agreement is reached, settlement shall be made through diplomatic channels.

7. Immediately upon the signing of this agreement, a joint committee composed of representatives of the Government of the Republic of China and of the United States will be established to aid and will consist of six members, three apointed by each Government. Two of the United States representatives will be members of MAAG. At its first meeting after establishment the committee will elect its chairman from among the appointed members of the committee, will proceed to the consideration of such agenda. After the first meeting the committee will meet weekly at the call of the chairman.

0068

AGREEMENT BETWEEN THE PARTIES TO THE NORTH ATLANTIC
TREATY REGARDING THE STATUS OF THEIR FORCES

APTICLE VIII

2. - (a) In the case of damage caused or arising as stated in paragraph 1 to other property owned
by a Contracting Party and located in its territory,
the issue of the liability of any other Contracting
Party shall be determined and the amount of damage
shall be assessed, unless the Contracting Parties
concerned agree otherwise, by a sole arbitrator
selected in accordance with sub-paragraph (b) of
this paragraph. The arbitrator-shall also decide
any counter-claims arising out of the same incident.

(f) Nevertheless, each Contracting Party
waives its claim in any such case where the damage is
less than: -

Belgium:	B.fr. 70,000.	Lusembourge	: L.fr. 70,000.
Canada :	$1.460.	Netherlands	: Fl. 5,320
Denmark:	Kr. 9,670	Norway	: Kr. 10,000.
France :	F.fr. 490,000.	Portugal	: Es. 40,250.
Iceland:	Kr. 22,800.	United Kingdom	: Ł 500.
Italy :	Li. 850,000.	United States	: $1,400.

Any other Contracting Party whose property has been
damaged in the same incident shall also waive its claim
up to the above amount. In the case of considerable
variation in the rates of exchange between these cur-
rencies the Contracting Parties shall agree on the
appropriate adjustments of these amounts.

한·미국 간의 상호방위조약 제4조에 의한 시설과 구역 및 한국에서의 미국군대의 지위에 관한 협정(SOFA)
전59권. 1966.7.9 서울에서 서명 : 1967.2.9 발효(조약 232호) (V.5 체결 교섭, 1959)   75

일본국과 아메리카합중국 사이의 상호협력과 안전보장
조약 제 6 조에 기한 시설, 구역 및 일본국에 있어서의
합중국 군대의 지위에 관한 협정 (毎日新聞 一月一日字)

過去文書로 一般文書로 再分類

전문 : (현행협정의 전문을 없애고 대신 상호협력과 안전보장조약 제 6 조를 인용해서 협정체결의 취지를 명백히 함)

제 1 조 : (합중국 군대의 구성원, 군속, 가족의 정의)

현행과 같음

제 2 조 : (시설 및 구역의 사용과 공동사용)

현행협정 제 2 조와 비교하면 조문상으로는 다소 변경되었으나 실질적으로 큰 변화는 없다. 제 1 항은 (A) (B)의 두 항으로 나누어 짐. (A)항에서는 현행협정에 있는 "이 협정의 효력발생일 까지 아직 양 정부가 합의에 도달하지 못한 때"를 삭제 함. "오까자끼" "러스크" 교환공문이 신 협정발효와 동시에 효력을 상실함으로 동 교환공문에 기한 "양국의 합의에 달하지 못한" 기지사용은 없어지게 되었기 때문이다. 이 새로운 제 2 조에서는 협정발효시에 사용하고 있는 기지는 이미 양정부의 정식 합의를 얻은것으로 되어 있다.

제 2 항 및 제 3 항은 현행과 거이 동문. 제 4 항 (미일 공동사용)은, 현행 제 4 항의 "사격장 및 연습장과 같은"을 삭제하고 그 대상의 범위를 확장함. 또한 공동 또는 임시사용의 경우, 합동위원회의 결정을 얻는 형식을 취할것을 명백히 함.

제 3 조 : (기지관리권)

현행 제 3 조의 1 의 "기지관리권의 절대성"의 인상을 준 조면은 다소 완화 됨. 기지에 관해서는, 현행조문에 있는 "권리, 권력 및 권능을 가진다를"필요한 모든 조치를 취한다" 하고 되었다. 또한 기지에 관한 " 범위 또는 관계되는 "경로 또는 관계 "로 개정 됨.

0070

제 1 당의 기지주변에의 광대권의 명사에 대해서는, 일본정부를 용어여,그의 암예다에서 명사되겠금 다쇼 표연이 왕료 되었다.

제 2 당은 연행 제 1 - 성한 거의 동임어나, 연답대 2 당의 최우의 부분(전기, 전자점시의 발해예망을 여운 입시런 표시)을 삭제다고, II이 예냥에 관다여 일본점부와 협의다여 일본점무는 이의 선처를 약속안때마는 취지가 규여겼다.

제 4 교 : (시섬 및 구역의 반환과 이어 따균 보상법 뷰구표시)
  연덤과 감음.

제 5 교 : (답명국관대다의 선박, 남공기 등의 춤입국)
  제 1 당은 연뎅과 감음. 제 2 당(선박, 남공기, 사냥, 군인, 군속, 가족의 국내이동)는 연뎅과 거이 감으나, 도또사용로구정 둥이 추가되었다. 제 3 당은 연뎅과 감음.

제 6 교 : (답금고용관여 및 통신)
  연형과 감음.

제 7 교 : (옹신 등의 공익사업이용권)
  연뎅과 감음.

제 8 교 : (기상업무)
  연뎅 제 8 교와 동문이나, 연뎅(A)의 괄호내의 (X 및 T)를 삭제다고 연뎅(B)의 비동암기상예비용 II 기상접II으로 고침.

제 9 교 : (군인, 군속 및 그 그족의 춤입국)
  1, 2, 4, 6앙은 연뎅과 감음. 제 3 앙(군인의 춤입국) 은 연뎅과 거이 감으나, II임본점부 당국의 요청이 있는 때에는 답공국 군때의 구성원은 언제든지, 그가 유때어는 신분증명서를 쩌시어지 않으면 안됨 대고, 쩌시의무를 명무더한 신1앙이 부가되었다. 이외에, 제 6 앙이 신섭되었다. 이 앙은 II임본국이 군때의 구성원 또는 군속의 자국어 영역으로 부어 송훈을 요청다고, 또한 군때의 구성원, 군속, 및 가족에 대여여 회겨명명을 내년 겅우에는,

한·미국 간의 상호방위조약 제4조에 의한 시설과 구역 및 한국에서의 미국군대의 지위에 관한 협정(SOFA) 전59권. 1966.7.9 서울에서 서명 : 1967.2.9 발효(조약 232호) (V.5 체결 교섭, 1959)

합중국정부는 이들을 자국의 영역내에 받아 들이고, 기타 일본국의 외국에 송출하는데 대하여 책임을 진다"라는 취지를 명기했다.

제 10 조 ; (운전면허 및 차량표지)

현행과 같음.

제 11 조 ; (관세)

북대서양조약기구의 일반협정과 "본"협정과 같이 개정되었다. 현행 제 11 조와 비교해서 특히 달라진 점은 다음의 3 가지 점이다.

(1) 합중국군대의 입국의 경우에는 세관검사를 받지 않는 것이 현행조항의 규정이었으나, 개인으로서 입국하는 경우에는 세관검사를 받도록 되었다.

(2) 현행조항에서는 미군용우편의 우편물은 세관검사를 받지 않는 것으로 되어 있으나, 신조항에서는 군용우편이라도 사용(私用)우편물은 검사를 받는다.

(3) 종래 검사를 받지 않든 미군의 군용화물 중에, 사용품만은 세관검사를 받도록 되었다.

제 12 조 ; (조달)

특히 노무관계에 대하여서는 실질적으로 변화 했다. 중요한 개정은 다음의 3 가지 점이다.

(1) 노무 및 납품 그리고 공사계약의 조달은 원칙적으로 직접조달방식으로 한다. 따라서 현행 제 1 항에 "이러한 납품 및 공사계약에 관해서는, 양국정부의 합의에 의해서, 일본정부를 통하여 조달할수 있다"라고 추가 되었다.

(2) 현행협정 제 16 조에 의해서, 합중국군 당국의 직용노무자(直用勞務者)(PX 등)도 간접고용노무자로 전환 됨.

(3) 보안해고에 의한 피해고자가 재판소의 부당노동행위의 판결에서 승소한 경우에는, 미국측은 이들을 재고용하지 않도록, "양국정부의 합의하는 기간"(NATO 와 같이 1 년간, 단 이것은 협정에 명문화 하지 않고, 의사록에 확인 됨)에 상당한

0072

임금은 지불되도록 됨.

제 13 조 : (과세)

국연군 법령과 관련하여 약간의 자구의 수정은 있으나,
실질적으로는 현행과 변동이 없다.

제 14 조 : (특수계약자)

현행협정의 점에 실질적으로 크게 변화 됨. 제 1 항은 현행
제 1 항과 같음. 제 2 항은 신설됨. 이 항에서는 특수계약자를
지정하는 경우, 미국 혹은 일본정부와 협의하여 결정하도록 되어있는
이외에 이 업자가 (1) 계약사업을 종료한 경우 (2) 제 14 조
이외의 사업에 종사한 경우 (3) 일본국 법령에 위반한 부정
행위를 행한 경우에는 그의 자격에서 생기는 우전은 면책된다는
것을 명기함.

제 15 조 : (PX   등 및 식당 등 세율의 차금에 대한 제 기관)

제 4 항을 제외하고는 현행과 같음. 제 4 항은 새로이
지방자연세 등의 납부의무를 부가하여 규정하고 있다.

제 16 조 : (법령존중의무)

현행과 같음.

제 17 조 : (형사재판권)

1963 년 9 월 29 일 동경에서 서명된 현행협정 제 17 조
개정의정서에 있는 제 17 조에 거의 그대로 신협정의 제 17 조가
됨. 이 의정서와 다른 점은 다음의 2 가지 점이다.

(1) 제 11 항에 II이 협정의 제 24 조가 적용되는 현대영어가
일어난 경우에는 규정이 있으나 제 24 조가 삭제되므로 이 근거
법규를 개정함. 신 조약 제 4 조의 현대영어가 일어난 경우 우고 됨.

(2) 새로이 제 12 항이 신의되어 검과규정을 명시 i 함.

제 18 조 : (민사청구권)

전반적으로 개정되어 실질적으로나 체재상으로나 북대서양
조약과 같은 우임한 조항이다. 즉 북대서양조약 일반협정의

0073

제 8 조는 그대로 신 협정 제 18 조에의 제 1 항으로부터 제 10 항
이 되고 있다. 연맹 제 18 조에 비교해서 육이 변경된 점은 다음의
3 가지 점이다.

(1) 연맹에서는, 합동국군대와 일반 접수산하의 공무집행 중에 일어
난 손해, 부상 및 사망에 관한 보상청구권은 상호간에 받기마로 있다.
이것을 신 협정에서는 "합동국군대와 지위대(구담사자의 방위대)다는
호연기사이에 삼으 받기다가기로 됨.

(2) 중재인 제도를 새로이 설정. 중재인은 1 인으로서 "양당사자의
합의에 따라여, 사법관계의 상급의 지위를 가지거나, 또는 가편
임이 있는 일본국민 중에서 선정한데(본고 2항 B)고 되어 있다.
또으 "중재인이 명한 여다한 재점도 구당사자에 대하여 구속력을
가지는 최종적인 것으로 한데고 규정됨.

또한 신협정 제 18 조- 8 당에서는 "합동국 군대의 구성원 피용자,
군속 및 일본국의 방위대의 구성원, 피용자의 불법행더 또는 부작위
가 공무집권 중에 행아여졌느냐의 여부, 또한 어느 임방의 당사자의
방위대의 차량이 허가 없이 사용되었느냐의 여부에 관하여 분쟁이
일어난 경우에는 본고 2 B 에 의하여 임명된 중재인에 부와다기로
다며, 이 점에 관한 중재인의 검정은 최종적이며 검정적인 것으로 한데
고 규정하여 중요한 편만을 부여다로 있다.

(3) 연맹 제 18 조 중 전편으로 삭제된 부분은 제 1 당 및 제 4 당의
전부와 제 3 당의 A 의 "청구가 있은 날로부터 1 년이내에 제기다는
것으로되의 3 가지 점이다. 다른 부분은 구구 신협점제 18 조에
잔입되고 있다. 이외에 북매서임으약의 일반협점 제 18 조 이외에
다음의 3 가지 점이 부가되어 있음.

(1)제 11 당, 본고에 있어서 사용된 "방위대"의 용어는, 일본국내에
있어서는 자위대, 합동국에 있어서는 군대를 의미한다.

(2) 제 12당, 본고 2 및 5 는 연맹에 의한 손해에대하여서는 적용
되지 않는다.

0074

(3)제 18 항, (경과규정 약관)

제 19 조, (수입 관세)

제 20 조, (군표)

제 21 조, (군 사우 편국)   모두 연령과 같음

제 22 조, (역내위은면)

　　　모연을 말학했음. 미국측이 임은검사에 신청다고 동의를 얻어
운남 1것급 개정됨.

제 23 조, (재산의 안전보장)

　　　연령과 같음.

제 24 조, (방어지출금)

　　　연령제 25조에 대답하는 것으로, 방어분담금조 말반을 삭제함.

제 25 조, (합동위면의)

　　　제 1 항에 약간의 자구소점이 있음 박 연령 제 26 조와
같음.

제 26 조, (방호조망)

　　　연령 제 27 조와 비도대서, 경과구정을 명확히 다 그 항이
보가되고 그외 약간의 자구의수정이 있으나, 실질적으로는 연령과
다답이 없음.

제 27 조, (개정절차)

　　　연령 제 28 와 같음.

제 28 조, (으벽기간)

　　　연비 제 29 조와

0075

한·미국 간의 상호방위조약 제4조에 의한 시설과 구역 및 한국에서의 미국군대의 지위에 관한 협정(SOFA)
전59권. 1966.7.9 서울에서 서명 : 1967.2.9 발효(조약 232호) (V.5 체결 교섭, 1959)

81

COMPARATIVE DESCRIPTION OF SUBSTANTIVE PROVISIONS
IN
INTERNATIONAL AGREEMENTS REGARDING FACILITIES AND AREAS

	The Objects	Method to Obtain The Objects	US Liability to: Rent For Private or Public Property	Damage To Property	Injury or Death	Time of Return	US Obligation relating to Restoration of Property upon return
::							
1955 ROK Draft	Facilities and Areas necessary to carry out the mission and purpose of the United Nations	Through agreement in Joint Committee composed of one representative of each party	To be agreed in Joint Committee. No specific provision is given in the Draft (Art. X)	Yes	Yes	By agreement or when facilities or areas are no longer needed	No obligation but sympathetic consideration shall be given on private property
Present Draft	Same as above but facilities and areas located in front line area are excluded	Same as above	Yes	Yes	Yes	Same as above	US will give proper or due consideration instead of sympathetic.
Jap-US Administrative Agreement	Facilities and Areas necessary for the purpose of Security Treaty	Same as above	To be agreed in Joint Committee. No specific provision is given in the Agreement.	Yes	Yes	When Facilities or areas are no longer needed	No obligation
Philip-US Base Agreement	Bases listed in Annex A. Bases listed in B subject to agreement. Other bases subject to agreement.	-	Yes	Yes	Yes	99 Years	-
Iceland-US Defense Agreement	Facilities as mutually agreed to be necessary	-	No	-	-	Upon 12 months' notification	-
Netherlands-US Defense Agreement	Areas and utilities including access road as agreed to be necessary	-	No	-	-	Upon termination of NATO Treaty or by Agreement between parties	-
US-UK Agreement on Bahama Long Range Proving Ground	Sites for the operation of the Flight Testing Range	UK will provide the Site after consultation with USA	Yes	Yes	Yes	When the Site is no longer needed	-
Germany-US-UK-France Convention on Rights and Obligations	Accommodation, Transportation, Communication, Other public services	Requirement for accommodation shall be presented to German authorities. When requirement is agreed by Germany and Forces concerned, it shall be carried out by German authorities	-	-	-	-	-

	a lve of each party			longer needed	s _ e given on private property
Present Draft Same as above but facilities and areas located in front line area are excluded	Same as above	Yes	Yes	Same as above	US will give proper or due consideration instead of sympathetic.
Jap-US Administrative Agreement Facilities and Areas necessary for the purpose of Security Treaty	Same as above	To be agreed in Joint Committee. No specific provision is given in the agreement.		When Facilities or areas are no longer needed	No obligation
Philip-US Base Agreement Bases listed in Annex A. Bases listed in B subject to agreement. Other bases subject to agreement.	-	Yes	Yes	99 Years	-
Iceland-US Defense Agreement Facilities as mutually agreed to be necessary	-	No	-	Upon 12 months' notification	-
Netherlands-US Defense Agreement Areas and utilities including access road as agreed to be necessary	-	No	-	Upon termination of NATO Treaty or by Agreement between parties	-
US-UK Agreement on Bahama Long Range Proving Ground Sites for the operation of the Flight Testing Range	UK will provide the Site after consultation with USA	Yes	Yes	When the Site is no longer needed	-
Germany-US-UK-France Convention on Rights and Obligations Accomodation, Transportation, Communication, Other public services	Requirement for accomodation shall be presented to German authorities. When requirement is agreed by Germany and Forces concerned, it shall be carried out by German authorities	-	-	-	-
Austria-US (Payment of Occupation Cost) Real estate Utilities Services Supplies	-	Yes	-	-	-

0077

Comparative Tables

0078

Revised Draft US-Japan Administrative Agreement	US-Japan Administrative Agreement

Article II

(Use of Facilities and areas by American forces in Japan)

1. (a) Japan, based on Article 6 of the Security Treaty, agrees to grant to the United States the use of facilities and areas in Japan. Agreement as to specific facilities and areas, shall be concluded by the two Governments through the Joint Committee provided for in Article XXVI of this Agreement. "Facilities and areas" include existing furnishings, equipment and fixtures necessary to the operation of such facilities and areas.
(b) The Facilities and areas which have been used by the United States at the time of the termination of the Administrative Agreement based on Article III of the Security Treaty will be the facilities and areas agreed upon by the two Governments based on (a).

3. The facilities and areas used by the United States armed forces shall be returned to Japan whenever they are no longer needed

1. Japan agrees to grant to the United States the use of the facilities and areas necessary to carry out the purposes states in Article I of the Security Treaty. Agreements as to specific facilities and areas, not already reached by the two Governments by the effective date of this agreement, shall be concluded by the two Governments through the Joint Committee provided for in Article XXVI of this Agreement. "Facilities and areas" include existing furnishings, equipment and fixtures necessary to the operation of such facilities and areas.

3. The facilities and areas used by the United States armed forces shall be returned to Japan whenever they are

0079

- 2 -

for the purposes of this Agreement and the United States agrees to continually consider the necessity of facilities and areas .... (No Revision ?)

4. (a) When facilities and areas are temporarily not being used by the American armed forces, interim use may be made by the Japanese Government or they may be allowed to be used by Japanese nationals provided that the two Governments agree through the Joint Committee that such use would not be harmful to the purpose for which the facilities and areas are normally used by the United States armed forces.

(b) With respect to such facilities and areas which are to be used by the United States armed forces for limited periods of time, the Joint Committee shall specify in the agreements covering such facilities and areas the extent to which the provisions of this Agreement shall apply.

Article III
(Use of facilities and areas,)

1. The United States shall have the right to carry out any measures within the

---

no longer needed for the purposes of this Agreement, and the United States agrees to keep the needs for facilities and areas ....

4. (a) When facilities and areas such as target ranges and maneuver grounds are temporarily not being used by the United States armed forces, interim use may be made by Japanese authorities and nationals provided that it is agreed that such use would not be harmful to the purposes for which the facilities and areas are normally used by the United States armed forces.

(b) With respect to such facilities and areas as target ranges and maneuver grounds which are to be used by the United States armed forces for limited periods of time, the Joint Committee shall specify in the agreements covering such facilities and areas the extent to which the provisions of this Agreement shall apply.

Article III

1. The United States shall have the rights, power and authority within

0080

the facilities and areas which are necessary or appropriate for their establishment, use, operation, defense or control. The United States shall also have such rights, power and authority over land, territorial waters and airspace adjacent to, or in the vicinities of such facilities and areas, as are necessary to provide access to such facilities and areas for their support, defense and control. In the exercise outside the facilities and areas of the rights, power and authority granted in this article, there should be, as the occasion requires, consultation between the two Governments through the Joint Committee.

2. The United States agrees that the above-mentioned rights, power and authority will not be exercised in such a manner as to interfere unnecessarily with navigation, aviation, communication, or land travel to or from or within the territories of Japan. All question relating to frequencies, power and like matters used by apparatus employed by the United States designed to emit electric radiation shall be settled by mutual arrangement. As a temporary measure the United States armed forces

facilities and areas which are necessary for their establishment, operation, defense or control. When the Japanese Government is requested by the American armed forces to provide more convenient access to such facilities and areas for their support, defense and control, the Japanese Government will take necessary measures to satisfy such a request within the bounds of related domestic laws concerning land, territorial waters and airspace adjacent to, or in the vicinities of such facilities and areas after consultations between the two Governments through the Joint Committee.

The United States shal also have the right to carry out necessary measures for the fulfillment of the abovementioned objectives after consultations between the two Governments through the Joint Committee.

2. The United States agrees that the abovementioned measures stipulated in (1) will not be carried out in such a manner as to interfere unnecessarily with navigation, aviation, communications; or land travel to or from or within the territories of Japan. All questions relating to frequencies, power and like matters used by apparatus employed by the United States designed to emit electrical waves shall be settled by mutual arrangement. The Japanese Government will take rational measures within

0081

the bounds of related domestic laws that will prevent or eliminate any interference to electronic communications devices which are necessary to the American armed forces.

Article IX
(Entry and exit)

1. The United States shall have the right to bring into Japan members of the United States armed forces, the civilian components, and their dependents under condition that they adhere to the provisions mentioned in this article.

6. In case the Japanese Government requests the expulsion from Japanese territories of members of the American armed forces and civilian components, or issues expulsion orders to former members of the American armed forces, former civilian components or the dependents of members of the American armed forces, civilian components, former members of the American armed forces and former civilian components, the United States authorities will have the responsibility to receive such persons in its territories as well as to see that they are transported out from Japan.

shall be entitled to use, without radiation interference from Japanese sources, electronic devices of such power, design, type of emission, and frequencies as are reserved for such forces at the time this Agreement become effective.

Article IX

1. The United States shall have the right to bring into Japan for purposes of this Agreement persons who are members of the United States armed forces, the civilian component, and their dependents.

0082

Article XI
(Customs and customs clearance)

5. Customs examination shall not be made in the following cases;

   (a) Units and members of the United States armed forces entering or leaving Japan under orders.

   (b) Official documents under official seal and mail in United States postal channels.

   (c) Military cargo shipped on a United States Government bill of landing.

Article XII
(Procurement)

4. Local labor requirements of the United States armed forces or the various organs stipulated under Article XV shall be met with the assistance of the Japanese authorities.

6. When Japanese courts pass judgments to the effect that employment contracts had not been terminated by the issuance of notices ending employment the Japanese and American authorities shall consult with each other to protect workers from dismissals. In case the consulatations

Article XI

5. Customs examination shall not be made in the following cases;

   (a) Units and members of the United States armed forces under orders entering or leaving Japan.

   (b) Official documents under official seal;

   (c) Mail in United States military postal channels and military cargo shipped on a United States Government bill of landing.

Article XII

4. Local labor requirements of the United States armed forces or civilian com- ponent shall be satisfied with the assistance of the Japanese authorities.

6. Members of the civilian components shall not be subject to Japanese laws or regulations with respect to terms and conditions of employment.

0083

do not succeed and continued employment is not carried out, the American Government shall bear the burden of the Japanese Government for a certain period of time.

Article XIV
(Specific contractors.)

2. The designation mentioned in (1) shall be made after consultation with the Japanese Government except in case it is impossible to hold competitive biddings due to reasons stemming from security cosiderations, technological qualification of the concerned administrations, the lack of material, machinery or service which do not come up to American standards, or from American defense restrictions.

The abovementioned designation shall be cancelled by the United States Government in the following cases:

(a) When contracts concluded with the United States for the American armed forces terminate.

(b) When it is proved that persons who are working in Japan for the American armed forces or affiliated enterprises, are also engaged in business activities other than those related to the American armed forces.

(c) When such persons are found to be engaging in illegal activities under Japanese laws.

0084

Article XVIII
(Waiving of claims.)

1. Each party shall waive all its claims against the other over any damage to properties that are owned by each country and used by ground, maritime or air-defense force of each country, in the following cases:

(a) In case the damage was caused by a member or employee of the defense forces of the other country in the performance of his official duty.

(b) In case the damage has been sustained by vehicles, vessels or aircraft owned by the other party during use by its defense forces in the performance of official duties.

Both parties shall mutually waive their claims over salvage operations, provided that the rescued vessel or cargo are owned by the other party and used by its defense forces during performance of official duties.

2. (a) The evaluation of the damage sustained in Japan under the circumstances mentioned in (1) by properties of either country, other than those mentioned above, shall be made by a mediator selected in accordance with (6) unless the two Governments otherwise agree upon.

Article XVIII

1. Each party waives all its claims against the other party for injury or death suffered in Japan by a member of its armed forces, or a civilian governmental employee, while such member or employee was engaged in the performance of his official duties in cases where such injury or death was caused by a member of the armed forces, or a civilian employee of the other party acting in the performance of his official duties.

2. Each party waives all its claims against the other party for damage to any property in Japan owned by it, if such damage was caused by a member of the armed forces or a civilian governmental employee of the other party in the performance of his official duties.

0085

official duties.

The mediator, in this case, shall locate the responsibility for the damage, estimate its value and also, examine the counterclaims arising from the same case.

(b) The mediator mentioned in (a) shall be selected by agreement of both governments from among Japanese citizens who have held in the past, or hold at present, high judiciary positions.

(c) The decision of the mediator shall be ultimately binding to both parties.

(d) The amount of compensation determined by the mediator shall be shared in accordance with provisions (i), (ii) and (iii) under (e), Section (5).

(e) The amount of compensation to be paid to the mediator shall be agreed upon between the two Governments and the compensation, together with expenses necessary for the mediator to discharge his duties, shall be paid by the two Governments at an equal ratio.

(f) However, the parties shall waive their claims whenever the amount does not exceed U.S. $1,400, or ₩504,000. In the event of large fluctuations in the exchange rates between the two currencies, both Governments shall make adjustments, by agreement, to the above-mentioned amounts.

3. In applying the provisions 1 and 2 to vessels "owned by the parties," they shall include vessels stripchartered, strip-requisitioned and seized by the nations concerned.

3. Claims, other than contractual, arising out of acts or omissions of members of, or employees of the United States armed forces in the performance of official duty or out of any other act, omission or occurrence for which the United States armed forces is legally responsible, arising incident to non-combat activities and causing injury, death, or property damage in Japan to third parties shall be dealt with by Japan in accordance with the following provisions:

(a) Claims shall be filed within one year from the date on which they arise and shall be considered and settled or adjudicated in accordance with the laws and regulations of Japan with respect to claims arising from the activities of its own employees.

(b) Japan may settle any such claims, and payment of the amount agreed upon or determined by adjudication shall be made by Japan in Yen.

(c) Such payment, whether made pursuant to a settlement or to adjudication of the case by a competent tribunal of Japan, or the final adjudication by such a tribunal denying payment, shall be binding and conclusive.

(d) The cost incurred in satisfying claims pursuant to the preceding subparagraphs shall be shared on terms to be agreed by the two Governments.

0087

(e) In accordance with procedures to be established, a statement of all claims approved or disapproved by Japan pursuant to this paragraph, together with the findings in each case, and a statement of the sums paid by Japan, shall be sent to the United States periodically, with a request for reimbursement of the share to be paid by the United States. Such reimbursement shall be made within the shortest possible time in Yen.

4. Each party shall have the primary right, in the execution of the foregoing paragraphs, to determine whether its personnel were engaged in the performance of official duty. Such determination shall be made as soon as possible after the arising of the claim concerned. When the other party disagrees with the results of such determination, that party may bring the matter before the Joint Committee for consultation under the provisions of article XXVI of this Agreement.

5. Claims against members of or employees of the United States armed forces arising out of tortious acts or omissions in Japan not done in the performance of official duty shall be dealt with in the following manner:

4. Each party shall waive all claims to the other party with regard to injuries and deaths caused to members of its defense forces during their execution of official duties.

5. As regards claims (excluding those those subject to contracts and provisions under 6 and 7) arising from damages caused in Japan to a third person other than the Japanese Government as a result of intentional or unintentional accidnets caused during performance of duties by members or employes of the U.S. military forces or other intentional or unintentional accidents for which the U.S. armed forces are legally

0088

responsible, Japan shall dispose of them according to the following provisions.

(a) The claims shall be instituted, examined and settled or referred to court pursuant to Japanese laws and regulations concerning claims arising from acts of the Japanese Self-Defense Forces.

(b) Japan shall be able to settle any of the claim mentioned above, and the amount agreed upon or decided upon by judgment shall be paid in Japanese Yen.

(c) The judgment by an authorized Japanese court regarding payment (whether according to settlement by agreement or by judgment of an authorized Japanese court) or nonpayment shall be ultimately binding to both parties.

(a) The Japanese authorities shall consider the claim and assess compensation to the claimant in fair and just manner, taking into account all circumstances of the case, including the conduct of the injured person, and shall prepare a report on the matter.

(b) The report shall be delivered to the United States authorities, who shall then decide without delay whether they will offer an ex gratia payment, and if so, of what amount.

(c) If an offer of ex gratia payment is made, and accepted by the claimant in full satisfaction of his claim, the payment themselves and inform the Japanese authorities of their decision and of the sum paid.

(d) Nothing in this paragraph shall affect the jurisdiction of the Japanese courts to entertain an action against a member or employee of the United States armed forces, unless and until there has been payment in full satisfaction of the claim.

8. In case it is not clear whether any intentional or unintentional acts by a member of the U.S. Security Forces or their civilian component was done

in the performance of his official duty
or not, or whether a vehicle involved in
the accident was one authorized by the
U.S. Security Forces or not, the decision
shall be made by the mediator to be
chosen on the basis of the Section 2 (b)
The decision to be made by the chosen
mediator shall be final.

9. (a) The U.S. shall not request exemption
of a member of the U.S. Security Forces
or their civilian component from the right
of trail by a Japanese court with the exception
of cases stipulated in 5 (f).

(b) The U.S. shall seize private movable
property (excepting movable property used
by the U.S. Security Forces) located within
the facilities and areas used by the U.S.
Security Forces at the request of Japanese
court in case such property must be seized
under the Japanese laws and hand it over to
the Japanese Government.

(c) The U.S. and Japanese Government authorities
shall cooperate in gathering evidences in
order to commit a claim under this article to
a fair trial and disposal.

Article XXII
(Enlistment of U.S. citizens into reserve
list.)

The U.S. Government can enlist eligible
American citizens in Japan applying for

Article XXII

The United States shall have the
right to enroll and train all eligible

0090

admission into the U.S. armed forces'
reserve organizations and train them
again.

Article XXIV
(Expenses for maintaining U.S. Security
Forces.)

(b) Stipulations for the joint defense
cost have been eliminated.

The current provisions for defense
consultations in Article XXIV have been
eliminated.

United States citizens, residing in
Japan, in the reserve organizations
of the armed forces of the United
States, except that the prior consent
of the Japanese Government shall be
obtained in the case of persons
employed by the Japanese Government.

Article XXV

2. It is agreed that Japan will:

(b) Make available without cost to
the United States, until the effective
date of any new arrangement reached
as a result of periodic reexamination,
an amount of Japanese currency equivalent
to $155 million per annum for the
purpose of procurement by the United
States of transportation and other
requisite services and supplies in Japan.
The rate of exchange at which Yen
payments will be credited shall be the
official per value, or that rate
considered most favorable by the United
States which on the day of payment is
available to any party, authorized by
the Japanese Government or used in any
transaction with any party by the
Japanese Government or its agencies or
by Japanese banks authorized to deal in
foreign exchange, and whichm if both
countries have agreed per-values with
the International Monetary Fund, is not
prohibited by the articles of Agreement
of the Fund.

0091

조 약 조 사 자 료 — *19*

단기 4292 년 4 월 27일

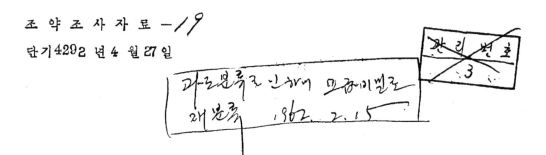

과.-로.문류로 인하여 ... ...

...   1962. 2. 15

제 명 : 주한 미국 주둔군이 사용하는 토지, 건물 및 시설에
         관한 한미간의 협정안의 검토

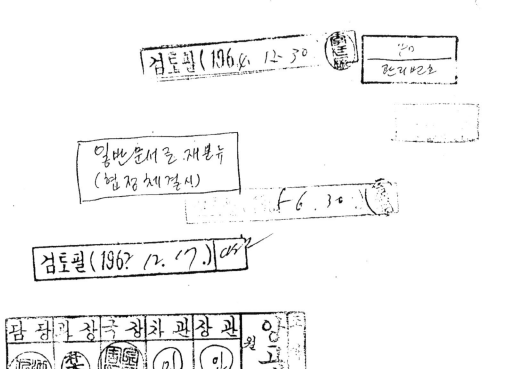

검토필(196 . 12. 30)

일반문서로 재분류
(협정 체결시)

검토필(196? 12. 7.)

외 무 부 정 무 국

0092

주한 미국 주둔군이 사용하는 토지 건물 및
시설에 관한 한미간의 협정 체결을 위한
검토

목   차

0093

10. Agreement relating to the facilties assistance between Italy and USA
11. Mutual Defense Assistance agreement between China and USA
12. Agreement between the parties to the NATO regarding the status of their forces
13. Agreement relating to the principles applying to the provision of aid in the prosecution of the War between Australia and USA
14. Agreement regarding settlement for war accounts and claims between Austria and and USA
15. Agreement relating to the payment of occupation costs between Austria and USA
16. Agreement regarding construction of military installation and facilities in China between China and USA
17. Defense agreement between Iceland and USA
18. Agreement relating to a special program of facilities assistance between Italy and USA
19. Agreement relating to the settlement of costs for claims arising under Article 18 of the administrative agreement between the Japan and USA
20. US-Netherlands agreement relating to stationing of US forces
21. UK-USA agreements on the lease of bases

0094

1. 서 론

주한 미국군이 사용하는 토지, 건물 및 시설에 관한 한미간의 협정안은 이미 1955년에 우리정부에서 미국측에 정식으로 제의한 "주둔군 지위에 관한 한미간의 협정안"에도 포함되어 있으나 전기 1955년 초안과 같은 전면적 협정의 체결이 지연되고 있는 현단계에서는 우선 부분적으로 시급한 문제부터라도 하나하나 독립시켜 우선적으로 해결하여 주둔군의 법적지위를 규제하여야 하고 이러한 입장에서 개별협정을 체결한다면 우선 주둔군이 사용하고 있는 토지, 건물 및 시설에 관한 전기 1955년 초안의 관계조항을 토대로 하여 이를 구체적으로 협정화하는 것이 시급하다. 따라서 본 협정의 초안에 있어서는 가급적으로 전기 1955년도 초안의 관계조항을 독립시키되 그에 대한 수정을 피하고, 단지 초의 구체적인 내용을 포괄적으로 규정함을 원칙으로 합이 타당하다고 생각된다. 즉 이 협정은 전면협정에서 구체적으로 표현되지 않은 부분을 부연하여 독립협정으로 할수 있게 하는데 그 목적이 있다. 전기 1955년 초안에서 구체적인 표현이 되지 못한 부분을 크게 구분하면, 첫째로 협정의 대상물에 관하여 어디에 있는 무엇을 사용케하느냐? 하는점과, 둘째로 이러한 사용에 대한 경제적대가는 어떻게 지불되는가? 하는 점과, 셋째로 이러한 경제적대가는 대물 및 대인피해에 대한 적용에 있어서 무엇을 기준으로 하는가? 하는 것이라고 할수 있겠다.

제2차 세계대전 이후 집단안전보장체제의 구상하에 미국은 세계 우방국가내에 군대나 또는 군사기지를 광범하게 배치하고 있고 이러한 배치에 따라 주둔군 및 기지에 관한 많은 협정을 체결하고 있으나 대부분의 경우에 있어서 우리나라에 대한 주둔과는 달리 특정적역만의 사용을 규제하고 있는 점에서 한미간의 협정안과는 그 체결배경 내지 입장을 달리하여 결국 사용을 허

한·미국 간의 상호방위조약 제4조에 의한 시설과 구역 및 한국에서의 미국군대의 지위에 관한 협정(SOFA)
전59권. 1966.7.9 서울에서 서명 : 1967.2.9 발효(조약 232호) (V.5 체결 교섭, 1959) **101**

가함에 있어서 일률적으로 어떠한 조건을 규정하고 있다고 할 수 없는 것이 특색이다. 미국 주둔군의 사용토지, 시설, 및 건물이 비교적 광범하다는 점에 있어서는 한미간의 입장은 미일협정의 입장과 대소 같다고 할수 있으나 이것 역시 다음과 같은 점에 있어서 상이한바 있다.

1). <u>정치적면에 있어서 보면</u>, 미국은 한국에 대하여 독립 초기로 부터 계속하여 국내적안정을 도모하기 위하여 한국정부에 대하여는 호의적인 고려를 하여왔고 또. 일본은 미국의 점령하에 있었든 반면 미국은 한국의 독립을 물심양면에서 적극적으로 협조하였을 뿐 아니라 국민의 사유재산을 보호하여야 하는 정부의 보상대책에 대하여 어떤 나라보다도 물질적 원조를 공여하여야 할 입장에 있으며,

2) <u>군사적면에서 보면</u>, 미국은 일본에서는 전략적인 고려만 하면 되는 반면에 한국에서는 전략적 인 고려 이외에 전술적인 고려까지 하여야 한다는 점인바 이는 환언하면, 한국에 있어서는 미국군의 토지, 건물 및 시설에 대한 선택권이 일본에서 보다 중요시된다는 것이다. 즉 한국은 작전지역한기 때문에 작전지대에 대하여서는 협정의 고려대상외에 두지않을수 없다. 또한 <u>전투기간에 사용한 것에 대하여서는 이것을 일일히 법적으로 계약을 체결하고 빌린것이 아니고 계엄령하에서 사용한 것이기 때문에 그 근거가 모호한 점이 많다.</u> 또한 일본에는 비교적 많은 군사시설 및 기지조건을 갖춘 객체가 많으나 한국에 있어서는 그런한 선택조건이 적다. 특히 항구 및 비행장에 대하여는 거의 모든 것을 반군 반민으로 사용하지 않을수 없는 지리적 요건이 있다.

0096

0002

　　이상의 고찰에서도 알수 있는 바와 같이 주둔군의 사용중인
토지, 건물 및 시설에 관한 협정은 각각 체약국의 입장에 따라
다른 것이다.

　　주둔군이 사용하는 토지 및 건물 시설에 관한 협정의 체결
에 있어서 첫째로 문제되는 것은 이것이 현재 주둔군이 사용중
인 것에 대한 반환을 초래하거나 또는 기정상태에 중대한 변화
를 주기위한 것이 아니고 단지 그 사용에 있어서의 법적규제를 명
백히 하기 위한 것이라는 점을 강조하여 이에 대한 미국측의 불신
이나 오해를 감소하기 위하여서는 종태에 사용하든 또는 현재 사
용중인 것에 대하여서는 이의 사용을 계속 허가하고 이 협정이 체
결된 후에 발생하는 토지, 건물 및 시설에 대하여서만 그 사용허

0003

0037

가 여부와 사용조건을 규제하자는 것을 명시할 필요가 있다. 즉 본 협정 체결 이전에 사용한 토지, 건물 및 시설에 대한 사용료는 별도의 청산협정으로 해결하고 앞으로의 사용료에 대하여서만 이 협정을 통하여 해결하자는 것을 명백히 할 필요가 있고 이와 유사한 방법은 미국과 오스트리아 간의 협정에서도 그 예를 볼수 있다. 즉 1947년 이전에 사용한 사용료의 청산협정과 그 후의 사용료는 별개협정으로 체결하였다. 이는 말할것도 없이 기존 체제를 인정하는 안정성을 존중하는 신중한 입장이라고 할수 있다. 그러면 이러한 전제하에서 이 협정에서 규제하여야 할 제반문제와 그에 대한 각국의 조약예를 보고저 한다.

0004

2. 주한 미국 주둔군이 사용하는 우지, 건물 및 시설에
   관한 한미간의 협정 체결에 있어서 고려하여야 할
   제문제 및 이에 대한 국제협정 예

   이 협정을 체결하는데 있어서 문제되는 점은 1 에서도
제기한 바와 같이 <u>대상물은 무엇이고, 어되에 있는 것이 포함</u>
<u>되는가 ? 둘째로 이에 대한 경재적대가는 지불하는가 않는가?</u>
<u>즉 국유재산, 공공단체의 재산 및 사유재산에 대한 경재적대가</u>
<u>의 지불을 하는가 않하는가? 셋째로 한다면 무엇에 관하여</u>
<u>또는 누구에 대하여 무엇을 기준으로 하여 피해보상을 하는가?</u>
하는 것인바 이를 각개의 경우로 나누어 국제협정과 비교하여
고찰하면 다음과 같다.

(1). 협정의 객체

      협정의 객체는 밀일협정 제2조, 일본과 유엔과의 협정
제 5 조와 같이 " ......목적의 수행에 필요한 시설 및 구역의
사용 ......", " 시설 및 구역은 당해 시설 및 구역의 운영에
필요한 현존의 섬비, 비품 및 정착물을 포함한다"고   합이
적당할 것이다. (초안 제 3 조)

      그러나 전기한바와 같이 협정의 대상이 되는 객체를 포괄
적으로 규정한다고 하드라도 아직 우리나라의 실정에 있어서는
어되에 있는 시설에 관하여 본 협정을 적용하는가 하는 문제는
해결되지 않는다. 따라서 협정에는 위치상의 문제를 규정하여
야 하는바, 본협정이 대상으로 하는 객체의 위치중 작전지대내
에 있는 것에 대하여서는 한국의 군사적 필요성을 강조하여 이
를 제외하는 것이 타당할 것이다.

0005   0099

끝으로 사용시기도 문제되는 바 작전기간중에 사용한 것과 휴전협정 체결이후에 사용한 것에 대한 것은 이를 구별함이 타당한 것이며 휴전협정을 체결한 이후의 것이라도 이 협정 체결이전의 것과 이 협정 체결이후에 이 협정에 의거한 사용에 관한 것은 이를 명확히 구별하여 이 협정 체결이전의 것은 청산협정을 통하여 일시적인 해결을 하고 이후에 사용한 것에 대하여서는 합동위원회가 이의 심의 결정을 한다는 것을 원칙으로 합의 기존상태의 안정성을 유지하는데 있어서 중요할 것이다.

2. 경재적대가

이 협정을 체결하는 주요목적중의 하나가 토지, 건물 및 시설에 대한 보상금을 받을수 있게 하는것인 이상 어떠한 것에 대하여 그 사용료 및 보상을 받는가 하는 것은 중요한 문제가 아닐수 없는 것이다.

우리나라가 1955년에 제시한 초안 제3조에는 이에 관한 구체적규정이 없이 단지 사유재산에 대한 동정적인 고려를 한다는 것밖에 규정되고 있지 않아 구체적으로 공공단체의 재산에 대한 보상이 포함되는지, 또는 보상액은 손해액의 전액인지 그 일부인지도 규정하지 않어 이 협정의 구체적운영을 모호하게 하고 있다.

따라서 금번 본 협정을 체결함에 있어서는 전기 의문을 제거하기 위하여 사유재산은 지방자치단체의 재산까지 포함한다는 점과 배상액은 손해액의 전액에 상당한다는 점을 명시할 필요가

0006   0100

있다. 즉 공공단체의 재산은 어떠한가 하는 점인바 이는 사인에 대한 보상에 있어서와 같이 보상을 지급하여야 할것이다. 왜냐하면 지방자치단체는 재산의 주체가 되는 것이고 그 중에는 수익을 위한 재산이 포함될 뿐만아니라 수익재산에 대하여서는 지방자체단체가 대개 사인과 동일한 지위에서 소유하고 있으므로 이는 사법상의 재산이며 법률에 특별한 규정이 없는한 이에는 사법상의 규정이 적용되는 것이다.

다음에 보상금의 액수를 피해액의 전액으로 하느냐 또는 피해액의 일부로 하느냐 하는문제 인바, 이에 대하여서는 초안 제3조에서 단지 동정적인 고려를 한다고 하였을뿐 하등의 규정을 하지 않았기 때문에 이에 관한 다소의 부연이 필요할 것이다. 즉 미비협정 제22조에 의하면 피해액 전액을 미국측이 보상하고 있고 이 피해액은 단지 사용불능에 의한 피해액에 그치는 것이 아니라 그 토지, 건물 및 시설을 수용당함으로서 타처로 이동하는메에 소요되는 경비까지 포함한다고 하여 비율빈정부의 입장에서 보면 비율빈정부의 예산은 이에 대하여 전혀 사용되지 않아도 좋게 되어 있고,

[검게 가려진 부분] 우리나라의 경우에 있어서는

이러한 보상액의 지불의무가 협정상 규정되어 있지 않기 때문에, 언제 종료될지도 모르는 휴전협정하에서 국민의 사유재산에 대한 보상대책도 없어 막연하게 미국측의 호의적 한도만을 기다리지 않으면 안되는 현재의 입장을 하루 속히 탈피하고 미국군의 사용에 관한 재비용의 념출원천을 확정하는 것이 필요한 것은 재론을 요치않는바 이다. 그러면 구체적으로 어떠한 조건을 부여함이 좋고 타국의 대미협정은 어떠한가를 보면 다음과 같다.

0007

0101

먼저 경제적대가에 관한 것을 대여시의 경제적대가와 반환시의 경제적대가로 대별하고 대여서의 경제적대가를 다시 임대료문제와 물체의 개조에 대한 경제적대가 및 기타의 경제적대가로 구분하고, 반환시의 경제적대가를 원상회복 및 객체의 개조에 대한 경제적대가로 구분하여 고찰함이 적당할 것이다.

(가) 대여조건

(ㄱ) 임대료문제 : 각국이 체결한 조약중에는 임대료나 사용료를 지불하지 않을 것을 규정한 것도 많다. 무료제공을 규정한 조약례는 미국이 센트 루시아와 체결한 협정 제3조, 미국이 영국과 체결한 바하마협정 제23조, 미국과 중국간의 협정 제3조 및 미국과 사우디 아라비아간의 협정 제4조등이다. 즉 이들 협정은 명시적으로 임대료를 받지않는다고 규정하고 있다.

이와는 반대로 임대료문제를 전혀 명시하지 않은 협정으로는 미국이 이타리아와 체결한 방위협정 제4조, 미국이 벨기이와 체결한 협정 제2조가 그 예라고 할수 있다.

(ㄴ) 징발시의 손실보상 : 센트 루시아협정 제3조에서는 사용에 대한 보상의무가 없다고 명시하고 있으나 미일협정, 바하마협정 및 다하란협정에서는 손실보상의 의무가 있다고 명시하고 있지는 않으나 미비협정 제23조는 사용에 연유하는 경비, 손실 및 비용등을 합리적으로 보상할 것을 명시하고 있다.

(ㄷ) 개조에 대한 대가 : 객체에 대한 개조에 대하여는 사전에 동의를 얻을 필요가 있는가에 대하여 명기한 협정은 없으나 이것은 객체에 대한 경제적가치를 증가시키는 경우에는 개량을 방해할 필요가 없는 까닭이라고 보아야 할것이며, 개조 또는 신축에 관한 조건을 규정한 협정으로서는 미비협정 제17조는 신축물을 미국의 재산으로 간주 하고 협정 폐기일잔에이들 재산을 비율빈의 관세면제

0008

0102

특권하에 미국으로 이전시킬수도 있는 것으로 규정하고 있고, 센트루시아협정 제3조는 사용자측의 개량권을 인정하는 반면 재사용의 목적을 저해하지 않는 조건으로 개량할수 있을 뿐이라고 명시하고 있다.

███████████████████████

(ㅁ) 기타조건 : 기타조건으로서는 첫째로 그 기지내의 광물권을 유보한 미비협정 제24조의 규정이 있고 둘째로 사용을 허가받은 객체를 제3국의 사용에 공여하는 것을 금지한 것으로서는 미비협정 제25조와 미일협정 제17조 (비밀조항)인바 이는 주목을 끄는 조항이라고 할것이다.

(나) 반환시의 경제적 대가

(ㄱ) 원상회복의 의무 :

반환시의 원상회복의 의무는 대체로 없는 것이 국제협정의 예인바, 미일협정 제4조나 미비협정 제22조는 모다 이 원칙을 명시하고 있다. 이에 대한 예외로서는 다하란협정 제16조가 있다. 즉 이것은 반환시에는 완전히 이용할수 있는 상태로의 회복을 명시하고 있다.

(ㄴ) 개량 증축에 대한 보상 :

토지나 건물을 일정한 목적을 위하여 사용함에 있어서 그 이용의 효과를 증진시키기 위하여 불가피하게 가하게 되는 객체에 대한 개량 또는 증축에 대하여서는 그 반환시에 그 객체의 경제적가치의 증가에 해당하는 만큼의 금액을 보상하는가의 문제는 미비협정 제 17조, 미일협정 제4조, 센트 루시아협정 제4조에서 모다 명시적으로 보상의무가 없는 것을 확인하고 있다.

(다) 우리나라의 입장

이상의 제국 체협정의 예를 보아 우리나라의 입장을 상기 분류에 의거해서 검토하면 다음과 같다.

0009

0103

객체에 대한 개량 또는 경제적가치 증가를 가저오는 조
치는 초안 제3조 의 3의 나에서 이에 대하여 사용자측이 아무런 보상
의 의무가 없다고 명시하고 있는바 이는 그 데로 살려두는 것이 국제
협정의 예에 비추어 당연하다고 할수 있다.

반환에 관하여서는 첫 째로 초안 제3조의 11의 나에서
ll 한국과 통합사령부는 일방당시자의 요청이 있을 경우에는 ....
..... 그러한 시설과 구역의 반환 또는 추가적을 합의할줄 있다고ll
하였고 또한 다에서느 반환의 필요성을 검토케하였기 때문에
원사회복의 의무와 개량증축에 대한 조건종 원상회복의 의무를 미
국측에 있는 것을 확인할 필요가 있다.

0010   0104

3. 대인 및 대물피해에 대한 보상의 기준

전기 2 에서검토한 바와 같이최소의 토지, 건물 및 시설의 수용 및 이에 따르는 보상에 대하여 미군측이 책임을 진다면, (특별한 합의하에 하며 양정부의 어떠한 비율에 의한 공동부담으로 할수 있을 것임)우리 초안 제3조에 규정된 미군의 사용으로 인한 혜손의 보상의 범위를 확대하여 첫째로 기지의 신설비에 관한 보상, 둘째로 기지 사용중에 발생하는 사고에 대한 보상 (예를 들면 비행기의 추락에 의한 인명 및 재산에 대한 보상, 시설내의 사고로 인한 그 인근 주민의 인명 및 재산에 대한 보상) 셋째로 원상회복에 대한 보상으로 구분하되 이러한 모든 보상에 대한 범위는 초안 제3조에 규정되어 있는 사인 에 대한 것을 국유재산 이외의 모든 재산 (즉 지방자치단체의 재산 포함)이라고 확장하여 이의 적용에 관한 해석상의 분쟁을 사전에 봉쇄함이 좋을 것이다. 물론 사인의 재산에는 지방자치단체의 재산등도 포함된다는 것이 우리 국내법에는 명시되어 있으나(지방자치단체의 재산의 수익성, 지방자치법 제123조 ; 국유재산법 제20조) 이를 명확히 할 필요가 있기때문이다. 또한 제3조에서 보상의 경우에도 이를 동정적고력(sympathetic consideration)라고 만 규정하여 그 산출근거를 명확히 하기 위하여 정당한 (due) 또는 적당한 (proper) 라는 용어로 바꿈이 좋을 것이다. 실례로 보아도 영국, 불란서, 독일등에서는 실제의 시가보다 그 가를 지불하여 주둔지의 국민감정을 완화하기 위하여 미국측이 노력하고 있는 것만 보아도 그 노력의 실례가 됨줄로 생각한다. 본합에서 문제되는 점은 기지 사용중에 발생하는 사고에 대한 보상 즉 예를 들면 비행장부근에서 비행기의 추락으로 인한 인명이나 재산에 대한 피해 또는 건물, 시설내의 부주의의 사고로 인한 폭발로 인근 주민의 생명 또는 재산에 대한 피해인바 이것에 대하여서도 외국에서는 보상을 받고 있다. 예를 들면 독일같은 곳에서는 연습후의 도로나 광량에 대한 보수책임까

0011   0105

지 부담하고 있는것은 우리에게 좋은 자료가 된다. 즉 주둔군이 사용하는 토지, 건물 및 시설에 대한 경제적 대가에 대하여서는 우리정부가 국민에 대하여 지급하는 보상의 모든 항목을 포함하여야 하는 것이 이론상 타당하며, 위 가격의 결정은 합동위원회에서 시가를 기준으로 하여 시가보다 불리하지 않은 조건으로 보상하는 것을 원칙으로 함이 좋을 것으로 생각되며, 이에 대하여서는 사유재산보호의 원칙이라는 민주주의 기본원칙의 정신을 따라가면 문제가 생기지도 않을 것으로 생각한다.

끝으로 분쟁해결의 방법에 대하여서는 이를 일차적으로 합동위원회의 심의사항으로 규정하고 합동위원회에서 해결하지 못한 점에 대하여서는 이를 정부간의 협의에 위임하는 각국 조약례를 따름이 좋을 것이다.

0012   0106

3.　주한 미국군의 지위에 관한
　　　　한미간의 협정 교섭 경위

　　　1950년 6월 25일, 공산괴뢰의 남침이 발발하자, 국제
연합 안전보장이사회는 동년 6월 25일, 6월 27일 및 7월 7일자
결의에 의거하여 통합사령부하에 국제연합군이 한국에 주둔하고
있으나, 1953년 7월 27일자로 체결된 휴전협정에 의거하여 ,
실제 전투는 종식되고 군사작전에 수반되는 긴박상태가 완화되었으
므로 국제연합군의 한국내 배치에 수반되는 제 문제에 관하여 우리나라
국민과 국제연합군 인원간의 오해를 최소한으로 감소하고 반대로
상호간의 협조를 최고도로 증진시키는 방법중의 하나로서 우리나라
정부와 통합사령부로서 행동하는 미합중국간에 주한 미국군의 지위에
관한 행정협정을 체결할 필요를 한미양정부가 공히 인정하고
다음과 같은 교섭을 해왔다.

　　　1) 1953년 8월 7일자로 이 대통령과 "덜레스" 미국무장관
은 공동성명을 통하여 " ... 우리 양국정부는 한미 상호방위조약이
발효하게된 이후 미국이 한국에 주둔하고 있게될 군대의 지위 및
우리들의 공동사업을 수행하는데 필요한 한국측 시설과 인원의
사용에 관한 협약을 즉시 상의하고자한다 ..."고 천명하여 주둔군의
법적 지위를 규제하는 협정이 곧 체결될 것을 선언하였다.

　　　2) 1954년 12월 2일에 조정한 외무부장관 서리는
주한 미국대사 앞으로의 각서에서 주둔군의 지위에 관한 협정의
체결전의 잠정적 조치로서 "한국 세관업무에 관한 한미간의 협정"
을 체결할 것을 제의하였다. (1955년 1월 27일자로
주한 미국대사는 안에 대한 회한을 보내면서 이 문제를 신중 검토
하겠다고 말하였을 뿐 어후 하등 적극적인 진전이 없었다)

0013

0107

한·미국 간의 상호방위조약 제4조에 의한 시설과 구역 및 한국에서의 미국군대의 지위에 관한 협정(SOFA)
전59권. 1966.7.9 서울에서 서명 : 1967.2.9 발효(조약 232호) (V.5 체결 교섭, 1959) 113

3) 1955년 4월 28일 변창관을 주한 미국대리대사 앞으로의 각서에서 주한 미국군의 지위를 전반적으로 규제하는 협정의 체결을 제의하는 우리나라 정부측에서 그간 예의 검토한 협정안을 송부하는 동시에 이에 대한 미국측의 동의를 촉구하였다. (당시의 우리정부측 초안 별첨 5).

4) 우리 정부의 전기 제의에 대하여 미국측은 본국 정부에서 검토중이라는 점을 확보하였을 뿐 하등 반응이 없었다.

5) 1957년 1월 5일자로 조정환 외무부장관은 주한 미국대사 앞으로의 각서에서 교섭개시를 촉구하는 동시에 본 협정을 체결하는 데에 미국의 국제연합 가맹국정부와의 사전교섭에 과도한 시간소비가 된다면 우리정부는 조속한 협정 체결을 위하여 대한민국을 일방으로하고 미국을 타방으로하는 단독 협정의 체결에 응할 용의가 있다는 것을 통고하였다. (본 각서에 대하여 미국 대사는 본국정부의 훈령을 대기중이라는 것을 밝혔고, 동 년 6월 29일에 외무부장관은 미국 대사에게 교섭개시를 독촉하였음).

6) 미국정부의 태도가 전기한 바와 같이 미온적임에 정부는 때마침 우리나라를 방문한 허어터 미국무차관에게 "우리정부의 수차의 체의에도 불구하고 미국측은 아직 특별한 이유를 제시하지도 않으면서 교섭개시를 치연시키고있는 점을 강조하고, 미군사령관 렘니쩌장군의 1955년 7월 26일자 공한에서 지적한 점 즉, 한미통상항해조약 및 한미투자보장협정이 체결된 후에 교섭을 개시하자는 점, 및 시간 및 사전교섭상의 난점을 피하기위하여 미국만을 당사자로 하는 한미간의 협정 형식으로 하자는 점에 대하여서는 한미통상항해조약은 체결되었고 또한 투자보장협정은 곧 될 것이라는 점과, 미국과의 단독협정 형식을 찬성한다는 점을 제시하고 현한 협정의 조속한 교섭개시를

0014

0108

촉구하였다. (1957년 9월 10일자).

7) 1957년 10월 10일 주한미국대사는 조정환 외무부 장관과의 회담에서 "공위물 청산협정"과 같은 형식으로 주둔군의 지위에 관한 전면적 협정을 지양하고 개별적으로 각 문제에 관하여 협정을 체결하는 것이 좋다는 의견을 개진하였음데 1957년 11월 26일에 조정환 외무부장관은 전기 미국대사의 재의를 환영한다는 전제하에 "주한 미국군의 지위에 관한 협정을 구매, 과세, 관세에 관한 협정, 청구권 청산 협정, 주둔군이 사용하는 시설 및 지역에 관한 협정, 출입국에 관한 협정, 형사재판관할권에 관한 협정으로 분리하여 체결할 것과 이에 대한 교섭개시를 제의하였다.

8) 전면적협정의 지양과 개별적 협정의 체결을 제의한 우리정부와 전기 각서에 대한 미국측의 태도는 다시 지극히 미온적인 반응으로 환원하였다.

9) 1958년 9월 18일 미국대사는 조정환 외무부장관을 방문하고 미국측의 태도를 구두로 다음과 같이 개진하였다.

   (1) 전투상태는 중지되었으나 아직 완전한 평화상태는 되지않았다는 점을 강조하고 특별히 형사재판권에 관한 대전협정 (1950년 7월 12일 서명)에 수정을 가하기 가하지 않는다는 보장을 한국측이 한다면 기타 문제에 관한 개별 협정에는 즉시 응할 용의가있다.

10) 1959년 3월 25일, 다우링 미국대사는 조정환 외무부 장관을 방문하고 미국내의 현안 협정 체결에 대한 반응은 지극히 약할 뿐더러, 전면적 협정을 체결하여도 미국 상원의 비준동의를 받기는 거의 불가능하다는 점을 강조하고 "주한 미국의 인역 물자 처리에 관한 협정에 있어서와 같이 개별적 협정으로 추진하되

한·미국 간의 상호방위조약 제4조에 의한 시설과 구역 및 한국에서의 미국군대의 지위에 관한 협정(SOFA) 전59권. 1966.7.9 서울에서 서명 : 1967.2.9 발효(조약 232호) (V.5 체결 교섭, 1959) 115

미국 국방성은 아직 이 문제에 관하여 미온적이므로 주한 미군
사령관 뎃커장군을 통하여 미국 국방성에 호의적 권고를 하도록
촉구하여, 개별협정으로라도 한 건씩 우선 시급한 것부터
처리하고, 이렇게 함으로서 아직 규제되지못한 주둔군의 지위를
법적으로 해결하는 것이 좋을 듯하다는 것을 개진하였고, 우리
정부도 아직 형사재판권에 관한 하등의 언질을 줌이 없이 처리
할 수 있는 것부터 해결하는 것이 좋을 것으로 해석하고있음.

0016

4 (1) 징발에 관한 특별조치령이 말하는 "비상 사태"
는 지금도 계속되고 있다고 보는가 ?

먼저 결론부터 말하자면 이 "비상사태"는 지금도
계속되고 있다고 보아야 할것이다. 왜냐하면 한국은 현재
전시하에 있으며 관계하에 어떻 것은 "비상 사태"하에 있
다는 것을 의미하기 때문이다.

그러면, 한국이 현재 전시하에 있다는 이유는 무엇인가.
그 이론적 근거로서는 한국 휴전의 성격을 들어야 할것인데,
첫째로 : 국제법상, 휴전은 실전(hostility)의 일시적
중단이며 이 휴전기간은 전시로 규정하는 것이 학자들간의
통설이다. 또한 휴전기간중 국제법상의 제 관계 및 국내법
상의 제 관계는 전시로 규정되며 그 기간은 아무리 길다
하드래도 그 동안의 법적 관계는 전시법의 적용을 받는 것
이다(Oppenheim, International Law, Vol. II, 8th Ed.,p.547)   )
둘째로 : 국제관행은 거의 예외없이 휴전기간을 전시로 규정
하고 있다. 즉 1944년 11월 3일 "불란서"의 1
재판소(Court of Cassation)은 "휴전이란 적대행위를 일시적
으로 정치시킬뿐 그 자체 전쟁상태를 종결시킨 것이
아니다"고 판시(判 示)한 후 피고를 사형에 처한 적이
있었고(이 한기, "한국휴전의 제 문제" 국제법학회 론고
제 3호, (1958), 41면) 또한 "이스라엘"과 "에짚
트"간의 휴전협정이 체결된 4년후인 오늘에 있어서도 양국간
에 있어서는 전쟁상태가 종결되지 않았음이 명백하다. (이 한기
전기 론고 제 48면 참조)
셋째로 : 우리나라의 관례는 현 휴전기간을 전시라고 판시
하였다. 즉, 단기 4289년 1월 11일, "강 문봉
중장 사건"의 재판 관할권을 재정함에 있어서 고등군법회의
는 현 휴전기간을 전시라고 규정하고 이 재판관할권이 군법
회의에 있음을 밝혔다.   0017

한·미국 간의 상호방위조약 제4조에 의한 시설과 구역 및 한국에서의 미국군대의 지위에 관한 협정(SOFA)
전59권. 1966.7.9 서울에서 서명 : 1967.2.9 발효(조약 232호) (V.5 체결 교섭, 1959)

참고 : 단기 4290년 7월 21일 국방부는 "군
       징발조치에 대한 법령조회의 건"(국방 관 제
       4260호 단기 4290년 7월 21일자)에 관
       하여 이를 법무부에 문의하였던바 법무부의 견해는
       "현재 한국은 전시로부터 이탈치 못하였으므로
       아직 비상사태가 법적으로 계속되고 있어 전기 조치령
       은 지금도 그 효력이 있다고 하였다. (법무 제
       302호 단기 4291년 1월 23일자, 대 국방
       부 장관 공문)

<u>넷째론 : 한국 휴전은 그 체결당사국인 공산주의자가 이를
그들의 재침략을 위한 준비 기간으로 알고 있는 까닭에
설지에 있어서도 이를 전시라고 봄이 타당하다.</u>

        즉 북한 괴뢰를 조종하는 "쏘련"은 조약을 정치적
기회주의와 결부시켜

        "조약에는 강국이 약국에게 무력 또는 경제압박을
        통하여 강제한 것과 당사자 쌍방을 위하여 체결된
        것과의 2개가 있다.   전자는 이것을 강제한 강국
        의 실력이 존속하는 기간동안만 이행되며 후자는 쌍방
        의 이익이 존재하는 동안만 이행된다" (이 한기
        전기 론고 제79면)

라고 규정하고 있고 또한 이의 증명으로서 그들은 한국 휴전
협정에 위반한 사례가 많았으므로   이 휴전협정의 기간은
사실상 전시인 것이다.   그들은 이 휴전협정이 그들의
이익과 배치할 때에는 언제나 이 협정을 폐기할 것이니
이는 평화를 가져오기 위한 휴전이 아니었고 단지 전쟁을
위한 휴전이다.

0018

- 8 -

0112

(2) ||유엔|| 군이 사용하고있는 토지 건물에 대한 고찰

아국은 건국 초기에 있어서 소련이 조종하는 북한괴뢰의 무력 침공을 받어 일찍이 볼수없는 국난에 봉착하게 된 까닭에 대통령은 ||징발에 관한 특별조치령||을 발포하게 되었고 또한 이러하여 징발된 토지 및 건물등은 그 침략을 막기위하여 사용 되게 되었다. 따라서 이렇게 징발된 토지 및 건물등은 ||유엔|| 군에도 제공할것을 약속하기에 이르렀다. (대한민국과 통일사명 부간의 경제조정에 관한 협정, 제3조 제13항 참조) 그러나, 이러한 근거에서 제공된 ||유엔||군 사용의 각 토지 및 건물중에는 그것이 무단히 사용되고 있는것이 허다할뿐만 아니라 그들이 사용중인 이러한 재산에 대하여는 단지 추상적인 근본 원칙이 있을뿐 상세한 규정이 결여되어있고 또한 아래와 같은 여러 이유를 고려할때 이 협정의 체결은 시급한 국가적 요청 이 않일수없다.

가. 한국휴전의 장기성 :

한국휴전은 평화를 전제로한 휴전이 아니고, 또한 우려나라에는 북진통일없이 평화가 있을수없는 까닭에 외세(소련의 지배)가 잔류하는 한 평화가 옳수없으나, 그들은 좁처럼 한국에서 떠날 려는 증표가 없는 까닭에, 한국휴전은 장기화 될것이 예상된다. 또한 우려나라는 미국과 체결한 || 상호방위조약||에서, ||각당 사국은 각자의 행정관리하에 . . . 합법적으로 드려갔다고 인정되는 영토에 있어서|| 무력공격을 받어야 비로서 ||각자의 헌법상의 수속에 따라|| 상호 무력원조를 한다 (제3조)고 하고, 또한 ||국제연합에 배처되는 . . . 무력행세를 삼가할것을 약속한다 (제1조)라고하여 공산 침략군에 선수를 부여한 것이 니, 사실상 그들이 선공할때까지 상당한 기간의 소오될 것이다. 따라서, 한국과 ||유엔||군은 ||유엔||군의 사용하고 있는 토지 및 건물에 관한 조약을 체결하여야 한다.

0113

나. ||유엔|| 군이 사용중인 토지에 관한 협정의 결여는 쌍방

우호관계에 해가 된다.

||유엔||군의 토지 및 건물의 무계 약 사용은 쌍방의 보상에 관한

의견 차이로 인하여, 앞으로 분쟁에 이를 가능성이 현저하며,

이는 지금 해결하지 않으면 앞으로 쌍방 우호증진에 큰 해가

될 우려가 있다.

다. ||대한민국과 통일사령부간의 경제조정에 관한 협정|| (일명

||마이야||협정)은 실지 한국의 ||건전한 경제수립||에 위협이 되고있다.

한국으로 부터 ||유엔||군이 대여받고 있는 모든 토지 및 건물은

||마이야||협정 제 3 조 제 13 항에 의한 것이나, ||유엔||군측은

왕왕 이들 토지 및 건물시설을 무료 제공할것을 주장하고 있는

바 (1956년 6 월 18 일 ||유엔||군사령부 참모장 하모니장군이

김현철 재무부장관에게 보내온 공한, 1957년 4 월 16 일자

극동군 사령관 공한) 전계 무료제공에 관한 규정은 현존치않을

뿐며, 임제의 착취 및 6. 25동란의 황폐로부터 허머기는

한국은 이를 부담할 능력이 없다. 뿐만 아니라, 앞으로도

||유엔||군이 이것의 무료제공을 고집합으로서 이에 관한 세척

규정의 설정을 거부한다면, 이는 ||마이야||협정 전문이 지향하는

정신 즉 ||대한민국의 주권을 침략함이 없이... 한국민의 고난을

구제하며, 대한민국의 건전한 경제를 수립 유지하기 위하여..

. ||에도 배치되는 것이다. 따라서 빈약한 한국경제의 육성을 위

위하여 그들은 이 협약을 체결하여야 한다.

0020

0114

5.

별첨 : 국제연합군이 사용중인 징발재산목록 및 보상금관계 자료

출처 : 국방부 관재과

7. 국제연합군이 사용중인 징발재산과 보상금 별표 ④)

토지　111,686,328평　　81,218,068,062환

건물　63,918평　　6,277,994,500환

물자　91,646점　　339,639,370환

계　　87,835,701,932환
（　615,713,379弗）

단, 위의 수자와 금액은 개략적인 수자임. 실지조사후 정확한 수자를 산출코자함.

징발 해제수량

토지　62,049,397평

건물　201,921평 (1530동)

계　62,251,308평

8. 국제연합국이 한국 재산을 사용할수있는 법적근거

대한민국과 통일사령부간의 경제조함에관한 협정(4285년 5월 24일 한국정부 대표 백두진, 미국정부 대표 마이야가 서명함. 이를 마이야협정 이라 略稱함.) 제3조 13항에 의거 한국정부는 징발에관한 특별조치명의 규정한바에의하여 국제연합군에게 징발제공하여왔음.

마이야협정 제3조 13항

한국국민을 제외한 통일사령부의 개인 또는 기관에대하여 전기 국제연합의 제결의에 의하여 부여되어있거나 또는 차후 상방 또는 일방의 관계기구에의하여 공식 또는 비공식으로 협약될 특권, 면제, 편의을 부여한다.

9. 국제연합군에 징발제공한 재산의 보상대책

가. 국제연합군에게 징발제공된 경위

6.25동란후 국제연합군이 작전상 필요로하는 부동산은 한국 법령 징발에관한 특별조치명을 적용하여 한국 육군 참모총장과 국제 연합군 사령관간의 작전임무수행상 협의에의하여 육군 참모총장이 징발제공하여왔으며 4287년 7월 15일자로 국제연합군 사용 재산에관한 업무를 육군으로부터 국방부에 이관되었음.

18

0021　　　　　　　0115

국제연합군의 부동산 사용요청은 계엄령이 해제된 이후에도 계속되므로 합법징발은 하지않고있으나 재산소유자의 동의가 있을 때만 특별히 사용 승인하여 제공하고있음.

나. 대미 절충 경우

(1) 1951.5.17자로 콜터장군이 미대통령에게 보내온 공한에는 II미군을 포함한 국제연합군은 공공용의과 물자 급 시설등의 사용료 청산관계를 후일 한국정부와의 협의하에 해결하도록 미육군성과 재무성의 지시가 있었다고 하였음.

(2) 1954.8.5 한국 경제사절단이 도미시 145,322,706,070환 (1954.6.30현재)을 요구절충하여 미국조야의 여론을 환기시켜 이를 조사하고저 미국정부 관계관이 래한목적으로 일본 동경에 도착한바 때마침 유류소동으로 미측 관계관은 래한을 중지 귀국하였음.

(3) 1955.5.23 손원일장관께서 도미사절시 167,953,529,360환 (1955.5.30현재)을 요구함.

(4) 1955.9.16자로 파자스장군 (국제연합군 참모장)이 김현철 재무부장관에게 보내온 공한에의하면 청산관계를 3단계로 제안 하여왔음. 3단계란,

ㄱ. 1단계   휴전까지의(1953.7.27) 전단가.

ㄴ. 2단계   휴전기간(1953.7.27)부터 한국정부 관계 부서와 협정을 체결하는 날까지의 기간.

ㄷ. 3단계   협정 체결일로부터의 기간.

이상 3단계로 나누어서 휴전기간이전의것은 청산불 가능하나, 협정체결일부터의것은 청산 가능하다고 시사하였음.

(5) 1955.12.15 재무부장관실에서 국제연합군이 사용한 전기, 수도, 부동산등의 보상에대하여 한미간 회의를 개최할시 요청 함. (미국대표 루모니장군)

(6) 1956.6.18 루모니장군 (국제연합군사령부 참모장)이 김현철 재무장관에게 보내온 공한에의하면 부동산의 사용료청산을 삭제 할것을 제안하여왔으나 차에대하여,

(7) 1956.8.7자로 김현철장관께서 루모니장군에게 보낸공한 에는 아래와같이 제안하였음.

ㄱ. 휴전기간 이전의 모든 사용료청산은 후일에 협의할것을

0022   0116

전제로 보류

ㄴ) 부동산 사용료 청산은 후일 협의 기로 보류.

(8) 1956.9.9 미8군 사령관에게 앞으로 유엔군이 필요한 재산을 획득 함시는 사용료를 지불 하지 않은한 획득할수 없을것이며 현재까지 사용중인 재산의 보상도 부담하여야 한다는 협의 문을 발송한바 미8군 사령관 화이트 장군은 1956.9.22일자로 유엔군 사령부에서 상세한 회신을 받도록 회신이 있었음.

(9) 1956.11.26 유엔군 사령관 렘니저 장군으로부터 회답이 유 한즉 교 워결정 (연합국 참전국 간의 협의 대상) 하기 위하여 미육군성에 상신 하였다함.

(10) 1957.1.17 자로 극동군 사령관에게 재차 요청하였으며 1957.4. 16일자로 불가하다는 회신이 왔음.

(11) 1957.3.15 김용우 장관 도미시 76,843,372,236환 (4288.12.31 현재)을 오구 하였음.

(12) 1958.3.3 백육군 참모총장 도미시 87,835,701,932환 (4290.12. 31 현재)을 오구 하였음.

다. 대책

(1) 현재까지의 공한 또는 요미사절을 통한 절충 방법은 결과적 으로 하등의 성과를 보지 못 하였으므로 우선 미국정부에 대 하여 보상촉구공한을 보내고 본건 유엔군 사용 징발 재산 보상 문제를 전문적으로 혼의 절충 하기 위한 관계부처 합동으로 구성된 자문위원회를 설치하여 추진 해결토록 하여야 함.

(2) 전기 추진 방법에 의하여도 별다른 반응이 없을시는 다음 방안에 의거 시행함.

ㄱ) 유엔군에 징발재산 제공을 제한함.

ㄴ) 한국정부 예산에 유엔군 사용 징발재산의 보상금을 계상 신청함.

(3) 피징발자로 하여금 미측에 진정케하여 대상지의 애로사실 을 반영케하고 또한 국내 보도에 반영게 한후 대외 통신 에 반영케함.

0023

0117

별표 4

UN군사용에 나온 수량 및 보상금

재판년도 / 항목		42283 (1950)	42284 (19-1)	42285 (1952)	42286 (1953)	42287 (1954)	42288 (1955)	42289 (1956)	42290 (1957)	계	비고
토지	면적 평										X 보상액은 국가선박운임 간접기업에 의함
	이										
	환										2. 각협공 가격과 단가
	$										A. 1950년 1:18환
건물	면적 평										B. 1환년 1:2환
	5/표										C. '1952 1:60
	환										D. '1954 1:…
	$										E. 1956 1:5…
물품	건수										3. 1애비차 = 1224… 1환 = 38 5/…
	환										
	$										
계	환										
	$										

0118

6. Relevant Article excerpted from the
Draft Administrative Agreement on the
Facilities and reas to be used by the
United States Forces in Korea proposed
on April 28, 1955.

<u>ARTICLE III</u>

1. (a) (i) Korea agrees to grant to the Unified Command the
use of the facilities and areas necessary to carry out the mission
and purposes of the United Nations forces in Korea.

(ii) Agreements as to facilities and areas to be used
by the United Nations forces in accordance with this
agreement shall be concluded by the two Parties through the
Joint Committee provided for in Article XVII of this Agreement.

(iii) Until such agreements are concluded between the two
Parties the United Nations forces shall continue to use such
facilities and areas as are being used at the time this
Agreement becomes effective.

(b) At the request of either Party, Korea and the
Unified Command shall review such arrangement and may
agree that such facilities and areas shall be returned
to Korea or that additional facilities and areas may be
provided.

(c) The facilities and areas used by the United
Nations forces shall be returned to Korea whenever they
are no longer needed for purposes of this Agreement, and
the Unified Command agrees to keep the needs for
facilities and areas under continual observation with
a view towar such return.

(d) When facilities and areas such as target

0025   0119

ranges and maneuver grounds are temporarily not being
used by the United Nations Forces. Interim use may be made
by Korean authorities and nationals in accordance with
the decision made by the Joint Committee provided for
in Article XVII of this Agreement.

    2. (a) The Unified Command shall have the
rights, power and authority within the facilities and areas
which are necessary or appropriate for their establishment, use, operation, or defense. The Unified Command
shall also have such rights, power and authority over
land, territorial waters and airspace adjacent to,
or in the vicinities of such facilities of such facilities and areas, as are necessary to provide access to
such facilities and areas for their support and defense.
In the exercise outside the facilities and areas of the
rights, power and authority granted in this Article
there should be, as the occasion requires, consultation
between the two Parties through the Joint Committee.

    (b) The Unified Command agrees that the above
mentioned rights, power and authority will not be exercised
in such a manner as to interfere unecessary with
navigation, aviation, communication, or land travel to
or from or within the territories of Korea. All questions
relating to frequencies, power and like matters used by
apparatus employed by the United Nations forces designed
to emit electric radiation shall be settled by mutual
arragement. Pending such arrangement, the United Nations
forces shall be entitled to use, without radiation
interference from Korean sources, electronic devices of such
power,

0026

0120

design, type of emission, and frequencies as are reserved for such forces at the time this Agreement becomes effective.

(c) Operations in the facilities and areas in use by the United Nations forces shall be carried on with due regard for the public safety.

3. (a) The Unified Command is not obliged, when it returns facilities and areas to Korea on the expiration of this Agreement or at an earlier date, to restore the facilities and areas to the condition in which they were at the time they become available to the United Nations forces, or to compensate Korea in lieu of such restoration. In case of private property demolished by such use, the Unified Command shall pay sympathetic consideration to its restoration.

(b) Korea is not obliged to make any compensation to the Unified Command for any improvements made in the facilities and areas or for buildings or structures left thereon on the expiration of this Agreement or the earlier return of the facilities and areas.

4. (a) Vessels and aircraft operated by, for, or under the control of the United Nations forces for official purposes shall be accorded access to any port or airport of Korea free from toll or landing charges. When cargo or passengers not accorded the exemption of this Agreement are carried on such vessels and aircraft, notification shall be given to the appropriate Korean authorities, and such cargo or passengers shall be entered in accordance with the laws and regulations of Korea.

(b) When the vessels mentioned in paragraph 4 (a) enter Korean ports, approapriate notification shall, under normal conditions, be made to the proper Korean authorities. Such

0027

0121

vessels shall have freedom from compulsory pilotage, but if a pilot is taken pilotage shall be paid for at appropriate rates.

5. (a) All civil and military air traffic control and communications systems shall be coordinated in accordance with the decision made by the Joint Committee.

(b) Lights and other aids to navigation of vessels and aircraft placed or established in the facilities and areas in use by the United Nations forces and in territorial waters adjacent thereto or in the vicinity thereof shall conform to the system in use in Korea. The Korean and the United Nations forces authorities which have established such navigation aids shall notify each other of their positions and characteristics and shall give advance notification before making any changes in them or establishing additional navigation aids.

6. The United Nations forces may use all public utilities and services belonging to the Government of Korea under conditions no less favorable than those applicable to the armed forces of Korea.

7. Korea and the United Nations forces shall cooperate in meteorological services through exchange of meteorological observations climatological information and seismographic data.

0122

대한민국과 통합사령부하의 국제연합군와
지위에 관한 행정협정안

(발체)

제 3 조

1. (ㄱ) (1) 한국은 통합사령부에 대하여 한국에 있어서 국제
연합군의 사명과 목적을 수행함에 필요한 시설과
구역의 사용을 허가함에 동의한다.

(2) 본 협정에 의하여 국제연합군이 사용할 시설 및
구역에 관하여는 본 협정 제 17조에 규정된
합동위원회를 통하여 양당사자간에 합의 결정하
기로 한다.

(3) 양 당사자간에 여사한 합의가 성립되기까지는
국제연합군은 본 협정발효시에 사용중인 시설 및
구역을 계속 사용한다.

(ㄴ) 한국과 통합사령부는 일방당사자의 요청이 있는 경우
에는 여사한 약정을 재검토하여야 하며 그러한 시설과
구역의 한국에의 반환 또는 추가적 제공에 관하여
합의 할 수 있다.

(ㄷ) 국제연합군에 의하여 사용되고 있는 시설과 구역을
본 협정의 목적상 불필요하게 되는 경우에는 한국에
반환되어야 하며 통합사령부는 여사한 반환을 목적으로
하여 시설과 구역의 필요성을 계속적인 검토하에 두는데
동의한다.

(ㄹ) 사격장 및 연습장등의 시설과 구역이 국제연합군에 의하여
임시적으로 사용되지않을 경우에는 본 협정 제 17조에
규정된 합동위원회의 결정에 의하여 한국당국과 국민이
이를 임시사용할 수 있다.

0029

0123

2. (가) 통합사령부는 시설 및 구역내에서 설정 사용 운영 또는
방어에 필요 또는 적절한 권리 권력 및 권능을 가진다.

통합사령부는 또 여 사한 시설과 구역에 인접한 또는
그 부근의 토지 영수 및 공간에 대하여 그 보급지원과
방어를 위하여 여사한 시설과 구역에의 출입과 관의를
... 하여 ... 합의자간 ... 합의 ... 있어야 한다.

(나) 통합사령부는 전기의 ... 권리 권력 및 권능을 한국영역
의 ... 한국영역내에서의 ... 항공 항공 ... 또는
지상교통을 불필요하게 저해하는 방법으로는 행사하지
않음에 동의한다.

국제연합군에 의해서 사용되는 전파 방사의 장치가
... 있는 주파수 전력 및 용량의 사항에 관한 모든
문제는 상호합의에 의하여 해결되어야 한다.

여사한 합의어 있을 ... 는 국제연합군은 본 협
력 발생시의 ... 하고 있는 전력, 설계, 방사의 형
및 주파수의 전자장치를 한국측으로 부터의 방사방해로
사용할 ... 것.

(다) 국제연합군이 사용하고 있는 시설과 구역내에 있어서의
활동은 공공안전을 적당히 고려하여 행하여져야 한다.

0124

0030

130 주한미군지위협정(SOFA) 서명 및 발효 2

3. (ㄱ) 통합사령부는 본협정의 만료시 또는 그 이전에 시설과 구역을 한국에 반환할 경우 당해시설 및 구역을 국제연합군의 사용에 제공된 당시의 상태로 복구시키거나 또는 그 원상회복 대신에 배상할 의무가 없다. 사유재산이 그러한 사용으로 말미암아 훼손된 경우에는 통합사령부는 그 원상회복에 호의적인 고려를 하여야 한다.

(ㄴ) 한국은 본 협정 만료시 또는 그 이전에 시설 및 구역이 반환되는 경우에 그 시설과 구역에 가하여진 개량 또는, 거기에 잔류된 건물, 기타 공작물에 대하여 통합사령부에 아무런 보상을 할 의무가 없다.

4. (ㄱ) 국제연합군에 의하여 국제연합군을 위하여 또는 국제연합군의 관리하에 공적목적으로 운항되는 선박 및 항공기는 입항료 또는 착륙료를 부과됨이 없이 한국의 여하한 항구 또는 공항에도 기항할수있다. 본협정에 의한 면제를 받지않는 화물이나 여객이 여사한 선박이나 항공기에 적재운송된 경우에는 한국의 관계당국에 통고되어야 하며 그러한 화물이나 여객은 한국의 법령에 따라 입국되어야한다.

(ㄴ) 제 4 조 (ㄱ)에 규정한 선박이 한국항구에 입항할 시에는 통상상태에 있어서는 한국의 관계당국에게 적당한 통고를 하여야 한다. 여사한 선박은 강제인항료를 면제된다. 단 항도를 받는 경우에는 적당한 율의 항도료를 지불하여야 한다.

5. (ㄱ) 모든 비군용 및 군용항공 교통관리와 통신체계는 합동위원회의 검열에 의거하여 조정된다.

(ㄴ) 국제연합군이 사용하는 시설 및 구역내와 그에 인접한 영수 또는 그 부근에 설치 또는 설비된 등화 및 기타 선박과 항공기의 항행보조시설은 한국에서 사용되는 제도에 일치하여야 한다. 여사한 항행보조시설을 설치한 한국과 국제연합군당국은 그 위치와 특성을 상호통고하여야 하며 계속 그를 옮기거나 또는, 다른 보조시설을 추가설치하려고 할때에는 이를 실시하기 전에 사전통고를 하여야 한다.

6. 국제연합군은 한국정부에 손해보는 모든 공익사업과 공공역무를 한국군에게 적용되는 조건보다 불리하지않은 조건으로 사용할 수있다.

7. 한국과 국제연합군은 기상관측 기후학상의 정보 및 지진관측의 자료의 교환을 통하여 기상업무에 있어서 상호협조한다.

0031
0125

ADMINISTRATIVE AGREEMENT

UNDER ARTICLE III OF THE SECURITY TREATY
BETWEEN THE UNITED STATES OF AMERICA AND JAPAN

ARTICLE II

1. Japan agrees to grant to the United States
the use of the facilities and areas necessary to carry
out the purposes stated in Article I of the Security
Treaty. Agreements as to specific facilities and
areas, not already reached by the two Government by the
effective date of this Agreement, shall be concluded
by the two Governments through the Joint Committee
provided for in Article XXVI of this Agreement.
"Facilities and areas" include existing furnishings,
equipment and fixtures necessary to the operation of
such facilities and areas.

2. At the request of either party, the United
States and Japan shall review such arrangements and
may agree that such facilities and areas shall be
returned to Japan or that additional facilities and
areas may be provided.

3. The facilities and areas used by the United
States armed forces shall be returned to Japan whenever
they are no longer needed for purposes of this Agreement,
and the United States agrees to keep the needs for
facilities and areas under continual observation with
a view toward such return.

4. (a) When facilities and areas such as
target ranges and maneuver grounds are temporarily
not being used by the United States armed forces,
interim use may be made by Japanese authorities and
nationals provided that it is agreed that such use

0126

would not be harmful to the purposes for which the
facilities and areas are normally used by the United
States armed forces.

(b) With respect to such facilities and
areas as target ranges and maneuver grounds which
are to be used by the United States armed forces for
limited periods of time, the Joint Committee shall
specify in the agreements covering such facilities
and areas the extent to which the provisions of this
Agreement shall apply.

ARTICLE IV

1. The United States is not obliged, when it
returns facilities and areas to Japan on the expiration
of this Agreement or at an earlier date, to restore
the facilities and areas to the condition in which
they were at the time they became available to the
United States armed forces, or to compensate Japan in
lieu of such restoration.

2. Japan is not obliged to make any compensation
to the United Stats for any improvements made in the
facilities and areas or for the buildings or structures
left thereon on the expiration of this Agreement or
the earlier return of the facilities and areas.

3. The forgoing provisions shall not apply to
any construction which the United States may undertake under special arragements with Japan.

0033

0127

공   란

Article XVIII

1. Each party waives all its claims against the other party for injury or death suffered in Japan by a member of its armed forces, or a civilian governmental employee, while such member or employee was engaged in the performance of his officia l duties in cases where such injury or death was caused by a member of the armed forces, or a civilian employee of the other party acting in the performance of his official duties.

2. Each party waives all its claims against the other party for damage to any property in Japan owned by it, if such damage was caused by a member of the armed forces or a civilian governmental employee of the other party in the performance of his official duties.

3. Claims, other than contractual, arising out of acts or commissions of members of, or employees of the United States armed forces in the performance of official duty or out of any other act, commission or occurrence for which the United States armed forces is legally responsible, arising incident to non-combat activities and causing injury, death, Japan in accordance with the following provisions:

(a) Claims shall be filed within one year from the date on which they arise and shall be considered and settled or adjudicated in accordance with the laws and regulations of Japan with respect to claims arising from the activities of its own employees.

(b) Japan may settle any such claims, and payment of the amount agreed upon or determined by adjudication shall be made by Japn in yen.

0035   0129

(c) Such payment, whether made pursuant to a settlement of to adjudication of the case by a competent tribunal of Japan, or the final adjudication by such a tribunal denying payment, shall be binding and conclusive.

(d) The cost incurred in satisfying claims pursuant to the preceding subparagraphs shall be shared in terms to be agreed by the two Governments.

(e) In accordance with procedures to be established, a statement of all claims approved or disapproved by Japan pursuant to this paragraph, together with the findings in each case, and a statement of the sums paid by Japan, shall be sent to the United States periodically, with a request for reimbursement of the share to be paid by the United States. Such reimbursement shallebehmadetwithin the shortest possible time in yen.

4. Each party shall have the primary right, in the execution of foregoing paragraphs, to determine whether its personnel were engaged in the performance of official duty. Such determination shall be made as soon as possible after the arisint of the claim concerned. When the other party disagrees with the results of such determination, that party may bring the matter before the Joint Committee for consultation under the provisions of Article XXVI of this Agreement.

5. Claims against members of or emplyees of the United States armed fordes arising out of tortious acts or ommissions in Japan not done in the performance of official duty shall be dealt with in the following manner:

9 (a) The Japanese authorities consider the claim and assess compensation to the claimant in a fair and just manner, taking into account all the circumstances of the case, including

0130

the conduct of the unjured person, and shall prepare a report on
the matter.

(b) The report shall be delivered to the United States
authorities, who shall then decide without delay whether they
will offer _ex gratia_ payment, and if so, of what amount.

(c) If an offer of ex gratia payment is made, an accepted
by the claimant in full satisfaction of his claim, the United
States authorities shall make the payment themselves and inform
the Japanese authorities of their decision and of the sum paid.

(d) Nothing in this paragraph shall affect the jurisdiction of the Japanese courts to entertain an action against
a member or employee of the United States armed forces, unless
and until there has been payment in full satisfaction of the
claim.

6. (a) Members of and civilian employees of the United
States armed forces, excluding those emplyees who have only
Japanese nationality, shall not be subject to suit in Japan
with respect to claims specified in paragraph 3, but shall be
subject to the civil jurisdiction of Japanese courts with respect
to all other types of cases.

(b) In case any private movable property, excluding that
in use by the United States armed forces, which is subject to
compulsory execution under Japanese law, is within the facilities
and areas in use by the United States armed forces, the United States
authorities shall upon the request of Japanese courts, possess
and turn over such property to the Japanese authorities.

(c) The United States authorities shall cooperate
with the Japanese authorities in making available witnesses and
evidence for civil proceedings in Japanese tribunals.

0037

0131

7. Disputes arising out of contracts concerning the procurement of materials supplies, equipment, services, and labor by or for the United States armed forces, which are not resolved by the parties to conciliation, provided that the provisions of this paragraph shall not prejudice any right which the parties to the contract may have to file a civil suit.

0132

0038

A G R E E M E N T

BETWEEN THE UNITED STATES OF AMERICA AND THE REPUBLIC
OF PHILIPPINES CONCERNING MILITARY BASIS.

ARTICLE I

1. The Government of the Republic of the Philippines (hereinafter referred to as the Philippines) grants to the Government of the United States of America (hereinafter referred to as the United States) the right to retain the use of the bases in the Philippines listed in Annex A attached hereto.

2. The Philippines agrees to permit the United States, upon notice to the Philippines, to use such of those bases listed in Annex B as the United States determines to be required by military necessity.

3. The Philippines agrees to enter into negotiation with the United States at the latter's request, to permit the United States to expand such bases, to exchange such bases for other bases, to acquire additional bases, or relinquish rights to bases, as any of such exigencies may be required by military necessity.

4. A narrative description of the boundaries of the bases to which this Agreement relates is given in Annex A and Annex B. An exact description of the bases listed in Annex A, with metes and bounds, in conformity with the narrative descriptions, will agreed upon between the appropriate authorities of the two governments as soon as possible. With respect to any of the bases listed in Annex B, and exact description with metes and bounds, in conformity with the narrative description

22

0039   0133

of such bases, will be agreed upon if and when such
bases are acquired by the United States.

ARTICLE II
MUTUAL COOPERATION

3. In the interest of international security
any bases listed in Annexes and B may be made available to the Security Council of the United Nations on
its call by prior mutual agreement between the United
States and the Philippines.

ARTICLE XXII
CONDEMNATION OR EXPROPRIATION

1. Whenever it is necessary to acquire by condemnation or expropriation proceedings real property belonging to any private persons, associations or corporations
located in bases named in Annex A and Annex B in order
to carry out the purposes of this Agreement, the Philippines will institute and prosecute such condemnation
on expropriation proceeding in accordance with the
laws of the Philippines. The United States agrees to
reimbures the Philippines for all the reasonable
expenses, damages and costs thereby incurred, including
the value of the property as determined by the Court.
In addition, subject to the mutual agreement of the two
Governments, the United States will reimburse the Philippines for the reasonable costs of transportation and
removal of any occupants displaced or ejected by reason
of the condemantion or expropriation.

2. Prior to the completion of such condemnation
or expropriation proceedings, in cases of military
necessity the United States shall have the right to
take possession of such property required for military

0040   0134

purposes as soon as the legal requisites for obtaining possession have been fulfilled.

3. The properties acquired under this Article shall be turned over to the Philippines upon the expiration of this Agreement, or the earlier relinquishment of such properties, under such terms and conditions as may be agreed upon by the two Governments.

ARTICLE XXIV
MINERAL RESOURCES

All minerals (including oil), and antiquities and all rights relating thereto and to treasure trove under, upon, or connected with the land and water comprised in the bases or otherwise used or occupied by the United States by virtue of this Agreement, are reserved to the Government and inhabitants of the Philippines; but no right so reserved shall be transferred to third parties, or exercised within the bases without the consent of the United States. The United States shall negotiate with the proper Philippines authorities for the quarrying of rock and gravel necessary for construction work on the bases.

ARTICLE XXV
GRANT OF BASES TO A THIRD POWER

1. The Philippines agrees that it shall not grant, without prior consent of the United States, any bases or any rights, power, or authority whatsoever, in or relating to bases, to any third power.

2. It is further agreed that the United States shall not, without the consent of the Philippines, assign, or underlet, or part with the possession of the whole or any part of any base or of any right, power or authority granted by this Agreement, to any third power.

24   0041

0135

UNITED KINGDOM

THE BAHAMAS LONG RANGE PROVING GROUND

Agreement and exchange of notes signed at Washington,
July 21, 1950; entered into force July 21, 1950.

A G R E E M E N T

BETWEEN THE GOVERNMENT OF THE UNITED STATES OF AMERICA
AND THE GOVERNMENT OF THE UNITED KINGDOM OF GREAT
BRITAIN AND NORTHERN IRELAND CONCERNING A LONG RANGE
PROVING GROUND FOR GUIDED MISSILES TO BE KNOWN AS "THE
BAHAMA LONG RANGE PROVING GROUND"

ARTICLE X

The Government of the United States of America
shall have the right to employ and use all utilities,
services and facilities, harbors, roads,. . .belong-
ing to or controlled or regulated by the Government
of the Bahama Islands or the Government of the United
Kingdom on such conditions as shall be agreed between
the Contracting Governments.

ARTICLE XXIII

FREEDOM FROM RENTS AND CHARGES

Except as provided in Articles XVII and XXII
the Sites shall be provided, and the rights of the
Government of the United States of America under this
Agreement shall be made available, free from all rent
and charges to the Government of the United States of
America.

0042

0136

AIR BASE AT DHAHRAN

AGREEMENT EFFECTED BY EXCHANGE OF NOTES SIGNED AT MECCA AND
AT JIDDA JUNE 18, 1951 ; entered into force June 18, 1951.

4.   In accordance with paragraph 23 of the existing Dhahran
Air field Agreement which states that all fixed installations
and other property used in operation and maintenance of the
Airfield will be returned to the Saudi Arabian Government
upon termination of the Agreement, and in view of the fact
that the said Agreement is being terminated and that such
installations and properties thereby revert to the Saudi
Arabian Government, and, due to the desire of the Saudi
Arabian Government to facilitate the errand of the Mission,
it agrees to place at the disposition of the Mission at
Dhahran Airfield, rent free, certain existing buildings
and installations as specified in the list agreed upon by
the appropriate authorities of the two Governments and
approved by the Saudi Arabian Minister of Defense.   This
list will be reviewed from time to time in the light of developing circumstances and requirements.

16.   Upon the termination of this Agreement, the Mission
will return to the Saudi Arabian Government in sound operating condition all fixed installations, properties and
equipment of which it makes use in the operation and
maintenance of Dhahran Airfield.

한·미국 간의 상호방위조약 제4조에 의한 시설과 구역 및 한국에서의 미국군대의 지위에 관한 협정(SOFA)
전59권. 1966.7.9 서울에서 서명 : 1967.2.9 발효(조약 232호) (V.5 체결 교섭, 1959)   143

PRINCIPLES APPLYING TO MUTUAL AID

IN THE PROSECUTION OF THE WAR

AGAINST AGGRESSION

————

PRELIMINARY AGREEMENT

BETWEEN THE UNITED STATES OF AMERICA

AND BELGIUM

Signed at Washington June 16, 1942

Effective June 16, 1942

ARTICLE II

The Government of Belgium will continue to contribute
to the defense of the United States of America and the
strengthening thereof and will provide such articles, services,
facilities or information as it may be in a position to supply.

0044

0138

The Executive Director of the Office of the United States
High Commissioner for Germany to the Minister of Finance
for the Federal Republic of Germany

OFFICE OF THE UNITED STATES HIGH COMMISSIONER FOR GERMANY

Office of the Executive Director

Bad Godesberg

Mehlemer Aue

March 24, 1953

MY DEAR MINISTER SCHAEFFER :

I am writing to you on behalf of Headquarters USAREUR in order to propose an agreement relative to the settlement of a certain category of occupation damage claims commonly known as Pre-1 July 1947 Claims. The proposal of USAREUR is as follows :

1. Headquarters USAREUR hereby authorizes the competent authorities of the Federal Republic of Germany to receive, process and pay, in accordance with existing occupation legislation and without reference to and U.S. agency, all claims for :

a. Damage caused as a result of acts or omissions committed in the territory of the Federal Republic and the Western Sectors of Berlin during the period from 1 August 1945 to 30 June 1947 inclusive by the United States Forces and authorities and other persons, agencies and organizations that acted on their behalf or authority or for whose acts or omissions the United States assumed responsibility.

b. Arrears of rentals accrued for the same period.

c. Damage caused to personal property not subject to requisition, in connection with real estate released during the period from the day following 30 June 1947 up to and including the day preceding 1 October 1952.

0045

0139

2.   The criteria to be utilized in the adjudication of the foregoing types of claims are those established by USAREUR Circulars Nos. 35, 57, 75 and 187.

3.   Headquarters USAREUR will make available to the competent authorities of the Federal Republic an amount of DM 6,400,000 for payment of the claims referred to under paragraph 1, a, b and c above.

The competent authorities of the Dederal Republic will provide such additional amounts from the Federal Budget, not chargeable as occupation costs, as may be necessary to satisfy the aforementioned claims, and will hold the U.S. authorities and Forces harmless against payment of any amount in excess of the DM 6,400,000 above provided for on account of the said claims.   The competent authorities of the Federal Republic agree that the U.S. Forces will have no further responsibility for claims covered by this agreement.

0046
29

0140

CONVENTION ON THE RIGHTS AND OBLIGATIONS OF FOREIGN FORCES AND
THEIR MEMBERS IN THE FEDERAL REPUBLIC OF GERMANY. Bonn, May 26, 1952
(as amended by Schedule II to the Protocol on the Termination
of the Occupation Regime in the Federal Republic of Germany
signed at Paris on October 23, 1954.

Article 17, (8.)   A Standing Commission shall be established,
to be composed of representatives of the appropriate authorities
of the Three Powers and of representatives of authorities of the
Federal Republic.   The duty of this Commission shall be to
guarantee effective coordination between civil and military
air activities.

Article 20. 1)   Installations and works directly serving
the purpose of defense, as well as safety installations, shall
be erected or adopted by the Federal Republic of Germany in
such amounts, areas and types as are needed for the common
defense.   Where there is a special need for security, the
Forces themselves may erect or adopt such installations or
works, provided that there is prior consultation with the
Federal Government.

30

0047   0141

SAINT LUCIA

LEASED BASES IN SAINT LUCIA

Agreement signed at Castries, Saint Lucia, July 29,
1952; entered into force July 29, 1952

TIAS 2673
July 29, 1952

A G R E E M E N T

concerning the utilization of leased base area

In Saint Lucia

ARTICLE II

Definition of Areas

The areas covered by this Agreement are those described
in paragraph 8 of the lease executed on the 29th March, 1950,
and in the schedules attached thereto.

ARTICLE III

Conditions of Occupation by the Government of Saint Lucia

(1) The Government of Saint Lucia shall have the right
to occupy and utilize for any purpose the areas mentioned in
Article ii hereof without liability for the payment to the
United States Government of rental or compensation for the use
thereof. This right shall extend to any license of the Government
of Saint Lucia without prior consent of the United States Government.

(2) The Government of Saint Lucia or its licensees shall
have the right to construct or carry out all needful
improvements to the said areas so long as such improvements
to the said areas so long as such improvements will not hinder
the expenditious reoccupation of these areas by the United
States Government for the purposes of the Bases Agreement.

0048

0142

(3) The occupation by the Government of Saint Lucia or any licensee thereof shall be accomplished in such manner as to cause no obstruction or permanent damage to existing bridges, roadways, runways and approach areas thereto, and drainage work allied thereto. This stipulation shall not impose a responsibility upon the said Government for damage thereto resulting from natural causes.

(4) The areas and the improvements thereto shall be open at all reasonable time for inspection by the military authorities of the United States or by their duly authorized agents.

ARTICLE IV

Reoccupation by the Government of the United States right to reoccupy and activate any portion or the whole of the areas covered hereby on giving thirty days' previous notice to the Government of Saint Lucia: provided that in the event of a war breaking out in which the United States is involved, : of or of any other overriding military necessity as determined by the Government of the United States of America, the United States Government shall have the right to reoccupy and activate immediately any portion or the whole of any of the areas aforesaid on giving 48 hours previous notice in writing to the Government of Saint Lucia.

(2) The United States Government shall not be liable to the Government of Saint Lucia or to any third party for any damage caused solely as a result of such reoccupation.

(3) In the event of reoccupation, the United States Government shall have the right to purchase from the Government of Saint Lucia any improvements constructed by the said Government of Saint Lucia or its licensees within

32

0049   0143

한·미국 간의 상호방위조약 제4조에 의한 시설과 구역 및 한국에서의 미국군대의 지위에 관한 협정(SOFA)
전59권. 1966.7.9 서울에서 서명 : 1967.2.9 발효(조약 232호) (V.5 체결 교섭, 1959) 149

the areas referred to in Article ii hereof. The purchase
price shall be mutually agreed-upon and in default of
agreement the price shall be settled by arbitration under
the provisions for arbitration contained in the Civil Code in
force in the Colony.

(4) In the event that improvements are not purchased
by the United States Government, the United States Government
may require the removal of any improvements constructed during the occupation of the Government of Saint Lucia under this
Agreement, without cost to the United States Government.

(5) The Government of Saint Lucia or any licensees
thereof shall begiven a period of time, consistent with
the exigencies of the military situation, for the removal
of any such improvements as are not desired for purchase
by the United States Government.

(6) The Government of Saint Lucia shall hold and save
the United States Government free from any cost arising
from third party claims as a result of such occupation.

ARTICLE V

Status of Previous Rights

(1) Nothing in this Agreement shall be construed to
deprive the Government of the United States of America of any
of its rights, privileges, immunities or exemptions
under the Bases Agreement or the Civil Aviation
Agreement.

(2) Nothing in this Agreement shall be construed to
confer upon the Government of Saint Lucia, with respect to
the use in place of any of the buildings or improvements
enumerated in Contract of Sale No. DA(a) - 96-505-Eng-114
dated the 94th August, 1949, any rights or privileges not

33

0050

0144

specifically granted by the said Contract of Sale or by
separate agreements made in pursuance of the provisions
thereof.

Done in duplicate at Casties in the Colony of Saint
Lucia of the Wind ward Islands this 29th day of July, 1952.

For the Government of the   For the Government of the
Colony of Saint Lucia,   United States of America.
Sindwar Islands.   CARL BREUER
                                   Consul of the United
                                     States of America
      F E DEGAZON
    Acting Administrator   (SEAL)
      (SEAL)

                                    Before me:

BEfore me:

한·미국 간의 상호방위조약 제4조에 의한 시설과 구역 및 한국에서의 미국군대의 지위에 관한 협정(SOFA)
전59권. 1966.7.9 서울에서 서명 : 1967.2.9 발효(조약 232호) (V.5 체결 교섭, 1959)

MUTUAL DEFENSE ASSISTANCE

CONSTRUCTION OF MILITARY INSTALLATIONS AND

FACILITIES

Agreement effected by~exchange of~Notes signed at
Taipei November 21, 1956, entered into force November
12, 1956.

2. The Government of the Republic of China,
at times appropriate to the orderly and economical
prosecution of the agreed construction work, and
without cost to the United States Government, its
Contractors or sub-contractors, will, on request,
place at the disposal of the Chief, MAAG, areas necessary
for carrying out the construction and related work
contemplated by these understandings. The term
"necessary areas" shall be understood to include, in
addition to the real estate on which construction
will be performed, rights to use of water available,
rights of entry for purposes of survey, and such
borrow areas, spoil areas, quarry sites and aggregate
production sites in streams or elsewhere as may be
necessary, together with rights of ingress and egress
and rights to remove such materials or deposit
excess materials as may be necessary to the agreed
construction work. Such "necessary areas" shall
cease to be at the disposal of the Chief, MAAG, upon
completion of the construction work contemplated by
these understandings.

3. The Government of the Republic of China will
hold the Government of the United States, its
Contractors and their sub-contractors harmless for
such destruction of any buildings, streets, roads,
public utilities and improvements of any kind on real

0052

0146

property placed at the disposal of the Chief, MAAG,
as necessary to the construction work contemplaced by
these understandings. Should any relocation of
facilities be required or resettlement costs be involved,
relocation and resettlement shall be accomplished by
the Government of the Republic of China at its own expense and at such time as not to interfere with the
orderly and economical prosecution of the work.

0053

0147

MUTUAL DEFENSE ASSISTANCE (facilities Assistance)
Agreement between the United States of America and
Italy, entered into force June 24, 1954.

c. It will furnish all of the land, buildings,
equipment, materials, and services required for the
additional production facilities, except for the
equipment and technical advice to be furnished by the
Government of the United States, and will take whatever
measures are required to accomplish the increase in
production facilities envisaged in the program.

(5) In carrying out the facilities assistance
program, the two Governments, acting through their
appropriate contracting officers, projects involved,
which will set forth the nature and amounts of the
contributions to be made by the Government of the
United States and the Government of Italy, the description and purpose of the facilities to be established,
and other appropriate details. Such arrangements may
include provisions for the procurement of equipment
to be furnished by the United States Government from
the Government of Italy under the offshore procurement
program, and the transfer of such equipment to the
Government of Italy in accordance with the provisions
of the Mutual Defense Assistance Agreement.

0054

0148

<u>MUTUAL DEFENSE ASSISTANCE</u>

AGREEMENT AMENDING THE AGREEMENT OF JANUARY 30 AND
FEBRUARY 9, 1951. Effected by exchange of notes
signed at Taipei October 23 and Nov. 1, 1952; entered
to force Nov. 1, 1952.

3. The Government of the Republic of China
agrees to furnish free of charge and without present
or future liability to the Government of the United
States or individual members of the MAAG, use of all
lands, buildings, services, personnel, utilities,
communication services, and vehicles which are to be
determined or have been dtermined or have been
determined by mutual agreement to be necessary and
reasonable for the efficient operation of the MAAG,
and which are incident to the official functions of
the MAAG or its member. Without prejudice to the mutual
agreement referred to in the preceding sentence, the
facilities to be extended to MAAG under the present
agreement shall include the use of lands and buildings
for office space, motor pools and storage areas;
necessary transport facilities to permit the free
ingrese and egress of official aircraft and naval vessels,
and the use without charge of air strips, air fields,
roads, ports and railroads by official aircraft, naval
vessels and or official vehicles, as well as the exemption
from payment of handling and stevedoring charges concerning goods and carges destined for MAAG or for the
members of MAAG; military vehicles necessary to supplement US vehicles for the official use of MAAG personnel;
utilities inclusing heat, light, water and telephones;
personnel such as laborers, interpreters and trans-

0055

0149

lators, custodial personnel, drivers and mechanics.

6. Claims for compensation for damages arising from acts of military members of MAAG shall be settled by agreement between the appropriate authorities of the Government of the Republic of China and the Government of the United States of America. In event that no such agreement is reached, settlement shall be made through diplomatic channels.

7. Immediately upon the signing of this agreement, a joint committee composed of representatives of the Government of the Republic of China and of the United States will be established to aid and will consist of six members, three apointed by each Government. Two of the United States representatives will be members of MAAG. At its first meeting after establishment the committee will elect its chairman from among the appointed members of the committee, will proceed to the consideration of such agenda. After the first meeting the committee will meet weekly at the call of the chairman.

ARTICLE VIII

2. - (a) In the case of damage caused or arising as stated in paragraph 1 to other property owned
by a Contracting Party and located in its territory,
the issue of the liability of any other Contracting
Party shall be determined and the amount of damage
shall be assessed, unless the Contracting Parties
concerned agree otherwise, by a sole arbitrator
selected in accordance with sub-paragraph (b) of
this paragraph. The arbitrator shall also decide
any counter-claims arising out of the same incident.

(f) Nevertheless, each Contracting Party
waives its claim in any such case where the damage is
less than: -

Belgium: B.fr. 70,000.	Lusembourge	:	L.fr. 70,000.
Canada : $1.460.	Netherlands	:	Fl. 5,320
Denmark: Kr. 9,670	Norway	:	Kr. 10,000.
France : F.fr. 490,000.	Portugal	:	Es. 40,250.
Iceland: Kr. 22,800.	United Kingdom	:	₤ 500.
Italy : Li. 850,000.	United States	:	$1,400.

Any other Contracting Party whose property has been
damaged in the same incident shall also waive its claim
up to the above amount. In the case of considerable
variation in the rates of exchange between these cur-
rencies the Contracting Parties shall agree on the
appropriate adjustments of these amounts.

0057   0151

Agreement relating to the principles applying to the
provision of aid in the prosecution of the war. (3 Sep 42)
(24 UNTS 196) (Exchange of Notes)

The Australian Minister to the Secretary of State

3.   The Government of Australia will provide as reciprocal
aid the following types of assistance to the armed forces of the
United States in Australia or its territories and in such other
cases as may be determined by common agreement in the light of
the development of the war:

    a. Military equipment, ...

    b. Other supplies, material, facilities and services
for the United States Forces except for the pay and allowances
of such forces, administrative expenses, and such local purchases
as its official establishments may make other than through the
official establishments of the Australian Government as specified
in paragraph 4;

    c. Supplies, materials and services ....

4.   The practical application of the principles formulated
in this note, including the procedure by which requests for aid by
either Government are made and acted upon, shall be worked out as
occasion may require by agreement between the two Governments ,
acting when possible through their appropriate military or civilian
administrative authorities. Requests by the United States Government for such aid will be presented by duly authorized authorities
of the United States to official agencies of the Commonwealth of
Australia which will be designated or established in Canberra and

0058

0152

in the areas where United States forces are located for the purposes
of facilitating the provision of reciprocal aid.

Agreement regarding settlement for war accounts and
claims incident to the operations of the US forces in
Austria during the period 9 April 1945 to 30 June 1947,
inclusive. (21 June 1947) (67 UNTS 90)

Article 1

3.   The Government of the United States agrees to pay the
sum of 308,382,590 Schillings to the Austrian Government in full
and final settlement of all obligations incurred by United States
Forces, agencies (Public or Quasi-Public) together with forces of
other nations operating under command of the United States Forces
in Austria, during the period 9 April 1945 to 30 June 1947, inclusive.

5.   The word claims as used covers all claims and includes
specifically but is not restricted to the followings:

a.   Claims for the loss, damage, destruction and use
of property, whether real, personal, or mixed and for supplies,
communication, transportation and other services, requsitioned,
ordered and used, arising out of the exercise or purported exercise
of belligerent, occupational or other rights and all other claims
of any type whatever against the United States by the Austrian
Government, nationals of Austria, or persons owning property in or
residing in Austria.

b.   Claims for rentals for real estate occupied during
the period 9 April 1945 to 30 June 1947, inclusive.

Article 4.

12.   The Austrian overnment further agrees that no amount
will be charged to the United States Forces in Austria for any
real properties, chattels appurtenat thereto or personal services

0060

0154

in connection therewith which shall be derequisitioned and vacated
by the United States Forces in Austria prior to 31 July 1947 or
for any claims arising out of the termination of employment.

0061   0155

Agreement relating to the payment of occupation costs
incident to the maintenance of United States Forces in
Austria subsequent to 30 June 1947. (21 June 1947)
(67 UNTS 100)

In order to assist the Government of Austria in the
restoration of its economic life and the return of its democratic
processes, the United States Forces in Austria hereby declares its
policy in regard to the payment of Occupation Costs in Austria:

Hereafter, the United States Forces in Austria will pay,
in United States dollars, for all real estate and chattels appurtenant thereto, utility service, services, and supplies furnished
for the maintenance of United States Forces in Austria.

To assist the United States Forces in Austria in the
accomplishment of this objective, the Austrian Government hereby
subscribes to the following procedures and agrees to furnish technical assistance necessary to implement the provisions stated below:

1. Payment for real estate and chattels apputenant
thereto, utility service, services and supplies furnished will be
made quarterly, or at such shorter intervals as may be deemed
desirable by the United States Forces in Austria in American dollars
by the United States Forces in Austria to the Austrian Government.
The United States Forces in Austria will present vouchers quarterly
or at such shorter intervals as may be deemed desirable by the
United States Forces in Austria on all items furnished together
with sufficient dollars at the agreed rate of exchange to cover
the amount included in the vouchers, for which the Austrian Government will acknowledge receipt and make proper payment against the

0062   0156

vouchers submitted and all claims arising under future agreements.

2. The rental value of real estate and chattels appurtenant thereto will be determined by adding (a) the annual furnished rental value in schillings of the real estate as determined by the

Federal Ministry of Finance of the Austrian Government as of 1 June 1947, (b) estimated annual schilling cost of electricity, gas and water, (c) estimated annual schilling cost of such inspections and services as may be required by Austrian law and dividing the total in schillings by twleve to determine the monthly rate. This monthly schilling rate will be then computed in dollars at the agreed rate of exchange. In any case where the rental value of the real estate incuding (a), (b) and (c) above and chattels appurtenant thereto may not have been estimated as of 1 June 1947, the Federal Ministry of Finance agrees to establish not later than 31 July 1947 a value in accordance with practices and similar valuations in effect as of 1 June 1947.

6. The Austrian Government agrees to maintain properties required for use by the United States Forces in Austria in a condition acceptable to the Commanding General, United States Forces in Austria. If, however, lack of materials or of articles necessary for proper maintenance of such properties prevent the Austrian Government from fulfilling its obligation in this respect, the United States Forces in Austria may make the necessary repairs and deduct the cost of same from the accrued and accruing rentals.

8. The United States Forces in Austria reserves all rights, titles, and interest in fixtures which are the property of the United States Government and which have been installed in real estate heretofore requisitioned, and in all fixtures hereafter installed and paid for by the United States Forces in Austria, except when

U063

0157

the value of the same shall be charged aginst the rental of the property in which installed or included in a single payment settlement to the Austrian Government of outstanding obligations.

10. The Austrian Government agrees that, without the express consent of the Commanding Genera United States Forces in Austria, or of the United States High Commissioner, no law it has heretofore enacted or may hereafter enact to ration and limit the use of electricity, gas and water shall apply to the use thereof by the United States Forces in Austria, but that those utilities will be furnished, without restriction other than those imposed by an act of God, in accordance with paragraph 3 thereof.

11. The Austrian Government further agrees that during the presence in Austria of representatives of the United States in connexion with the Occupation of Austria it will enter into agreements with any other United States Government agency now or hereafter requiring real estate and chattels appurtenant thereto, identical to this agreement unless more favorable terms are offered by the Government of Austria.

J064   0158

Agreement regarding construction of military installation
and Facilities in Taiwan (21 Nov 56) (Exchange of Notes)
(7 UNTS 3411)

2. The Government of the Republic of China, at times appropriate to the orderly and economical prosecution of the agreed
construction work, and without cost to the United States Government,
its Constractor or sub-contractors, will, on request, place at the
disposal of the Chief, MAAG, areas necessary for carrying out the
construction and related work contemplated by these understandings.
The term "necessary areas" shall be understood to include, in
addition to the real estate on which construction will be performed,
rights to use of water available, rights of entry for purposes of
survey, and such borrow areas, spoil areas, quarry sites and
aggregate production sites in streams or elsewhere as may be
necessary, together with rights of ingress and egress and rights
to remove such materials or deposit excess materials as may be
necessary to the agreed construction work. Such "necessary areas"
shall cease to be at the disposal of the Chief, MAAG, upon completion
of the construction work contemplated by these understandings.

3. The Government of the Republic of China will hold the
Government of the United States its Contractors and their sub-
Contractors harmless for such destruction of any buildings, streets,
roads, public utilities and improvements of any kind on real property
placed at the disposal of the Chief, MAAG, as necessary to the
construction work contemplated by these understandings. Should any
relocation of facilities be required or resettlement costs be
involved, relocation and resettlement shall be accomplished by the
Government of the Republic of China at its own expense and at such
time as not to interfere with the orderly and economical prosecution
of the work.

0065

0159

Defense Agreement pursuant to the North Atlantic
Treaty. (5 May 51) (205 UNTS 174)

Article 1

The United States on behalf of the North Atlantic Traty Organi-
zation and in accordance with its responsibility under the North
Atlantic Treaty will make arrangements regarding the defense of
Iceland subject to the conditions set forth in this Agreement.
For this purpose and in view of the defense of the North Atlantic
Treaty area, Iceland will provide such facilities in Iceland as
are mutually agreed to be necessary.

Article 2.

Iceland will make all acquisitions of land and other arrangements required to permit entry upon and use of facilities in
accordance with this Agreement, and the United States shall not
be obliged to compensate Iceland or any national of Iceland or
other person for such entry or use.

Agreement relating to a special program of facilities
assistance (24 June 1954) (Exchange of Notes) (235 UNTS 3)

As a result of these discussions, the following understandings were arrived at:

(1) The Government of Italy undertakes that in connection with the facilities assistance to be furnished by the
United States:

(a) It will not discriminate in the sale of propellants and explosives produced in facilities for which the
Government of the United States has provided assistance against
any North Atlantic Treaty country in terms of the price charged,
the quality made available, or delivery dates.

(b) It will maintain the additional facilities made
available through United States assistance so that they will
be in a condition to produce propellants and explosives promptly
when they may be required: but pending such time, equipment
furnished by the United States and such additional facilities
may be used for other purposes, provided such use will not interfere with the ready availability of such equipment and facilities for the production of propellants and explosives.

(c) It will furnish all of the land, buildings,
equipment, materials, and services required for the additional
production facilities except for the equipment and technical
advice to be furnished by the Government of the United States,
and will take whatever measures are required to accomplish
the increase in production facilities envisaged in the program.

(d) In order to safeguard the security of the increased
productive capacity so urgently needed for the mutual defense of
the North Atkantic Treaty countries, it will take appropriate

0067   0161

steps to prevent the employment in such additional facilities of
personnel who are Communists or affiliated with Communist-domina-
ted labor organization

     (2)

9   (3)

0068   0162

US-Japan

Agreement relating to the settlement of costs for claims
arising under paragraph 3 (d) of Article XVIII of the
Administrative Agreement of 28 February 1952.
(Exchange of Notes 23 March 1953) (185 UNTS 94)

American Ambassador to the Japanese
Minister for Foreign Affairs

Tokyo, March 23, 1953

Excellency:

I have the honor to refer to paragraph 3 (d) of Article
XVIII of the Administrative Agreement under Article III of
the Security Treaty between the United States of America and
Japan. The said paragraph provides that "the cost incurred in
satisfying claims pursuant to the preceding subparagraphs shall
be shared on terms to be agreed by the two Governments."

In order that the two Governments may reach agreement, as
contemplated by the said provision, on the sharing of the cost incurred in satisfying claims, I have been authorized by the
Government of Hapan that the cost incurred in satisfying claims
pursuant to paragraph 3 of Article XVIII of the said Administrative Agreement shall be shared in the proportion of 75 percent
chargeable to the United States and 25 percent chargeable to
Japan, retroactive to the date on which the Administrative
Agreement entered into force.

If the proposal made herein is acceptable to the Government of Japan, this Note and Your Excellency's reply shall be
considered as constituting an agreement, effective on the date
of Your Excellency's Note in reply, between the Government of
the United States and the Government of Japan as contemplated
by paragraph 3 (d) of Article XVIII of the Administrative Agreement. The Government of the United States undertakes to seek

0069

0163

the legislative action required to carry out this agreement.

Accept, excellency, the renewed assurances of my highest consideration.

Robert Murphy

0070

0164

US-Netherlands

Agreement relating to Stationing of United States Armed

Forces in the Netherlands (Exchange of Notes: 13 August

1954; entered into force: 16 Nov. 1954)

The American Ambassador to the Netherlands
Minister for Foreign Affairs

Excellencies:

I have the honor to refer to our recent discussions
regarding the manner in which our two Governments, as parties to
the North Atlantic Treaty, may further the objectives of Article
III of that Treaty to strengthen their individual and collective
capacity to resist armed attack through the stationing of
United States armed forces in the Netherlands.   I have the
honor to imform Your Excellencies that the Government of the
Netherlands an agreement on the following terms.

1. The Governments of the United States and the Netherlands agree that the United States Government may station its
forces in the Netherlads, as may be mutually determined, in
furbherance of the objectives of the North Atlantic Treaty.

4   2. The Netherlands Governments will, without cost to
the United States, provide land areas and utilities connections,
including access roads, agreed to be necessary for the purposes
of this agreement.   The other expenses involved in carrying out
this agreement shall be borne by the United States and the Netherlands Governments in proportions to be determined between them.
Use of the utilities and services required by the United States
forces will be facilitated by the Netherlads Government.

When at the expense of the United States Government, charges
for the use of such utilities and charges for services requested
and rendered will be no higher than those paid by the Netherlands
armed services.

3.   3. Title b removable equipment, materials and supplies
brought into, or acquired in, the Netherlands by or on behalf of h
the United States in connection with this agreement will remain
in the United States Government.
This property will be free from all duties, inspections and
other restriction, whether on import or export, and from all
taxes.   At the termination of any operation under this agreement, the United States will be compensated by the Netherlands Government for the residual value, if any, of installations developed
at the expense of the United States under this agreement.
The amount and manner of compensation shall be determined between
the appropriate authorities of the two Governments.

4. The provisions of the Agreement signed at London
on June 19, 1951, Between the Parties to the North Atlantic
Treaty Regarding the Status of Their Forces, together with such
understandings as the two Governments may reach concerning the
implementation of these provisions, shall govern the status of
United States forces in the Netherlands.

5.

6.

7.........

0072

0166

Agreement to permit the utilization of Five Islands (Nelson,
Caledonia, Pelican, Lenagan, and Craig and Rock) for recreational
purposes as well as for the maintenance of a quarantine station.
(Exchange of Note: 19 Nov 53 and 19 Jul 54) 5 UST 2364)

The American Consul General to the
Colonial Secretary for Trinidad and Tobage

I have the honor to refer to your letter of July 13, 1953,
in which your Government requested the United States Government to
permit the utilization of the Five Islands for recreational purposes
as well as for the maintenace of a quarantins Station.

I now have been instructed by my Government to inform
you that it has no objectionto the utilization of the Five Islands for
the purposes indicated, subject to the following terms and conditions:

1. The United States Government may reoccupy the areas in
the event of war or emergency upon 48 hours' notice, or at other times,
upon 30 days' notice;

2. The United States CGovernment shall be free from any liability
to pay compensation for claims arising during the Trinidad and Tobage
Government's occupationlor as a result of re-occupation by the United
States;

3. The Government of Trinidad and Tobago shall be free from
any liability to pay rent or cimpensation to the United States for the
use of the areas;

4. The Government of Trinidad and Tobago shall be free to
allow use of the areas by third parties;

5. The Government of Trinidad and Tobago shall consult with
the local United States authorities before constructing or carrying
out improvements in the area;

6. Improvements constructed or carnied our by the Government
of Trinidad and Tobago shall not be such as to hinder expeditious
reoccupancy of the areas by the United States Government;

0073

0167

7. In the event of reoccupancy, the United States Government shall have the right to purchase any improvements made by the Government of Trinidad and Tobago, or its licensees;

8. In the event of reoccupancy, the United States Government may require the removal, without cost to it, of any improvements not purchased;

9. Utilization shall cause no permanent obstruction of, or permanent damage to existing bridges, roadways, or any allied installations, but this is not to be construed as imposing any obligation on the Government of Trinidad and Tobago to maintain such facilities.

10. Access to the area shall not involve entrance to the United States Naval Station, or interference with the seadrome;

11. The United States Government shall have the right to inspect the areas at all reasonable times; and

12. All the present rights of the United States Government, except as modified by this arrangement, shall remain unimpaired.

US-UK

Agreement concerning a long-range proving ground for guided

missiles to be known as "the Bahamas Long Range Proving Ground"

and exchange of notes. (Washington 21 Jul 50)(1 UST 545)

The Government of the United States of America and the

Government of the United Kingdom of Great Britain and Northern

Ireland, with the concurrence of the Government of the Bahama

Islands,

Considering that it is the intention of the Government of

the United States of America to establish a Long Range Proving

Ground .....

Having decided that the said Proving Ground should be used by

the Government of the United States of America and the Government

of the United Kingdom of Great Britain and Northern Ireland for testing

the flight of guided missiles and associated equipment and for training

with such missiles and equipment, and

Have agreed as follows:

Article 3. Rights of way.

Article 4. Provision of sites.

Article22. Claims for compensation

1. The Government of the United States of America which shall

not be less than the summpayable under the laws of the Bahama Islands,

and to indemnify the Governments of the United Kingdom and of the

Bahama Islands and all other suthorities, corporations and persons

in respect of vaild claims arising out of:

a. The death or injury of any person, except persons

employed by the Government of the United Kingdom in connection with

the Bahamas Long Range Proving Ground, resulting from the establishment,

maintenance or use by the Government of the United States of America

of the Flight Testing Range;

0075

0169

b. damage to property resulting from any action of the Government of the United States of America in connection with the establishement, maintenance or use of the Flight Testing Range;

c. the acquisition of private property, or of rights affecting private property, to enable the Sites, or any rights of the Government of the United States of America under this Agreement, to be provided.

2. Compensation payable under sub-paragraph (1) (c) of this Article shall be assessed in accordance with the laws of the Bahama Islands.

3. For the purposes of this Article the laws of the Bahama Islands shall be the laws in force at the time of the signature of this Agreement, provided that any subsequent alteration of the said alws shall have effect if the Contracting Governments so agree.

Article 18

Removal of Property

Article 23

Freedom from Rents and Charges

Except as provided in Articles XVII and XXII the Sites shall be provided, and the rights of the Government of the United States of America under this Agreement shall be made available, free from all rent and charges to the Government of the United States of America.

Note: The US-UK Agreement relating to the extension of the "Bahamas Long Rang Proving Ground" for guided missiles by the Establishment of additional sites in Turks and Caicos Islands has the same prevísions as that of above. (4 UST 429)

The US UK Agreement concerning the extension of the Bahamas Lon Range Proving Ground by the establishement of additional sitesin Saint Lucia also has the same provisions as that of above. (7 UST 1939)

The US-UK Agreement concerning the extension of the Bahamas Long Range Proving Ground by the establishement of additional sites in Ascension Island has the same provisions (7 UST 1999)

0076   0170

Agreement for the establishement in Barbados of an occeanographic research station (Washington Nov 1. 1956) (7 UST 2901)

The Government of the United States of America and the Government of the United Kingdom of Great Britain and Northern Ireland, with the concurrence of the Government of Barbados,

Considering that the Government of the United States of America wishes to establish an Oceanographic Research Station in Barbados to be used in association with the Government of the United Kingdom for the purpose of ...

...

Have agreed as follows:

Article II

General Description of Rights

1. Subject to the provisions of this Article the Government of (the United States of) ~~The United States of~~ America shall have the right in the Site:

    a. to establish, maintain and operate on Oceanographic Research Station;

    b. to establishm maintain and use an instrumentation and communication system including radio, land lines and submarine cables for operational purposes in connection with the Oceanographic Research Station;

    c. to operate such vessels and aircraft as may be necessary for purposes connected directly with the operation of the Oceanographic Research Station.

Article III

Right of Way

The Government of the United Kingdom shall, with the concurrence of the Government of Barbados. provide to the Governments of the United States of America such rights of way as may be agreed to be necessary for the establishment, maintenance or use of the Oceanographic Research Station. The Cost of acquisition of any right of way over private property shall be borne by the Contracting Governments in such proportions as are agreed between them.

Article IV

Provisions of Site

1. The Government of the United Kingdom shall, with the
concurrence of the Government of Barbados, provide so long as this
Agreement remains in force such Site for the purpose of the
establishement and operation of the Oceanographic Research Station
as may be agreed between the Contracting Governments to be necessary
for that purpose. The cost of acquisition of private property or of
rights affecting provate property, to enable the Site to be provided,
shall be borne by the Contracting Governments in such proportions as
are agreed between them.

Article XVIII

Removal of Property

1. The title to any property placed on the Site (including
property affixed to the realty) and provided by the Government of the
United States of America for the purposes of this Agreement shall
remain in the Government of the United States of America.

2. At any time before the termination of this Agreement of
within a reasonable time thereafter, such property may, at the discretion
of the Government of the United States of America, be

    a. relocated within the Site, or

    b. removed therefrom, lor

    c. disposed of while on the Site on the condition

(unless otherwise agreed between the Government of Barbados and the
United States authorities) that it shall forthwith be removed therefrom.

3. Any ground from which such property is so removed shall, if
the Government of Barbados so require, be restored as far as possible
to its present condition by the Government of the United States of
America.

4. The Government of the United States of America will not,
in Barbados, dispose of any such property.

0078   0172

a. without the consent of the Government of Barbados, or

b. without offering the property for sale to that Government, if such offer is consistent with laws of the United States of America then in effect, or

c. before the expiration of such period, not being less than 120 days after the date of such offer, as may be reasonable in the circumstances.

5. Such property may be exported by the United States authorities free from any license, export tax, duty or impost.

6. Any such property not removed or disposed of as aforesaid within a reasonable time after the termination of this Agreement shall become the property of the Government of Barbados.

Article XXII

Claims for Compensation

1. The Government of the United States of America undertakes to pay adequate and effective compensation, which shall not be less than the sum payable under the law of Barbados, and to indemnify the Government of the United Kingdom and the Government of Barbados and all other Authorities, corporations and persons in respect of valid claims arising out of:

a. the death or injury of any person, except persons employed by the Government of the United Kingdom in connection with the Oceanographic Research Station, resulting from the establishment, maintenance or use by the Government of the United States of America of the Oceanographic Research Station;

b. damage to property resulting from any action of the Government of the United States of America in connection with the establishment, maintenance or use of the Oceanographic Research Station;

c. the acquisition of private property or of rights affecting private property (other than such property or of rights acquired under Article III or Article IV) to enable any rights of the Government of the United States of America under this Agreement to be exercised.

0173

_079

4

2. Compensation payable under sub-paragraph(I) (c) of this
Article shall be assessed in accordance with the law of Barbados.

3. For the purpose of this Article the law of Barbados shall
be the law in force at the time of the signature of this Agreement,
provided that any subsequent alteration of the said law shall have
effect if the contracting Governments so agree.

Article XXIII

Freedom from Rents and Charges

Except as provided in Articles XVII and XXII the Site
shall be provided, and the rights of the Government of the United
States of America under this Agreement shall be made available,
free from all rent and charges to the Government of the United States
of America.

INTERNATIONAL AGREEMENTS REGARDING FACILITIES AND AREAS

Object	Method to Obtain The Objects	US Liability to — Rent For Private or Public Property	US Liability to — Damage To Property	US Liability to — Injury or Death	Time of Return	US Obligation relating to Restoration of Property upon return
1955 ROK Draft	Facilities and Areas necessary to carry out the mission and purpose of the United Nations	Through agreement in Joint Committee composed of one representative of each party	To be agreed in Joint Committee too. No specific provision is given in the Draft		By agreement or when facilities or areas are no longer needed	No obligation but sympathetic consideration shall be given on private property
Present Draft	Same as above but facilities and areas located in front line area are excluded	Same as above	Yes	Yes	Same as above	US will give proper or due consideration instead of sympathetic.
Jap-US Administrative Agreement	Facilities and Areas necessary for the purpose of Security Treaty	Same as above	To be agreed in Joint Committee too. No specific provision is given in the Agreement.		When Facilities or areas are no longer needed	No obligation
Philip-US Base Agreement	Bases listed in Annex A. Bases listed in B subject to agreement. Other bases subject to agreement.	—	Yes	Yes	99 Years	—
Iceland-US Defense Agreement	Facilities as mutually agreed to be necessary	No	No	—	Upon 12 months' notification	—
Netherlands-US Defense Agreement	Areas and utilities including access road as agreed to be necessary	No	Yes	—	Upon termination of NATO Treaty or by Agreement between parties	—
UK-US Agreement on Bahama Long Range Proving Ground	Sites for the operation of the Flight Testing Range	UK will provide the Site after consultation with USA	Yes	Yes	When the Site is no longer needed	—
Germany-US-UK-France Convention on Rights and Obligations	Accomodation, Transportation, Communication, Other public services	Requirement for accomodation shall be presented to German authorities. When requirement is agreed by Germany and Forces concerned, it shall be carried out by	—	—		—

purpose of the
United Nations

Present Draft	Same as above but facilities and areas located in front line area are excluded	Same as above	Yes	Yes	Yes	Same as above	US will give proper or due consideration instead of sympathetic.
Jap-US Administrative Agreement	Facilities and Areas necessary necessary for the purpose of Security Treaty	Same as above	To be agreed in Joint Committee. No specific provision is given in the Agreement.			When Facilities or areas are no longer needed	No obligation
Phili-US Base Agreement	Bases listed in Annex A. Bases listed in B subject to agreement. Other bases subject to agreement.	—	Yes	Yes	Yes	99 Years	—
Iceland-US Defense	Facilities as mutually agreed to be necessary	—	No	—	—	Upon 12 months' notification	—
Netherlands-US Defense agreement	Area and utilities including access road as agreed to be necessary		No	—	—	Upon termination of NATO Treaty or by Agreement between parties	—
UK-US Agreement on Bahama Long Range Proving Ground	Sites for the operation of the Flight Testing Range	UK will provide the Site after consultation with USA	Yes	Yes	Yes	When the Site is no longer needed	—
Germany-US-UK-France Convention on Rights and Obligations	Accomodation, Transportation, Communication, Other public services	Requirement for accomodation shall be presented to German authorities. When requirement is agreed by Germany and Forces concerned, it shall be carried out by German authorities	?	—	—	—	—
Austria-US (Payment of Occupation Cost)	Real estate Utilities Services Supplies	—	Yes	—	—	—	—

0175

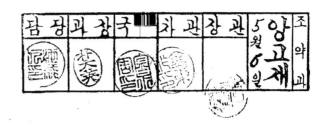

TO   : His Excellency the President

FROM   : Foreign Minister

SUBJECT   : Proposal to Start Negotiations for
               the Conclusion of Agreement concerning
               the Facilities and Areas to be Used by
               the U.S. Forces in Korea   /

        In view of the fact that the absence of an
equitable agreement on the status of U.S. forces
in Korea has caused various difficulties in the relations of U.S. forces and local Korean populace, the
Government has repeatedly requested the U.S. Government to conclude an Agreement which will regulate the
status of U.S. forces in Korea.

        The reaction of the U.S. Government, however,
has been ~~cool~~ *dilatory* toward our repeated requests and no
negotiation~~s~~ ~~on the~~ *for* conclusion of the above-mentioned
agreement ~~have~~ *has* been undertaken despite of our earnest
efforts on this question. The main reason for the
U.S. reluctancy to conclude a comprehensive Status
of Forces Agreement with the Republic of Korea seems
to be stemming from the U.S. hesitancy to turn over
to the Korean authorities a part of its jurisdictional
rights over U.S. military personnel stationed in Korea,
which it enjoys now by virtue of existing   agreement
between the two ~~countries.~~ *Government*

        Although the best policy of our Government is
to conclude a comprehensive Status of Forces Agreement with the U.S. side to regulate all problems
arising from the stationing in Korea of U.S. forces,

0176

and early settlement of this question at the present
time is not likely due to the above-mentioned attitude
of the U.S. side. Under the circumstances, the Ministry
finds it advisable to settle problems first on item-by-
item basis because any further delay on this matter
~~would be detrimental to~~ the interests of our Government.
As a matter of fact, such item-by-item approach has
already been employed by the Ministry when it concluded,
for instance, agreements on the problems of U.S. surplus
property and on the public utilities for the U.S. forces
in Korea.

It is recommended that the Ministry sends a note
to Ambassador Dowling draft of which is enclosed herein, proposing to commence negotiations for the conclusion of an agreement on the facilities and areas to be
used by the U.S. forces in Korea.

If the recommendation meets with Your Excellency's
approval, the Ministry will send the note to Ambassador
Dowling and its copy to General Decker, and shall
immediately proceed to draw up a detailed draft Agreement to be presented to the U.S. side as a basis of
negotiation.

Most respectfully,

The first item should be dealt with is an agreement on the facilities and lands that are used for the U.S. forces in Korea

(the draft of which is attached herewith)

0177

/ D R A F T /

Excellency,

I have the honor to draw your attention to the ~~subject~~ *the usage of the* ~~problem~~ of facilities and areas now in use by the U.S. forces in Korea.

As you may recall, most of the facilities and areas presently in use by the U.S. forces in Korea were furnished by the Korean authorities under the emergency state during and immediately after the outbreak of the Korean War. Under the then prevailing situation, no adequate agreement was concluded between the Government of the Republic of Korea and the Government of the United States of America to regulate various problems in relation to the use of facilities and areas by the U.S. forces in Korea.

Under the present circumstances, my Government feels that it would best serve the interests of *countries that are wholeheartedly engaged* both ~~the Korean and American authorities~~ in their joint efforts ~~for the defense~~ against the common enemy if the two Governments conclude an equitable agreement concerning the f acilities and areas ~~to be~~ *that are* used by the U.S. forces in Korea. In view of the fact that the absence of such an agreement in the past made it impossible to settle problems relating to the use of facilities and areas by the U.S. forces stationed in Korea, an agreement of this nature would ensure ~~that the joint defense efforts of the two Governments stand on a solid ground and reasonable framework.~~

0178

I wish ~~to propose,~~ therefore, that the representatives of ~~both~~ the Korean and U.S. Governments meet and discuss ~~on the~~ conclusion of an agreement which would cover at least the following points:

(1) The Korean Government will endeavor to materialize in the proposed agreement regulations to enable the United States forces in Korea to carry out their operation in most effective way;

(2) Both Governments will review the conditions by which the U.S. forces are using the facilities and areas in Korea; but the Korean Government will grant in ~~principle~~ the continued use by the United States forces of the facilities and areas presently in use ~~by such forces~~; and

(3) The United States Government will give due ~~sympathetic~~ consideration to owners of the properties offered to them.

I sincerely hope that the above proposal of my Government will receive favorable consideration by your Government and that on that basis the negotiations be commenced for the conclusion of an agreement on the subject matter at an early date.

Accept, Excellency, the renewed assurances of my highest consideration.

Chung W. Cho
~~Minist~~er

His Excellency Walter C Dowling
    Ambassador ~~of~~ ~~the United States of~~
    America

RECOMMENDATION KPO/186

관리 번호
제 42

검토필 (1962 12. 17. 464   검토필 (196 X. 12 - 30)

May 12, 1959

가결쓸측근 맞상비밀로재별목 1962. 2. 15

TO   : His Excellency the President

FROM   : Foreign Minister

SUBJECT : Proposal to Start Negotiations for
          the Conclusion of Agreement concerning
          the Facilities and Areas to be Used by
          the U.S. Forces in Korea

검토필 (196 5 6. 30)

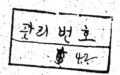

In view of the fact that the absence of an
equitable agreement on the status of U.S. forces in
Korea has caused various difficulties in the relations
of U.S. forces and local Korean populace, the Government has repeatedly requested the U.S. Government to
conclude an Agreement which will regulate the status
of U.S. forces in Korea.

The reaction of the U.S. Government, however,
has been dilatory toward our repeated requests and no
negotiation for conclusion of the above-mentioned
agreement has been undertaken despite of our earnest
efforts on the question. The main reason for the U.S.
reluctancy to conclude a comprehensive Status of Forces
Agreement with the Republic of Korea seems to be stemming from the U.S. hesitancy to turn over to the Korean
authorities a part of its jurisdictional rights over
U.S. military personnel stationed in Korea, which it
enjoys now by virtue of existing agreement between the
two Governments.

0180

- 2 -

Although the best policy of our Government is to conclude a comprehensive Status of Forces Agreement with the U.S. side to regulate all problems arising from the stationing in Korea of U.S. forces, and early settlement of this question at the present time is not likely due to the above-mentioned attitude of the U.S. side. Under the circumstances, the Ministry finds it advisable to settle problems first on item-by-item basis for it would better the interests of our Government. As a matter of fact, such item-by-item approach has already been employed by the Ministry when it concluded, for instance, agreements on the problems of U.S. surplus property and on the public utilities for the U.S. forces in Korea.

The first item that should be dealt with is an agreement on the facilities and lands that are used by the U.S. forces in Korea.

If the recommendation meets with Your Excellency's approval, the Ministry will send a note, the draft of which is attached herewith, to Ambassador Dowling and its copy to General Decker, proposing to commence negociations for conclusion of an agreement on the said subject.

Most respectfully,

0181

/D R A F T/

Excellency,

    I have the honor to draw your attention to the subject of usage of the facilities and areas now in use by the U.S. forces in Korea.

    As you may recall, most of the facilities and areas presently in use by the U.S. forces in Korea were furnished by the Korean authorities under the emergency state during and immediately after the outbreak of the Korean War. Under the then prevailing situation, no adequate agreement was concluded between the Government of the Republic of Korea and the Government of the United States of America to regulate various problems in relation to the use of facilities and areas by the U.S. forces in Korea.

    Under the present circumstances, my Government feels that it would best serve the interests of both countries that are wholeheartedly engaged in their joint efforts against the common enemy if the two Governments conclude an equitable agreement concerning the facilities and areas that are used by the U.S. forces in Korea. In view of the fact that the absence of such an agreement in the past made it impossible to settle problems related to the use of facilities and areas by the U.S. forces stationed in Korea, an agreement of this nature would ensure the joint defense efforts of the two Governments to be very fruitful and most satisfactory.

0182

I wish to propose, therefore, that the representatives of both the Korean and U.S. Governments meet and discuss for conclusion of an agreement which would cover at least the following points:

(1) The Korean Government will endeavor to materialize in the proposed agreement regulations to enable the United States forces in Korea to carry out their operation in most effective way;

(2) Both Governments will review the conditions by which the U.S. forces are using the facilities and areas in Korea; but the Korean Government will grant, in accordance of international precedents, the continued use by the United States forces of the facilities and areas presently in use; and

(3) The United States Government will give due consideration to owners of the properties offered to them.

I sincerely hope that the above proposal of my Government will receive favorable consideration by your Government and that on that basis the negotiations be commenced for conclusion of an agreement on the subject matter at an earliest date.

Accept, Excellency, the renewed assurances of my highest consideration.

/s/
Chung W. Cho
Minister

His Excellency
Walter C. Dowling
Ambassador of the United States
of America

0183

검토필(1962. 12. 17.) 인

발송

6月12日 金外務次官이
Dowling 大使를 招致하여
次官室에서 交

과로 분류로 포공비밀로 재분류
1962. 2. 17.

관리번호
41

June 10, 1959

검토필(196. 4. 12. 30.)

Excellency,

I have the honor to draw your attention to the subject of usage of the facilities and areas now in use by the U.S. forces in Korea.

As you may recall, most of the facilities and areas presently in use by the U.S. forces in Korea were furnished by the Korean authorities under the emergency state during and immediately after the outbreak of the Korean War. Under the then prevailing situation, no adequate agreement was concluded between the Government of the Republic of Korea and the Government of the United States of America to regulate various problems in relation to these facilities.

My Government feels that it would best serve the interests of both countries that are wholeheartedly engaged in their joint efforts against the common enemy if the two Governments conclude an equitable agreement regarding the same. In view of the fact that the absence of such an agreement in the past made it impossible to resolve problems related to the use of such facilities and areas, an agreement of this nature would improve the defense efforts of the two Governments.

I wish to propose, therefore, that the representatives of both the Korean and U.S. Government

0184

meet and discuss and later conclude such an agreement which could cover (1) regulations to enable the United States forces in Korea to carry out their operation in a most effective way; (2) set out the conditions under which the U.S. forces will be using the facilities and areas involved; (3) with the Korean Government granting, in accordance with international precedents, the continued use by the United States forces of such facilities and areas and (4) with the United States Government giving full consideration to owners of the properties.

I sincerely hope that the above will receive favorable consideration by your Government and that discussions could be commenced at the earliest date possible with end in view of concluding an agreement along the lines indicated above, without delay.

Accept, Excellency, the renewed assurances of my highest consideration.

Chung W. Cho
Minister

His Excellency
    Walter C. Dowling
        Ambassador of the United States
           of America

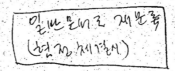

0185

외 무 부

4292 년 6 월 12 일

별첨 주한미국군이 사용하는 토지, 건물 및
시설에 관한 한미간의 협정 체결의 교섭개시를 요
청하는 각서는 4292년 6월 12일 차관 께서
다우링 주한 미국 대사를 초치하여 직접 수교하셨음.

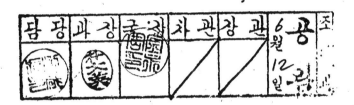

한·미국 간의 상호방위조약 제4조에 의한 시설과 구역 및 한국에서의 미국군대의 지위에 관한 협정(SOFA)
전59권. 1966.7.9 서울에서 서명 : 1967.2.9 발효(조약 232호) (V.5 체결 교섭, 1959)

approved as written

Excellency,

I have the honor to draw your attention to the subject of usage of the facilities and areas now in use by the U.S. forces in Korea.

As you may recall, most of the facilities and areas presently in use by the U.S. forces in Korea were furnished by the Korean authorities under the emergency state during and immediately after the outbreak of the Korean War. Under the then prevailing situation, no adequate agreement was concluded between the Government of the Republic of Korea and the Government of the United States of America to regulate various problems in relation to these facilities.

My Government feels that it would best serve the interests of both countries that are wholeheartedly engaged in their joint efforts against the common enemy if the two Governments conclude an equitable agreement regarding the same. In view of the fact that the absence of such an agreement in the past made it impossible to resolve problems related to the use of such facilities and areas, an agreement of this nature would improve the defense efforts of the two Governments.

I wish to propose, therefore, that the representatives of both the Korean and U.S. Governments meet and discuss and later conclude such an agreement which could cover 1) regulations to enable the United States forces in Korea to carry out their operation in a

0187

外務部 接受
4292.6.10

most effective way; (2) set out the conditions under which the U.S. forces will be using the facilities and areas involved; (3) with the Korean Government granting, in accordance with international precedents, the continued use by the United States forces of such facilities and areas and (4) with the United States Government giving full consideration to owners of the properties.

I sincerely hope that the above will receive favorable consideration by your Government and that discussions could be commenced at the earliest date possible with end in view of concluding an agreement along the lines indicated above, without delay.

Accept, Excellency, the renewed assurances of my highest consideration.

Chung W. Cho
Minister

His Excellency
Walter C. Dowling
Ambassador of the United States of America

0188

외 무 부

외정(조) 제　　　호

단기 4292년 6월 12일

예고문에 의한 일반문서로 재분류
1962. 12. 31

정 무 국 장

방 교 국 장 귀 하

보도자료 송부의 건

대미의 건별첨 자료를 보도자료로서 송부하오니 선처 하시기 바라나이다.

별 첨 : 주한 미국군이 사용하는 토지 건물 및 시설에 관한 한미간의 협정 체결을 위한 교섭에 관한 보도자료　1부

담 당	과 장	국 장	6월 12일	조약과
			양고지	

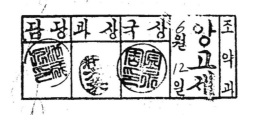

0189

정부는 한국 내에 주둔하고 있는 외국군대와 우리나라 국민간의 최대한도의 협조를 기하기 위하여 수년래 ‖ 주둔군의 지위에 관한 한미간의 협정 (흔히 행정협정 이라고 불린다) ‖ 의 체결을 촉구하는 한편 이의 실현을 위하여 예의 노력하여 왔는바, 이러한 전면적협정의 체결이 되기까지라도 시급한 문제부터 하나씩 해결하여야 할 것으로, 최근 외무부는 ‖ 주한 미국군이 사용하는 토지, 건물 및 시설에 관한 한미간의 협정 (가칭) ‖ 의 체결을 미국측에 대하여 제의한바 있다.

물론 어떠한 토지, 건물 및 시설을 대상으로 하느냐 또는 그러한 사용에 대한 경제적인 대가문제등을 어떠한 방법으로 해결하느냐 하는 문제는 앞으로의 교섭에 의하여 구체적으로 해결될 것이다.

0190

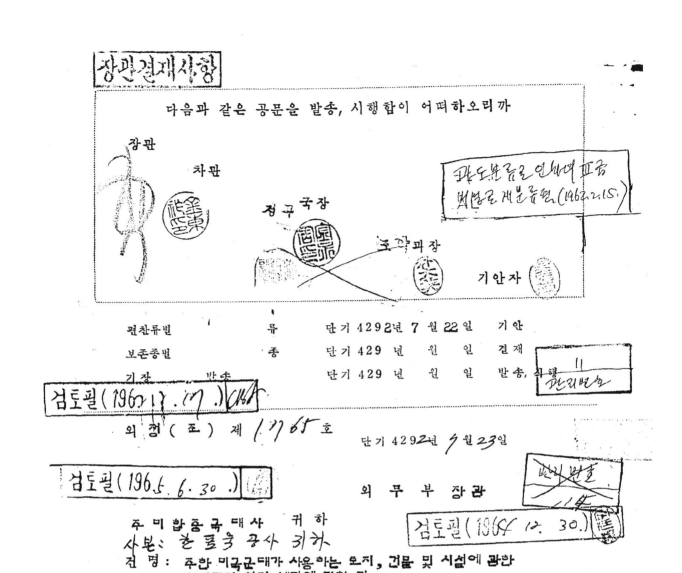

다음과 같은 공문을 발송, 시행함이 어떠하오리까

장관

차관

정구국장

조약과장

기안자

파도문등로 인사에 표금
법별로 재분등원 (1962.2.15.)

편찬류별		류	단기 4292년 7 월 22일	기안
보존종별		종	단기 429 년 원 일	결재
기장 발송			단기 429 년 원 일	발송

검토필 (1962.13. 19.)

외정 (조) 제 1765 호   단기 4292년 5 월 23일

검토필 (1965. 6. 30.)   외 무 부 장 관   검토필 (1964. 12. 30.)

주미합중국대사 귀하
사본: 손코옥 공사 귀하
건 명: 주한 미국군대가 사용하는 토지, 건물 및 시설에 관한
       한미간의 협정 체결에 관한 건

        머리의 건, 외정 제4432호 (단기 4290년 12월 16일자) 를 통하여
이미 귀하에게 통보한바 있으므로 귀하도 주지하는바와 같이, 주한 미국
군대의 지위에 관한 협정을 체결하기 위하여 정부는 과거 수년동안 여러
차례에 걸쳐 미국측에 교섭개시를 촉구한바 있었으나, 미국측에서는 이러한
포괄적인 협정 체결 교섭에 대하여 유리한 관심을 보여주지않았으며,
근래에는 오히려 미국 주둔군의 지위를 몇개의 협정으로 분리 규정함이
좋겠다고 시사하여온바 있었는데, (참조. 별첨1 교섭경위), 이러한 미국무성
의 태도는 미국군대의 지위에 관한 협정에 대하여 예민한 관심을 표시하고
있는 미국 국회 또는 일반 국민여론을 자극시키지 아니하며는 국내사정과
또한 상호간에 합의할수있는 사항부터 하나하나 개별적으로 처리하여
나가는것이 현명하겠다는 판단에 기초를 둔것으로 보여지는데, 우리의
목적을 달성하기위하여 정부는 이러한 개별협정 체결 제의를 수락하고, 위선

0191

현안중의 하나인 "주한 미국 군대가 사용하는 토지, 건물 및 시설에 관한 한미협정"을 체결하고저 준비를 진행시켜, 단기 4292년 6월 10일 에는 다울링 대사에게 협정 체결을 위한 교섭 개시를 제의하기에 이르렀아온바(참조. 별첨 5), 이 교섭 제의는 현재 국무성에 계속 되고있는데 우리의 노력은 서울과 와싱톤에서 유기적으로 행하여저야 하겠으므로, 귀하는 이러한 문제에 관하여 종래 미국측의 태도가 언제 나 소극적이었음을 양지하시와, 전기 우리측 제의에 대한 미국측의 동의를 획득하도록 예의 국무성 당국과 접촉하시며, 그 결과를 수시로 보고하시기 바라나이다. ~~본건 접촉활동의 실무는 한표욱 공사의 담당~~ ~~으로 합의 적정할것입니다.~~

이 상.

별 첨 :

1. 교섭 경위

2. 단기 4290년 9월 10일자로 "허어터"국무차관에게 전달한 한국정부 의 견해

3. 개별협정 체결 제안에 관한 단기 4290년 11월 13일자 외무부장관 공한

4. 개별협정 체결에 관한 한국정부의 견해를 전달하는 단기 4290년 11월 26일자 외무부장관 공한 및 주한 미국대사의 회한

5. "주한 미국군대가 사용하는 토지, 건물 및 시설에 관한 협정" 교섭 제의에 관한 단기 4292년 6월 10일자 외무부장관 공한 및 주한 미국대사의 회한

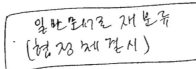
일반문서로 재분류
(협정 체결시)

별첨 1

고 섭 경 위

1. 단기4286년 8월 7일, 덕태용·변과 덥떼스국무장관은 공동성명을 통하여, 한미상호방위조약 효력발생후 주한미국군대의 지위에 관한 협정 체결을 위하여 즉시로 협의할것을 선언하였음.

2. 단기4287년 12월 2일, 우미정부는, 주한 유언군의 지위에 관한 협정이 체결되기전에 잠정적으로 ||한국 세관업무에 관한 한미협정||을 체결 할것을 미국측에 제의하였으나, 미국측의 반응이 없었음.(참조. 별첨2.)

3. 단기4288년 4월 28일, 우미정부는 주한 유언군의 지위를 전반적으로 규정하기위한 한국정부와 통합사령부간의 협정체결을 미국측에 제의하고, 이와 동시에 우티측의 협정안을 전달하였으나, 미국측은 여시 이에 대하여 반응을 보이지 않았음.(참조. 별첨2.)

4. 단기4290년 1월 5일, 우미정부는, 주한 유언군의 지위에 관한 협정을 체결함에 있어서 관계 연합국 정부간의 의견조정이 곤난하고 또한 사일을 오하는 경우에는 미국군대만의 지위 략도 규정하기위한 한미간의 단독협정을 체결할것을 미국측에 제의하고, 동년 6월 29일자로 이를 재차 촉구하였 음(참조. 별첨2.).

5. 단기4290년 9월 10일, 당시 내한중인 허허국무차관에게 각서를 수고하여, 그간의 교섭경위를 설명하고, 한미간의 협정체결을 촉구하였음(참조. 별 첨 2).

6. 단기4290년 10월 10일, 주한 미국대사는 외무부장관과의 회담에서, 포괄적인 협정 체결을 지양하고 적당한 사항에 관하여 미국군대의 지위를 부분적으로 규정하는 개별협정의 체결 가능성을 시사하였음.

7. 단기4290년 11월 13일, 우미정부는 전기 미국대사의 시사를 확인, 수탁하는 뜻을 미국측에 전달하고(참조. 별첨 3), 동년 11월 2ㅇ일 개별협정 체결에 관한 우미정부의 대체적인 방안을 제시하였음(참조. 별 첨 4). 그러나 미국측은 이에 대하여 여전히 소극적인 태도를 보였음.

0193

8. 단기 4291년 9월 18일, 주한 미국대사는 외무부 차관과의 회담에서, 한국에 있어서 전투상태는 중지되었으나 아직 완전한 평화상태로 회복하지않았음을 강조하고, 재판 관할권에 관한 단기 4283년 7월 12일의 한미 협정(대전협정)을 수정하지않는다는 한국측의 보장이 있을 경우에는 미국정부는 기타사항에 관하여 개별협정을 체결할 용의가 있다고 언명하였음.

9. 단기 4292년 3월 25일, 주한 미국대사는 외무부장관과의 회담에서, 미국군대의 지위에 관한 전면적인 협정은 미국 상원의 비준동의를 받기가 거의 불가능함을 강조하고, 개별협정 체결이 보다 더 용이할 것이라고 지적하였음. 우리측은, 이러한 미국측의 제의는 미국군인에 대한 재판관할권을 규정한 대전협정의 수정을 피하기위한것이라고 해석하고, 그러나 이 문제에 관하여는 하등의 언질을 주지않고서 개별협정 체결을 추진하기로 결정하였음.

10. 단기 4292년 6월 10일, 우리정부는 개별협정중 우선 ‖주한 미국군대가 사용하는 토지, 건물 및 시설에 관한 협정‖체결을 위한 한미간의 교섭 개시를 정식으로 제의하였음(참조. 별첨⑤).

이 상.

협정 체결시 일반문서로
재 분류

한·미국 간의 상호방위조약 제4조에 의한 시설과 구역 및 한국에서의 미국군대의 지위에 관한 협정(SOFA) 전59권. 1966.7.9 서울에서 서명 : 1967.2.9 발효(조약 232호) (V.5 체결 교섭, 1959) 201

Our friendly and understanding consultations demonstrate clearly the determination of the United States and the Republic of Korea to stand together in cordial cooperation to achieve our common objective, including the reunification of Korea.

We have today initialed a draft of a mutual-defense treaty. That treaty is designed to unit our nations in common action to meet common danger and it will cement the ties which have brought us together to combat in Korea the menace of Communist aggression.

Our two governments will actively proceed with the constitutional processes necessary to bring this treaty into full force and effect. These constitutional processes, in the case of the United States, require that the United States Senate consent to the ratification. The United States Senate, having adjourned this week, will not again be in regular session until next January. However, United States Senate leaders have been kept fully informed of the exchange of views which have led to the action we have taken today and it is our sincere hope that this will lead to prompt and favourable United States Senate action.

Between now and the date when the Mutual Defense Treaty can be expected to come into force and effect, our armed forces in Korea will be subject to the United Nations Command which will comply with the armistice terms. If, during this period, there should occur unprovoked armed attack by the Communist forces against the Republic of Korea in violation of the armistice, the UNC, including the Republic of Korea forces, would at once and automatically react, as such an unprovoked attack would be an attack upon and and a threat to the UNC itself and to the forces under its command. Such reaction to an unprovoked armed attack would not be a new war but rather a resumption by the Communist forces of the active belligerency which the armistice has halted. The UNC will be constantly alert against such an attack.

0195

0196

Our Governments will promptly negotiate agreements to cover the status of such forces as the United States may elect to maintain in Korea after the mutual-defense treaty comes into force and effect, and the availability to them of Korean facilities and services needed for the discharge of our common task. In the meantime, the Republic of Korea will continue to cooperate with the UNC and the status of UNC forces in Korea and the availability to them of Korean facilities and services will continue as at present.

The armistice contemplates that a political conference will be convened within three months, that is, prior to October 27, 1953. At that conference the United States delegation, in cooperation with the ROK delegation and other delegations from the UNC side, will seek to achieve the peaceful unification of historic Korea as a free and independent nation. We and our advisers have already had a full and satisfactory exchange of views which we hope and trust will establish a preparatory foundation for coordinated effort at the political conference.

If, after the political conference has been in session for 90 days, it becomes clear to each of our governments that all attempts to achieve these objectives have been fruitless and that the conference is being exploited by the Communist delegates mainly to infiltrate, propagandize or otherwise embarrass the Republic of Korea, we shall then be prepared to make a concurrent withdrawal from the conference. We will then consult further regarding the attainment of a unified, free and independent Korea which is the postwar goal the United States set itself during World War II, which has been accepted by the United Nations as its goal and which will continue to be an object of concern of United States foreign policy.

We recognize that the Republic of Korea possesses the inherent right of sovereignty to deal with its problems, but it has agreed to take no unilateral action to unite Korea by military means for the agreed duration of the political conference.

We contemplate that the projected three to four year program

0197

for the rehabilitation of the war ruined Korean economy shall be coordinated through the combined economic board, under the joint chair-
manship of the Korean and American representatives. This program
contemplates the expenditure of approximately one billion dollars of funds,
subject to appropriations thereof by the United States Congress. Two
hundred million dollars has already been authorized, out of prospective
defense savings.

We have exchanged preliminary views with respect to various problems
involving the maintenance and development of ROK land, air and sea forces.

We feel confident that the relationship thus established between
our two governments marks an important contribution to the developing of
independence and freedom in the Far East. With unshaking faith in the
principle of collective security, and with loyal adherence to the Charter
of the United Nations, we intend to move forward together toward the
achievement of our common objective--the restoration of a unified,
democratic and independent Korean nation.

There are no other agreements or understandings stated or implied
resulting from these consultations other than those herein contained.

일반 문서로 재분류 (1962. 2. 9)

0123

한·미국 간의 상호방위조약 제4조에 의한 시설과 구역 및 한국에서의 미국군대의 지위에 관한 협정(SOFA)
전59권. 1966.7.9 서울에서 서명 : 1967.2.9 발효(조약 232호) (V.5 체결 교섭, 1959) 207

별첨 2.

✓ <u>ROK views transmitted to U.S. Under Secretary Herter</u>

September 10, 1957

SUBJECT: Proposed Agreement on the Status of United
Nations or ~~United States Forces~~ in Korea.

The Government of the Republic of Korea, keenly
desiring to conclude an agreement which would define
the status of the United Nations armed forces in Korea,
with the Government of the United States of America
acting for the Unified Command in accordance with "The
Resolution on the Settlement of the Unified Command" of
the Security Council of the United Nations of July 7,
1950, initially proposed to the Government of the
United States of America through the Foreign Minister's
note of April 28, 1955, attached hereto as Annex A,
that negotiations should be opened for that purpose.

It is also recalled that, as there was no
positive reaction on the part of the United States
Government on the said matter, the Korean Government
again renewed its proposal to the United States through
the Foreign Minister's notes of January 5, 1957 and
June 29, 1957 respectively, copies of which are attached
hereto as Annex B and Annex C. No definite reply stat-
ing the position of the United States Government in
regard to these proposals has been received as yet.

Attention is invited to the note (Annex D hereto)
of General Lemnitzer of July 26, 1955 addressed to the
Foreign Minister, in which the former, in expressing
his views on the possibility of negotiations on the

0201

said Agreement, stated that the United States Government envisages difficulties in commencing negotiations immediately for two reasons:

1) It would be preferred by the United States Government that the negotiations for the proposed treaty of Friendship, Commerce and Navigation between the two countries as well as an agreement guaranteeing investments be completed before the initiation of negotiations for the agreement in question;

2) The Unified Command could not participate in negotiations for such an agreement without the prior consent of the allies within the Unified Command, and the task of obtaining such consent is time consuming.

As for the first reason mentioned above, the Korea-United States Treaty of Friendship, Commerce and Navigation has been already signed and is now only awaiting exchange of the instruments of ratification. As for the agreement guaranteeing investment, i.e. the so-called MSA Guarantee Agreement proposed by the United States Government, the Korean Government is preparing the final draft, and a definite agreement should be reached in the immediate future.

As for the second reason, the Government of the Republic of Korea is of the opinion that, as the United States forces in Korea actually constitute the preponderant components of the United Nations Forces under the Unified Command, the negotiations could be commenced first between the Korean Government and the United States Government regarding the status of the United States forces in Korea.

한·미국 간의 상호방위조약 제4조에 의한 시설과 구역 및 한국에서의 미국군대의 지위에 관한 협정(SOFA)
전59권. 1966.7.9 서울에서 서명 : 1967.2.9 발효(조약 232호) (V.5 체결 교섭, 1959) 209

3

Apart from the above-mentioned two reasons, it
is presumed that the reluctance on the part of the
United States Government to commence negotiations on
this subject is based on the fact that Korea is
technically still in a state of war. Needless to say,
however, active hostilities ceased in 1953, and the
danger of a recurrence of hostilities is not considered
imminent. It cannot be predicted how long the current
situation will last.

Under these circumstances, it is not realistic
to consider the current situation, which has lasted
so long, a state of war in a virtual sense. Therefore,
the Korean Government does not consider that anything
in the current situation in Korea prevents the Governments of the Republic of Korea and the United States
of America from entering into the relations which would
be established if the Agreement under reference be
concluded. As for the anxiety concerning the possible
recurrence of hostilities in Korea, there would be no
reason why the parties to the proposed Agreement
should not review the applicability of the provisions
concerned in such case.

What the Korean Government desires to conclude
with the United States is nothing but such agreements
similar to those concluded by the latter with NATO
powers in 1951 and with Japan in 1952 on the same
subject.

In the absence of such an agreement between the
Republic of Korea and the United States of America,
and in view of the then-prevailing conditions of war-
fare and urgent necessity, a modus vivendi, which

0203

partly defined the status of the United States forces
in Korea, came into being between the two governments
through the exchange of notes at Taejon on July 12,
1950 concerning the exclusive jurisdiction by court-
martial of the United States over its military
personnel in Korea. In view of the changed conditions
after the summer of 1953, the aforesaid provisional
arrangement of 1950 is no longer appropriate in its
nature nor sufficient to meet and solve adequately,
under the circumstances, all of the complicated problems and matters arising daily because of the stationing and disposition of United States forces in Korea.

In this connection, it is with regret that
numerous incidents must be mentioned which occurred
between the United States army personnel and local
civilians; in most cases, incidents caused by
delinquency on the part of members of the United
States forces in Korea, involving many casualties and
much damage to valuable property. All of such incidents, according to the provisional arrangement of 1950,
are exclusively within the jurisdiction of the United
States. The Korean Government especially fears that
such incidents, and the present way of application of
justice, may injure the friendly relationship existing
between the peoples of the two countries.

The Government of the Republic of Korea again
requests the Government of the United States of America
to give favorable consideration to the ~~proposal of the~~
proposal of the Korean Government so that negotiations
between the two governments may be commenced as early

한·미국 간의 상호방위조약 제4조에 의한 시설과 구역 및 한국에서의 미국군대의 지위에 관한 협정(SOFA)
전59권. 1966.7.9 서울에서 서명 : 1967.2.9 발효(조약 232호) (V.5 체결 교섭, 1959) 211

as possible. A prompt conclusion of the Agreement in question would undoubtedly serve to promote increased friendship between the peoples of the two countries.

0205

<u>A N N E X   A.</u>

April 28, 1955

Dear Mr. Charge d'Affaires:

I have the honour to initiate a proposal to conclude an Administrative Agreement between the Government
of the Republic of Korea and the Government of the United
States of America, and enclose herewith a draft of the
Agreement. With regard to this proposal, I would like
first to refer to my note dated December 2, 1954, concerning a conclusion of provisional agreement regarding
the functions of Korean customs authorities with respect
to the United Nations forces in Korea. Particular
reference was made in the note to the effect that such
customs agreement will remain in force pending conclusion of a General Administrative Agreement which shall
cover other subject also.

Having in mind that the United Nations forces
under the Unified Command are and will be disposed in
and about the territory of the Republic of Korea until
the objective of the United Nations in Korea will have
been achieved pursuant to the resolutions of the United
Nations Security Council of June 25, 1950, June 27, 1950
and July 7, 1950, it is the belief of the Korean Government that terms shall be provided, for the interests of
both parties, to govern the disposition of and render
convenience to the said forces in and about Korea, and
that they shall be determined through mutual agreement
between the Republic of Korea and the United States of
America acting as the Unified Command in accordance with
"The Resolution on the Settlement of the Unified Command"
of the Security Council of the United Nations of July 7,
1950. A practical and effective Administrative Agreement
to be concluded between the said two parties will help
minimize misunderstanding and maximize cooperativeness
between the Korean people and United Nations forces
personnel in Korea.

In the belief that a conclusion of the Agreement
is in the mutual interests, I wish to propose formally,
on behalf of the Government of the Republic of Korea,
that negotiation will be commenced between the representatives of Korean Government and the United States
Government. Upon the receipt of your consent, we will
proceed to decide the date and place of the conference,
which will be mutually agreeable.

Accept, dear Mr. Charge d'Affaires, the assurances of my highest consideration.

Enclosure: Draft of Administrative
            Agreement

Y. T. Pyun
Minister of Foreign
Affairs

The Honourable Carl W. Strom,
Charge d'Affaires,
Embassy of the United States of America
Seoul, Korea

0206

January 5, 1957

Excellency:

I have the honour to refer to the Foreign Minister's note addressed to Mr. Carl W. Strom, Charge d Affairs ad interim of the Embassy of the United States of America in Korea dated April 28, 1955 enclosing a draft of an Administrative Agreement between the Republic of Korea and the Unified Command for establishment of the Status of the United Nations Forces in Korea.

In the afore-said note, the Minister informed the Government of the United States of America of the desire of the Korean Government to commence negotiations with the United States Government for the said Status of Forces Agreement which will also define the former's customs functions as referred to in my letter of December 2, 1954.

To this proposal, however, no acceptance has been given as yet, although the American Charge d'Affairs notified in his replying note of May 9, 1955, that upon obtaining his Government's view on the said request, he would communicate with the Minister.

I hereby wish again to propose, on behalf of my Government, that negotiation be commenced at an earliest possible date between the representatives of the Korean Government and the United States Government. In connection with this re-proposal, I would like further to

His Excellency
    The right honourable
        Walter C. Dowling
            Ambassador of the United States of
                America to the Republic of Korea
                    Seoul, Korea

0207

refer to the note of July 26, 1955 addressed to the
Foreign Minister by General Lemnitzer advising on this
matter.

General Lemnitzer expressed his views on the
possibility of negotiating the said agreement in the
above note to the effect that the United States
Government envisages difficulties in commencing immediately negotiations for a proposed agreement for
the following two reasons:

The one reason was that it would be preferable
to the American Government that negotiations for a
proposed treaty of Friendship, Commerce and Navigation
between the two countries as well as an agreement
guaranteeing investments be completed before the initiation of negotiation for an agreement in question. The
other was that the Unified Command cannot participate
in negotiation of such agreement without the prior
consent of allies within the Unified Command and it is
anticipated that the task of obtaining such consent
will be difficult.

Attention, however, is paid to the fact that the
points indicated above constitute no longer difficulties
about negotiating the said agreement under the present
circumstances.

The Treaty of Friendship, Commerce and Navigation
has been already signed and is now waiting to be formally ratified. As regards the agreement guaranteeing
investments, discussions have been completed on
provisions of its draft and now the work of finalising

한·미국 간의 상호방위조약 제4조에 의한 시설과 구역 및 한국에서의 미국군대의 지위에 관한 협정(SOFA)
전59권. 1966.7.9 서울에서 서명 : 1967.2.9 발효(조약 232호) (V.5 체결 교섭, 1959) 215

it remains only. On the other hand, since allies within the Unified Command have been decreased in number into twelve nations and since the American forces form the predominant components of the United Nations Forces, there exist no difficulties, it is belived, in securing consent of other allies as to the matter.

And thus, even in case the consent of the other allies has not been obtained as yet, it is, therefore, proposed that negotiations be started first between both representatives of the Korean Government and the United States Government and that negotiations with other allies shall be carried on separately in accordance with terms to be agreed upon between Korea and the United States of America. It is sincerely requested that the concurrence of the United States Government be given to the wish of the Korean Government to commence negotiations for the agreement proposed.

Please accept, Excellency, the renewed assurances of my highest consideration.

Chung W. Cho
Minister of
Foreign Affairs

0203

June 29, 1957

My dear Mr. Ambassador:

I have the honor to remind your Government as
I have orally mentioned to you on several occasions,
that the conclusion of an Administrative Agreement
defining and setting forth in detail the status of
United States troops stationed in Korea is still
pending.

On April 28, 1955, our draft proposal of an
Administrative Agreement between this Government and
the Unified Command, to establish the status of United
Nations forces in Korea, was addressed to your Embassy.
On November 1, 1956, it was proposed that a separate
agreement be negotiated between representatives of this
Government and the United States Government, in case of
difficulty in obtaining early consent of the other
Allied Governments.

In the absence of such an administrative agreement,
a temporary agreement was made through the exchange of
Notes at Taejon, on July 12, 1950, concerning the exclusive jurisdiction by court-martial of the United States
over members of the United States Military Establishment
in Korea. This agreement, which is still in force, was
improvised to meet an emergency situation and is not
considered sufficient to meet effectively all the complex and complicated problems arising from the presence

His Excellency
    Ambassador Walter C. Dowling
        American Embassy,
            Seoul.

0210

of the United States troops in Korea.

This Government is strongly convinced that the early conclusion of a formal and detailed agreement on the status of United States troops in Korea would serve to strengthen cordial relations between our people and American military personnel, and would provide great satisfaction to the mutual cause and interest of both countries.

I wish to state again that this Government is most desirous of receiving the concurrence of the United States Government in order to commence negotiations for an administrative agreement along the lines of the proposal of April, 1955. Your Government's earliest favorable consideration of this matter is most sincerely desired.

Accept, Excellency, renewed assurances of my highest consideration.

Chung W. Cho
Minister of
Foreign Affairs

A N N E X   D.

Dear Minister Pyun:

Thank you very much for your letter of 13 June 1955, in which you acknowledge-receipt of General Taylor's letter of 14 May 1955, with the inclosures pertaining to customs functions of the Republic of Korea.

I have noted the desire of the Korean Government to commence negotiations with the Government of the United States for a Status of Forces Agreement between the Korean Government and the Unified Command. This matter is presently under study by the Departments of my government in Washington.

Current thinking on this matter is that it would be preferable that negotiations now in progress or pending be completed before the initiation of negotiations for an agreement of the type in question. Ambassador Lacy advises me that a proposed treaty of friendship, commerce and navigation between our respective governments is under consideration, as well as an agreement guaranteeing investments, and that he is anxious to complete these matters before taking up any other major negotiations.

I am sure you are also aware that the Unified Command cannot participate in a negotiations of any Status of Forces Agreement without the prior consent of our allies within the United Nations Command. It is anticipated that the task of obtaining this consent will be difficult and time consuming.

Sincerely,

/s/
L. L. LEMNITZER
General, United States Army
Commander-in-Chief

His Excellency Pyun Yung-Tai
    Minister for Foreign Affairs of
        the Republic of Korea

0212

Foreign Minister to United States Ambassador

November 13, 1957

Dear Mr. Ambassador:

    I wish to bring to your attention the question
of an Agreement on the status of the United States
Forces in Korea and to recent developments in our
efforts to solve problems arising between members
of the United States Forces and Korean nationals.

    Since the cessation of active hostilities in
1953, it has become increasingly clear that a <u>modus
vivendi</u> reached between our two Governments through
an exchange of notes at Taejon on July 12, 1950 allow-
ing the United States exclusive jurisdiction by court-
martial of members of the United States Forces in
Korea is not sufficient to cope with various complicated problems involving members of the United States
Forces and our people.

    This Government, keenly desiring to conclude
an agreement on the status of United States Forces in
our Country, initially proposed to your Government
through the Foreign Minister's note of April 28, 1955,
that negotiations be commenced for that purpose, and
later, having failed to receive any positive reaction
to this proposal, brought up the matter again on
several occasions. When the Under Secretary of State
visited Korea, a note on this question dated September
10, 1957, was presented to Mr. Herter in the hope that

0213

the matter would receive his favorable attention. A
copy of this note is enclosed.

In this connection, I am deeply interested in
a suggestion made by you at a meeting held in my
office on October 10, 1957 that there might be room
for reaching a separate agreement on particular items
as was done in the utilities problems" I deeply appreci-
ate your friendly and cooperative interest in these
problems and will be very happy to proceed with negotiations for separate agreements with your Government on
particular items; for instance, taxation, customs duty,
and criminal jurisdiction. I am confident such negotiations will lead to an acceptable solution to our common
problems.

With warmest personal regards, I remain,

Sincerely yours,

Chung W. Cho
Minister

His Excellency
Walter C. Dowling
Ambassador,
American Embassy,
Seoul

별첨 4.

<u>Foreign Minister to the United States Charge d'Affaires, a.i.</u>

November 26, 1957

Dear Mr. Charge d Affaires:

I refer to my letter of November 13, 1957
addressed to Ambassador Dowling, regarding the agreement
on the status of United States forces in Korea. In this
letter I suggested we commence negotiations to conclude
separate agreements on particular items such as taxation,
customs duties, etc., instead of concluding a full-scale
agreement.

In this connection, I have pleasure in forwarding
a memorandum on the position of my Government on the
separate agreements to be concluded between our two
Governments.

It would be greatly appreciated if you give
favorable attention to this memorandum.

With warmest personal regards, I remain

Sincerely yours,

Chung W. Cho
Minister

Mr. T. Eliot Weil,
Charge d'Affaires, a.i.,
American Embassy,
Seoul.

0215

MEMORANDUM

Considering the present stalemate which exists between Korea and the United States regarding the commencement of negotiations for the conclusion of a full-scale administrative agreement to govern the entire status of United States forces in Korea, it is recommended that several agreements between the two Governments be separately concluded so that the status of United States forces in Korea can be regulated as far as possible upon a mutually acceptable basis:

1) Agreement concerning Procurement, Taxation and Customs Duties of United States forces in Korea. (Ref. Art. 6, 7, 8, of Draft Administrative Agreement proposed by the Korean Government.)

2) Agreement concerning Settlement of Claims relative to the stationing of United States forces in Korea. (Ref. Art. 5)

3) Agreement concerning Facilities and Areas to be used by United States forces in Korea. (Ref. Art. 3, para. 10 of Art. 4, Art. 9, 10)

4) Agreement concerning Entry and Exit of United States forces in Korea. (Ref. Art. 2)

5) Agreement concerning Criminal Jurisdiction over Offences by United States forces in Korea. (Ref. Art. 4, 13, 14)

1.   Agreement concerning Procurement, Taxation and Customs Duties of United States forces in Korea.

It is vital for the Republic of Korea Government to check the smuggling conducted through the supply routes of United States forces in Korea. This agreement

한·미국 간의 상호방위조약 제4조에 의한 시설과 구역 및 한국에서의 미국군대의 지위에 관한 협정(SOFA) 전59권. 1966.7.9 서울에서 서명 : 1967.2.9 발효(조약 232호) (V.5 체결 교섭, 1959) 223

is one of the most urgent to be concluded between the
two countries. For the purpose of preventing and
checking the aforesaid smuggling, the Korean Customs
Officials wish to have access, for inspection purposes,
to the wharves and military airports, which are now
exclusively held and controlled by the United States
military authorities.

As for procurements, goods and services which
are required and can be obtained from local sources
for the subsistance of United States forces should be
procured in a manner most likely to help maintain Korean
economic stability, and least probable of adversely
affecting it, also in coordination with and, when
desirable, through or with the assistance of competent
authorities of Korea.

2. __Agreement concerning Settlement of Claims
relative to United States forces in Korea.__

This agreement is to govern civil jurisdiction,
particularly the settlement of claims arising out of
injuries and damages. It is aimed to clarify the
responsibility for injuries of and damages to Korean
nationals and their properties caused by United States
forces, and to facilitate settlement of the claims
arising out of such injuries and damages. On the other
hand, the Korean Government will undertake to make every
effort to protect United States forces and their members
from injuries to them and damage to their properties.

3. __Agreement concerning Facilities and Areas
to be used by United States forces in Korea.__

While the Korean Government is willing to grant
to United States forces the use of certain facilities

0217

and areas and certain rights, powers and authority necessary for carrying out their mission, this agreement is aimed to clarify the scope of exemption from the liabilities of compensation or restoration accruing from the use of such facilities and areas.

This agreement will also contain provisions in regard to military post office and non-appropriated fund organizations, and further, such provisions as will enable the Korean Government to make interim use of any of such facilities or areas of target ranges and maneuver grounds, which are temporarily not used by United States forces.

4. **Agreement concerning Entry and Exit of United States forces in Korea.**

This agreement will clarify the scope of exemption from Korean immigration laws and regulations for the members of United States forces, including civilian component and their dependents.

5. **Agreement concerning Criminal Jurisdiction over Offences by United States forces in Korea.**

It is to propose to the United States Government to amend the existing Taejon agreement of 1950 to suit the changed conditions caused by the cessation of actual hostilities. As for the amendment, efforts should be made to limit the jurisdiction of the United States court-martial over members of United States forces to such cases as have occurred in the course of execution of official duties, and further to make

한·미국 간의 상호방위조약 제4조에 의한 시설과 구역 및 한국에서의 미국군대의 지위에 관한 협정(SOFA) 전59권. 1966.7.9 서울에서 서명 : 1967.2.9 발효(조약 232호) (V.5 체결 교섭, 1959) 225

- 4 -

additional provisions for judicial cooperation, including joint search and investigation.

Ministry of Foreign Affairs
Seoul, Korea
November 26, 1957

0219

American Embassy
Seoul, Korea

December 3, 1957.

My dear Mr. Minister:

I have the honor to acknowledge receipt of your letter of November 26, 1957 with which was enclosed a memorandum concerning the position of your Government on the question of negotiating separate agreements on various subjects pertaining to the status of United States forces in Korea.

I have forwarded copies of your letter and enclosure to Washington for consideration by my Government.

I shall hope, in due course, to send you a further communication on the subject of your Government's memorandum.

With warmest personal regards, I am

Sincerely yours,

/s/
T. Eliot Woil
Charge d'Affairs ad interim

His Excellency
   Chung W. Cho
      Minister of Foreign Affairs
         Republic of Korea

0220

별첨 5

<u>Foreign Minister to the United States Ambassador</u>

June 10, 1959

Excellency,

I have the honor to draw your attention to the
subject of usage of the facilities and areas now in
use by the U.S. forces in Korea.

As you may recall, most of the facilities and
areas presently in use by the U.S. forces in Korea
were furnished by the Korean authorities under the
emergency state during and immediately after the
outbreak of the Korean War. Under the then prevailing
situation, no adequate agreement was concluded between
the Government of the Republic of Korea and the Government of the United States of America to regulate
various problems in relation to these facilities.

My Government feels that it would best serve
the interests of both countries that are wholeheartedly
engaged in their joint efforts against the common
enemy if the two Governments conclude an equitable
agreement regarding the same. In view of the fact
that the absence of such an agreement in the past
made it impossible to resolve problems related to the
use of such facilities and areas, an agreement of
this nature would improve the defense efforts of the
two Governments.

His Excellency
    Walter C. Dowling
        Ambassador of the United States of
            America

0221

I wish to propose, therefore, that the representatives of both the Korean and U.S. Government meet and discuss and later conclude such an agreement which could cover (1) regulations to enable the United States forces in Korea to carry out their operation in a most effective way; (2) set out the conditions under which the U.S. forces will be using the facilities and areas involved; (3) with the Korean Government granting, in accordance with international precedents, the continued use by the United States forces of such facilities and areas and (4) with the United States Government giving full consideration to owners of the properties.

I sincerely hope that the above will receive favorable consideration by your Government and that discussions could be commenced at the earliest date possible with end in view of concluding an agreement along the lines indicated above, without delay.

Accept, Excellency, the renewed assurances of my highest consideration.

Chung W. Cho
Minister

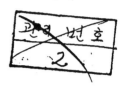

No. 983   ~~Seoul, June 15, 1959.~~
~~1962. 2. 15~~

Excellency:

I have the honor to refer to Your Excellency's note

of June 10, 1959, proposing negotiation and conclusion of

an agreement on the usage of facilities and areas now in

use by United States Forces in Korea.

I also have the honor to inform Your Excellency that

I have forwarded your proposal to the Department of State

for its consideration.

Accept, Excellency, the renewed assurances of my

highest consideration.

His Excellency

Cho Chong-hwan,

Minister of Foreign Affairs,

Seoul.

0223

59-18-4 (3)

미·문 PO-ㅛ(I)

N

駐美大第 92-434 號

檀紀四二九二年 八月 二日

大韓民國駐美國大使館

외무부장관 귀하

科名 한국군과

一. 미국군대가 사용할 토지, 건물 및 시설에 관한
   (대 외정(條)제一七六五호)

미국간의 협정체결에 관한 건

그간 대로공한으로 지시하신 바에 관하여서는

그 취지를 충분히 인식하고, 기회있을때 마다

국무성 당국의 의향을 타진하고 있는바, 八월

二六일 에도, 국무성 동북아국장 「데이비드, 베인」씨

=大韓民國駐美國大使館

0225

에게 본건 협정 체결을 위한 교섭개시를 촉구 한바 있는데, 국무성 당국이 아직·연구 검토중 이며 그것이 끝나는대로·연락하겠다는 대답이었기 동보하오며·앞으로 이에관한 진전이 있는대로 수시 보고 하겠음을 첨언 하나이다.

0226

EXCERPT COPY (from Minister Han's Report of August
27, 1959.)

· · · ·

Before leaving the State Department, Minister
Han inquired about our proposal of June 10, 1959 concerning the negotiation and conclusion of an agreement
on the usage of facilities and areas now in use by the
United States Forces in Korea. Mr. Bane replied to
this inquiry by saying that they hoped to be able to
comment on the proposal in the near future. It was his
understanding that informal negotiations for the conclusion of the Agreement had already beem considerably
discussed.

0227

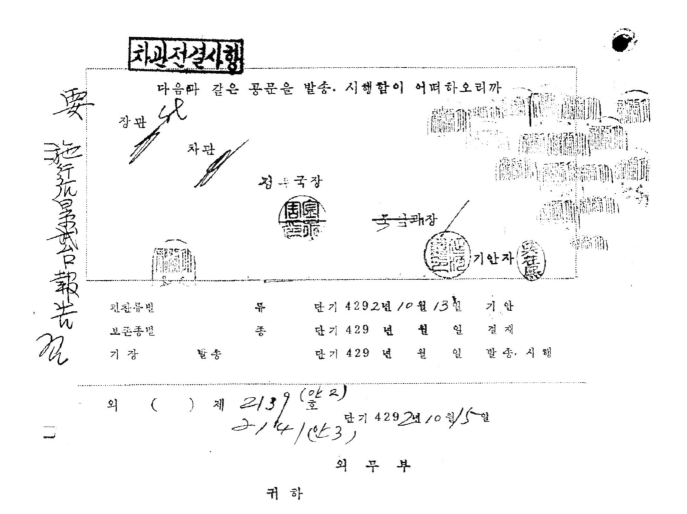

차관전결사항

다음과 같은 공문을 발송·시행함이 어떠하오리까

장관		차관			
			정무국장		구주과장 기안자

편찬류별	류	단기 4292년 10월 13일	기안
보존종별	종	단기 429 년 월 일	결재
기장 발송		단기 429 년 월 일	발송·시행

외 ( ) 제 2139 (안2)호
2141 (안3)   단기 4292년 10월 15일

외 무 부

귀 하

전 명: 주한 미국 군대가 사용하는 토지, 건물 및 시설에 관한
한미간의 협정 체결에 관한 건

품 의

머리의 건, 주한 미국 군대의 지위를 부분적으로 규정하기 위한
시도의 하나로서 단기 4292년 6월 10일자로 미국측에 제의한 바 있는
"주한 미국 군대가 사용하는 토지, 건물 및 시설에 관한 협정"체결을
촉진하기 위하여 다음과 같은 절차를 이행함이 어떠하온지 교재를
앙청하나이다.

절 차

안 (1) 미국측에 대한 교섭개시 촉구
안 (2) 주미대사의 외교활동 촉구
안 (3) 관계부처에 대한 의견 및 자료 요청

별 첨: (1) 협정 체결을 제의한 정부 각서 및 미국측의 접수통고
      (2) 주미대사에 대한 교섭추진훈령 사본
      (3) 주미대사의 중간보고 사본

0228

/D R A F T/

PT-21

      The Acting Minister of Foreign Affairs presents his compliments to the Charge d'Affaires ad interim of the United States of America and has the honor to refer to the Foreign Minister's note of June 10, 1959, proposing negotiation for conclusion of an agreement on the usage of facilities and areas now in use by United States forces in Korea.

      The Acting Minister would be ~~most~~ grateful if the Charge d'Affaires ad interim would meet promptly the desire of the Government of the Republic of Korea to commence the proposed negotiation.

      The Acting Minister avails himself of this opportunity to renew to the Charge d'Affaires ad interm of the United States of America the assurances of his high~~est~~ consideration.

October _15_ , 1959

Seoul

0229

안 (2)

의정 (조) 제 2159호

단기 4292 년 10 월 15 일
외 무 부 장 관

주미 대사 귀하
사본 : 한표욱 공사

건 명: 주한 미국 군대가 사용하는 토지, 건물 및 시설에 관한

한미간의 협정 체결에 관한 건

     (연: 의정 (조) 제 1765 호, 단기 4292 년 7 월 23 일)

     (대: 주미대 제 92— 434 호, 단기 4292 년 8 월 27 일)

     머리의 건, 연호공한으로 그 취지를 충분히 인식하실 ॥주한 미국
군대가 사용하는 토지, 건물 및 시설에 관한 한미 협정॥체결에 관하여
그간 대호공한 내용과 같이 계속적으로 외교교섭을 추진중으로 생각
되온데, 본건 협정교섭을 추진하라는 대통령 각하의 유시에 따라
금번 당부에서는 별첨 공한과 같이 미국측에 대하여 협정체결교섭
개시를 촉구한 바 있아오니, 귀하 께서도 이에 대한 미국측의 동의를
조속히 획득하기 위한 외교활동을 일층 더 적극적으로 추진하시고 그결과를보고
하시기 바라나이다.

별 첨 : 주한 미국 대사 대리에 보낸 외무부차관 공한 사본.

0230

안　　　(3)

외정 (조) 제 2141 호

단기4292년 10월 15 일

외 무 부 장 관

각 부 장 관
각 실 장 　귀 하
각 청 장

건 명: 주한 미국 군대가 사용하는 토지, 건물 및 시설에 관한
　　　한미간의 협정 체결을 위한 의견 및 자료 요청에 관한 건

　　　머리의 건, 단기4286년 12월 22일자 외정 제 2201호 및
단기4286년 12월 31일자 외정 제 2201호등으로 주지하시는 바와
같이, 정부는 그 동안 주한 미국 군대의 지위를 전반적으로 규제
하기 위한 한미협정 체결에 관하여 미국측과 오래 동안 접촉하여
왔으나, 미국측의 소극적 태도로 말미아마 우리측의 목적이 달성되
지 못 하였음에 비추어, 이러한 정돈상태를 타개하기 위한 하나의
시도로서, 당부에서는 미국 군대의 지위 중 한미간에 합의할 수
있는 사항을 개별적으로라도 해결하기로 하여, 위선 ‼주한 미국
군대가 사용하는 토지, 건물 및 시설에 관한 한미협정‼ 체결 교섭을
단기4292년 6월 10일자로 미국측에 제의하였는 바, 귀부(실, 청)가
직접 소유하고 있는 토지, 건물 및 시설과 소관하고 있는 기업체 및
개인이 소유하고 있는 토지, 건물 및 시설 중 미국 군대가 사용하였
거나 사용하고 있는 것의 목록 및 관계자료를 알려주시고 아울러
본건에 대한 귀견을 회시하여 주시기 바라나이다.

0231

Foreign Minister to United States Ambassador

June 10, 1959

Excellency,

I have the honor to draw your attention to
the subject of usage of the facilities and areas
now in use by the U.S. forces in Korea.

As you may recall, most of the facilities and
areas presently in use by the U.S. forces in Korea
were furnished by the Korean authorities under the
emergency state during and immediately after the
outbreak of the Korean War. Under the then
prevailing situation, no adequate agreement was
concluded between the Government of the Republic of
Korea and the Government of the United States of
America to regulate various problems in relation to
these facilities.

My Government feels that it would best serve
the interests of both countries that are wholeheartedly
engaged in their joint efforts against the common
enemy if the two Governments conclude an equitable
agreement regarding the same. In view of the fact
that the absence of such an agreement in the past
made it impossible to resolve problems related to the
use of such facilities and areas, an agreement of
this nature would improve the defense efforts of the
two Governments.

His Excellency
    Walter C. Dowling
        Ambassador of the United States of
        America

0232

I wish to propose, therefore, that the
representatives of both the Korean and U.S. Government
meet and discuss and latter conclude such an agreement
which could cover (1) regulations to enable the United
States forces in Korea to carry out their operation
in a most effective way; (2) set out the conditions ·
under which the U.S. forces will be using the
facilities and areas involved; (3) with the Korean
Government granting, in accordance with international
precedents, the continued use by the United States
forces of such facilities and areas and (4) with the
United States Government giving full consideration to
owners of the properties.

I sincerely hope that the above will receive
favorable consideration by your Government and that
discussions could be commenced at the earliest date
possible with end in view of concluding an agreement
along the lines indicated above, without delay.

Accept, Excellency, the renewed assurances of
my highest consideration.

Chung W. Cho
Minister

0233

No. 983   Seoul, June 15, 1959.

Excellency;

I have the honor to refer to Your Excellency's

note of June 10, 1959, proposing negotiation and

conclusion of an agreement on the usage of facilities

and areas now in use by United States Forces in Korea.

I also have the honor to inform Your Excellency

that I have forwarded your proposal to the Department

of State for its consideration.

Accept, Excellency, the renewed assurances of

my highest consideration.

                              /s/
                              Walter C. Dowling

His Excellency

  Cho Chong-hwan,

    Minister of Foreign Affairs,

      Seoul.

0234

외정 (조) 제   호

단기 4292 년 7 월 23 일

외 무 부 장 관

주 미 합 중 국 대 사   귀 하

사 본 : 한 표 육 공 사   귀 하

건 명 : 주 한 미 국 군 대 가 사 용 하 는 토 지 , 건 물 및 시 설 에 관 한

한 미 간 의 협 정 체 결 에 관 한 건

머 리 의 건 , 외 정 제 4432 호 (단 기 4290 년 12 월 16 일 자)를

통 하 여 이 미 귀 하 에 게 통 보 한 바 있 으 므 로 귀 하 도 주 지 하 는 바 와

같 이 , 주 한 미 국 군 대 의 지 위 에 관 한 협 정 을 체 결 하 기 위 하 여

정 부 는 과 거 수 년 동 안 여 러 차 례 에 걸 처 미 국 측 에 교 섭 개 시 를

촉 구 한 바 있 었 으 나 , 미 국 측 에 서 는 이 러 한 포 괄 적 인 협 정 체 결 교 섭 에

대 하 여 유 력 한 관 심 을 보 여 주 지 않 았 으 며 , 근 래 에 는 오 히 려 미 국

주 둔 군 의 지 위 를 몇 개 의 협 정 으 로 분 리 규 정 함 이 좋 겠 다 고 시 사

하 여 온 바 있 었 는 데 (참 조 · 별 첨 1 교 섭 경 위), 이 러 한 미 국 무 성 의

태 도 는 미 국 군 대 의 지 위 에 관 한 협 정 에 대 하 여 예 민 한 관 심 을

표 시 하 고 있 는 미 국 국 회 또 는 일 반 국 민 여 론 을 자 극 시 키 지

아 니 하 려 는 국 내 사 정 과 또 한 상 호 간 의 합 의 할 수 있 는 사 항 부 터

하 나 하 나 개 별 적 으 로 처 리 하 여 나 가 는 것 이 현 명 하 겠 다 는 판 단 에

기 초 를 둔 것 으 로 보 여 지 는 데 , 우 리 의 목 적 을 달 성 하 기 위 하 여

정 부 는 이 러 한 개 별 협 정 체 결 제 의 를 수 락 하 고 , 우 선 편 안 중 의

하 나 인 ‖주 한 미 국 군 대 가 사 용 하 는 토 지 , 건 물 및 시 설 에 관 한

한 미 협 정 ‖을 체 결 하 고 저 준 비 를 진 행 시 켜 , 단 기 4292 년 6 월

10 일 에 는 다 울 링 대 사 에 게 협 정 체 결 을 위 한 교 섭 개 시 를 제 의

하 기 에 이 르 렀 아 온 바 (참 조 · 별 첨 5), 이 교 섭 제 의 는 현 재

국 무 성 에 계 속 되 고 있 는 데 우 리 와 \~록 은 서 울 과 와 싱 톤 에 서

0235

유기적으로 행하여져야 하겠으므로, 귀하는 이러한 문제에 관하여

종래 미국측의 태도가 언제나 소극적이었음을 양지하시와, 전기

우리측 제의에 대한 미국측의 동의를 획득하도록 예의 국무성

당국과 접촉하시며, 그 결과를 수시로 보고하시기 바라나이다.

                                     이 상.

별 첨:

    1. 교섭 경위

    2. 단기 4290 년 9 월 10 일자로 "허테"국무차관에게 전달한
       한국 정부의 견해

    3. 개별협정 체결 제안에 관한 단기 4290 년 11 월 13 일자
       외무부 장관의 공한

    4. 개별협정 체결에 관한 한국 정부의 견해를 전달하는 단기
       4290 년 11 월 26 일자 외무부 장관 공한 및 주한 미국 대사
       의 회한

    5. "주한 미국 군대가 사용하는 토지, 건물 및 시설에 관한
       협정" 교섭 제의에 관한 단기 4292 년 6 월 10 일자
       외무부 장관 공한 및 주한 미국 대사의 회한

주 미 대 제 92─ 425 호

단기 4292 년 8 월 27 일

대 한 민 국 주 미 국 대 사

외 무 부 장 관   귀 하

건 명: 주한 미국 군대가 사용하는 토지, 건물 및 시설에
       관한 한미 간의 협정체결에 관한 건
       (대: 외정 (조) 제 1766 호)

　　　　머리의 건, 대호공한으로 지시하신 바에 관하여서는 그 취지를
충분히 인식하고 기회 있을때 마다 국무성 당국의 의향을 타진
하고 있는 바, 8 월 26 일에도 국무성 동북아 국장 ‖메이비드．
베인‖씨에게 본 건 협정체결을 위한 교섭개시를 촉구한 바
있는데, 국무성 당국이 아직 연구 검토 중이며 그것이 끝나는
데로 연락하겠다는 대답이었기 통보하오며, 앞으로 이에 관한
진전이 있는데로 수시 보고 하겠음을 첨언 하나이다．

0237

10/16 차관이 주한미주
대사대리 앞 께
무 교함 (印)

PT-21

      The Acting Minister of Foreign Affairs
presents his compliments to the Charge d'Affaires
ad interim of the United States of America and
has the honor to refer to the Foreign Minister's
note of June 10, 1959, proposing negotiation for
conclusion of an agreement on the usage of
facilities and areas now in use by United States
forces in Korea.

      The Acting Minister would be grateful if
the Charge d'Affaires ad interim would meet
promptly the desire of the Government of the
Republic of Korea to commence the proposed
negotiation.

      The Acting Minister avails himself of this
opportunity to renew to the Charge d'Affaires
ad interim of the United States of America the
assurances of his high consideration.

October 15, 1959

Seoul

한·미국 간의 상호방위조약 제4조에 의한 시설과 구역 및 한국에서의 미국군대의 지위에 관한 협정(SOFA)
전59권. 1966.7.9 서울에서 서명 : 1967.2.9 발효(조약 232호) (V.5 체결 교섭, 1959)   245

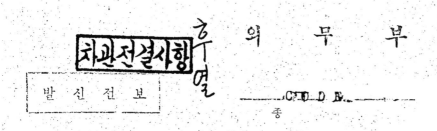

의 무 부

CODE

번호 MW-1032

일시 161150

TO: MINISTER HAN, KORIC WASHINGTON D.C.

RE WOIJONGJO NUMBER ONE SEVEN SIX FIVE DATED TWENTY
THREE JULY NINETEENFIFTYNINE ON PROPOSED NEGOTIATION
FOR AGREEMENT ON USAGE OF FACILITIES AND AREAS NOW
IN USE BY AMERICAN FORCES IN KOREA PD GOVERNMENT
STRONGLY DESIRES EARLIEST CONCLUSION OF AGREEMENT PD
MINISTRY TODAY URGED AGAIN AMERICAN EMBASSY TO
COMMENCE NEGOTIATION WITHOUT DELAY PD MAKE EFFORTS TO
GET PROMPT AND FAVORABLE REACTION OF WASHINGTON
AUTHORITIES PD DETAILS BY POUCH PD

VICE MINISTER CHOI

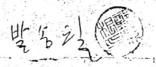

0239

At the request of Vice Foreign Minister Kyu
Hah Choi, U.S. Chargé d'Affaires Sam P. Gilstrap
called on the former at 8:30 a.m., October 16, 1959
at the former's office. Vice Minister Choi handed
to Mr. Gilstrap a note concerning the proposed
negotiation for agreement on the usage of facilities
and areas now in use by the U.S. Forces in Korea.
A copy of the note is enclosed herewith.

Vice Foreign Minister Choi, in handing the said
note to Mr. Gilstrap, stated that the proposal on
this matter was originally made by Foreign Minister
Cho in his letter to former Ambassador Dowling. It
was his understanding, Vice Minister Choi said, that
Ambassador Dowling at that time remarked to Foreign
Minister Cho that the Korean proposal appeared to
be quite reasonable and that he would transmit it
to Washington for its consideration and action. Vice
Minister Choi also stated that, when Ambassador Dowling
was received in audience by His Excellency the
President shortly before his departure for Washington,
His Excellency the President reminded Ambassador
Dowling again of the Korean proposal on this matter,
to which Ambassador Dowling answered that he would
invite his Government's due attention when he returned
to Washington.

Vice Minister Choi added that the Korean Government would render the fullest cooperation to the U.S.

Forces in Korea, but that he felt it necessary to
have certain agreement regulating the use of facilities and areas by U.S. Forces in Korea. The Korean
Government is ready, Vice Minister Choi said, to
enter into negotiation with the U.S. side on this
matter at any time.

Mr. Gilstrap stated that he heard from Ambassador
Dowling about the Korean proposal on this matter and
that he would be glad to bring the matter to the
attention of his Government for expeditious action.

0241

TO: FOREIGN MINISTER CHUNG W. CHO, ROKMISUN NEW YORK

RE PROPOSED AGREEMENT ON FACILITIES AND AREAS IN USE
BY AMERICAN FORCES IN KOREA PD DESIRING EARLIEST
CONCLUSION OF AGREEMENT CMA MINISTRY TODAY URGED
AGAIN AMERICAN EMBASSY TO COMMENCE NEGOTIATION OF
AGREEMENT WHICH MINISTRY PROPOSED LAST JUNE PD MINISTRY
ALSO INSTRUCTED KOREAN EMBASSY TO MAKE EFFORTS TO GET
PROMPT AND FAVORABLE REACTION OF WASHINGTON AUTHORITIES PD

VICE MINISTER CHOI

0242

/D R A F T/

ctɔber *17*, 1959

TO   : His Excellency the President

FROM   : Vice Minister of Foreign Affairs

SUBJECT: Agreement on the usage of facilities and areas
         now in use by United States forces in Korea

In accordance with Your Excellency's instructions,
I as Acting Minister of Foreign Affairs urged again
on October 15, 1959 ~~the~~ United States Charge d'Affaires *a. i.*
Sam P. Gilstrap to meet promptly the proposal of the Korean
Government to commence the negotiation for an agreement
on the usage of facilities and areas now in use by
United States forces in Korea which the Minister of
Foreign Affairs proposed to the United States
Ambassador on June 10, 1959.

At the same time, the Ministry also instructed
the Korean Embassy in Washington to make efforts in
order to get a prompt and favorable reaction of
Washington authorities on the said proposal.

For Your Excellency's reference, I enclose
herewith copies of the note to the United States
Charge d'Affaires of October 15, 1959 and the cable
instructions to the Korean Embassy on the subject.

Most respectfully,

과도분류오인받어 일반문서로
재분류됨 (1962. 2. 15)

0243

COPY

REPORT KPO/5&&

October 17, 1959

TO   : His Excellency the President
FROM   : Vice Minister of Foreign Affairs
SUBJECT : Agreement on the usage of facilities and areas
           now in use by United States forces in Korea

과도한규를 인하여 일반문서
로 재분류함 (1962, 2, 15)

In accordance with Your Excellency's instructions,
I, as Acting Minister of Foreign Affairs, urged again
on October 15, 1959 United States Charge d'Affaires
a.i. Sam P. Gilstrap to meet promptly the proposal of
the Korean Government to commence the negotiation for
an agreement on the usage of facilities and areas now
in use by United States forces in Korea which the
Minister of Foreign Affairs proposed to the United
States Ambassador on June 10, 1959.

At the same time, the Ministry also instructed the
Korean Embassy in Washington to make efforts in order
to get a prompt and favorable reaction of Washington
authorities on the said proposal.

For Your Excellency's reference, I enclose
herewith copies of the note to the United States Charge
d'Affaires of October 15, 1959 and the cable instructions
to the Korean Embassy on the subject.

Most respectfully,

0244

REPORT KPO/580

단기 4292년 10월 22일

박 찬 일 비서관 귀하

정 무 국 장

건 명. 주한 미국 군대가 사용하는 토지, 건물 및 시설에 관한
한미협정 체결에 관한 건

머리의 건, 협정 체결 교섭 개시를 요구한 우리정부의
제안을 미국측이 조속히 수락하도록, 금 10월 22일 주미대사관
에 별첨과 같이 재차 훈령하였아옵기 이에 보고하나이다.

이 상

0245

TO: AMBASSADOR YANG, KORIC WASHINGTON D. C.

ATTENTION: MINISTER HAN

RE WOEJONGJO NUMBER TWO ONE THREE NINE DATED

FIFTEEN OCTOBER NINETEENFIFTYNINE FOR AGREEMENT

ON USAGE OF FACILITIES AND AREAS IN USE BY AMERICAN

FORCES PD EARLIEST COMMENCEMENT OF NEGOTIATION

IS AGAIN ~~URGED~~ *INSTRUCTED* BY HIS EXCELLENCY THE PRESIDENT PD *Please*

TAKE MEASURES IMMEDIATELY TO GET PROMPT ACCEPTANCE

BY WASHINGTON AUTHORITIES OF KOREAN PROPOSAL PD *awaiting*

earliest ~~YOUR~~ REPORT ~~ON LOCAL DEVELOPMENT IS REQUESTED~~

~~WITHOUT DELAY~~ PD

                                    VICE MINISTER CHOI

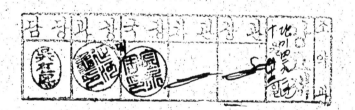

0246

駐美大第92-597號

檀紀四二九二年 十月二二日

大韓民國駐美國大公

件名 주한 미국군대가 사용하는 토지, 건물 및 시설에 관한

한미간의 협정 체결에 관한 건

(대 MW-〇三二호)

머리의 건 대로전문 및 외정조제 二三九호에

의거하여 전상진 一등서기관이 四九년 十월 二二일 본

이을 대리하여 미국 국무성 핫국담당 책임관 "레인"

씨를 방문하고 동 협정체결을 위한 교섭개시를 촉

=大韓民國駐美國大事官

22234

4292.10.29

0243

0247

구한 현지 등 협정체결 문제는 국무성 및 국방성

에서의 검토중이나 행사관할권문제를 제외한 기타

미주둔군에 관련한 전반문제에 관한 협정체결 문제와

결부하여 검토중이기 때문에 현재로서 밀톡 회답

일잘를 확언하기 곤난한 처지에 있다고하여 국무빙측으

로서는 약 개월이내에 밀톡의 태토를 결정할

수있도록 노력하고 있다고 하옵기 우선 현황을

회보하오니 양지하시기 바라나이다.

0244

0248

MINISTRY OF FOREIGN AFFAIRS
R. O. K.
CRO D H

INCOMING

TELEGRAM

WASHINGTON

NO. WM-1036

DATE. 231700

TO. KORPITAL AND VICE FOREIGN MINISTER

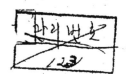

REUR MW-1047 WE HAVE CONTACTED STATE DEPARTMENT PD

OUR PROPOSAL IS UNDER ACTIVE CONSIDERATION BY THE

STATE AND DEFENSE DEPARTMENTS BUT DUE TO DIFFERENCES

OF OPINION, NO DEFINITE DATE CAN BE SET AT THIS

MOMENT BUT THE STATE DEPARTMENT IS TRYING TO MAKE A

DECISION WITHIN ONE MONTH PD

파우분쿠르 인사에
일반분서로 재분류
(1962. 2. 15)

KORIC

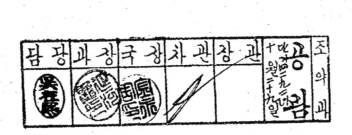

TIME RECEIVED

INFO. TO:

CLEARANCE:

CENSOR

0249

REPRODUCTION FROM
THIS COPY, IF
CLASSIFIED, IS
PROHIBITED

COMMUNICATIONS ROOM

외 무 부

번 호 WM-1049

일 시 271700

착 신 전 보

WASHINGTON

파도분류로인하여
일 반분서로 재분류함
(1962. 2. 15)

관리번호
~~125~~

TO: WOIMUBU

RE YOUR CODED MESSAGE FOREIGN MINISTER CHO AND I WILL SEE

SECRETARY OF STATE HERTER AND ASSISTANT SECRETARY OF STATE

PARSONS FRIDAY AFTERNOON AND DISCUSS ALL THESE MATTERS

FULLY INCLUDING:

STATUS OF AMERICAN ARMED FORCES IN KOREA.

EMERGENCY AID FUND FOR THE TYPHOON VICTIMS REQUESTING

IMMEDIATE ACTION.

KOREAN-JAPANESE CRISIS AND RELATIONS.

REUNIFICATION AND ADMISSION OF KOREA TO THE U.N.

AMBASSADOR YANG

비 고: 수 신 시 간:

검 인

0250

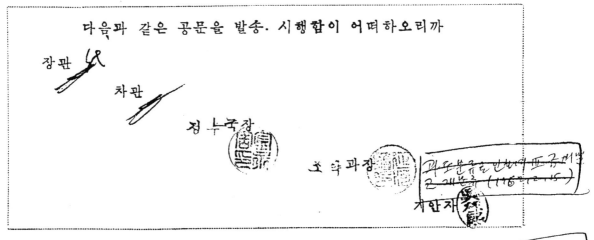

다음과 같은 공문을 발송·시행함이 어떠하오리까

장관

차관

정무국장

조약과장

치안자

편찬류별　　　　　　류　　　단기 429 2년 10월 30일　기안

보존종별　　　　　　종　　　단기 429 년　　월　　일　결재

기장　　　발송　　　　　　단기 429 년　　월　　일　발송·시행

과도문류로인하여
일반문서로재분류
1962, 2, 16

외 (　　) 제　　　호　　　단기 429 년　　월　　일

외　무　부　차　관

박 한 일 비서관　　　귀 하

전 명: 주한 미국 군대가 사용하는 토지, 건물 및 시설에 관한
　　　　한미협정 체결에 관한 건.

　　머리의 건, 주미대사관으로 부터 별첨과 같은 내용으로 국무성측과의

접촉에 관한 중간보고가 있었아옵기, 이를 보고하나이다.

　　　　　　　　　　　　이　상

0251

단기4292년 10월 30일

외 무 부 차 관

박 한 일 비서관 귀하

건 명: 주한 미국 군대가 사용하는 토지, 건물 및 시설에 관한
한미협정 체결에 관한 건.

여미의 건, 주미대사관으로 부어 별첨과 같은 내용으로
국무성측과의 접촉에 관한 중간보고가 있었아옵기, 이를 보고
하나이다.

이 상

0252

JUMIDAI No. 92-597

October 22. 1959

TO   : Vice Minister of Foreign Affairs

FROM   : Minister Han

SUBJECT   : Agreement on the usage of facilities and
            areas in use by United States forces in Korea

REFERENCE : Cable MW-1032

    Under the instructions through the cable MW-1032
and WOIJONGJO No. 2139, First Secretary Sang Jin Chyun
on my behalf visited Mr. Samuel O. Lane of Korea Desk
of the Department of State on October 21, 1959 and
urged the United States to commence negotiation on the
proposed agreement. Mr. Lane said that the Korean
proposal was under active study by both the Department
of State and the Department of Defense, but it was
difficult for him at that time to inform a definite
date of the United States reply, in view of the fact
that they were studying the Korean proposal together
with all the other problems relating to the status of
United States forces except criminal jurisdiction.
Mr. Lane added that the Department of State would make
efforts to decide the position of the United States
Government within a month.

0253

KORPITALI AND VICE MINISTER CHOI

IN CODE (FOREIGN MINISTRY)

COPY

RE YOUR NW-1047 WE HAVE CONTACTED THE STATE DEPARTMENT
AND OUR PROPOSAL IS UNDER ACTIVE CONSIDERATION BY STATE
AND DEFENSE DEPARTMENTS BUT DUE TO DIFFERENCES OF OPINION
NO DEFINITE DATE CAN BE SET AT THIS MOMENT BUT THE STATE
DEPARTMENT IS TRYING TO MAKE A DECISION WITHIN ONE MONTH.

KORIC

0254

한·미국 간의 상호방위조약 제4조에 의한 시설과 구역 및 한국에서의 미국군대의 지위에 관한 협정(SOFA)
전59권. 1966.7.9 서울에서 서명 : 1967.2.9 발효(조약 232호) (V.5 체결 교섭, 1959) 261

외비접수 NOV 3 1959

KOREAN EMBASSY
WASHINGTON, D.C

October 29 1959

과도분류로인바여
재분류함 (1962, 2, 15)

정리번호
126

Dear Minister Choi,

Enclosed is a copy of a memorandum prepared by
Mr. Chyun, our First Secretary, with reference to
the agreement on the usage of facilities and areas
now in use by U.S. forces in Korea.

Sincerely yours,

Pyo Wook Han
Minister

The Honorable
Kyu Ha Choi
Vice Minister
Seoul, Republic of Korea

Enclosure - 1

0255

KOREAN EMBASSY

WASHINGTON, D. C.

MEMORANDUM

To: Minister Han

From: First Secretary Sangjin Chyun

Subject: Proposed conclusion of an agreement on the usage
          of facilities and areas now in use by U.S. forces
          in Korea.

        In accordance with your instructions, I called
on Mr. Samuel O. Lane, Chief of the Korean Desk, State Depart-
      on Wednesday October 21,
ment, to convey our Government's desire to commence promptly
the proposed negotiation for the subject agreement pursuant to
the Foreign Ministry instructions dated October 15.

        I reminded Mr. Lane of the fact that more than
three months time had elapsed since the Korean Government formally proposed the conclusion to the American Embassy in Korea,
of an "agreement on the usage of facilities and areas now in use
by the U.S. forces in Korea", and urged the prompt acceptance by
the U.S. Government of our long pending proposal.

        In this regard, the Minister of Foreign Affairs
sent a note proposing negotiations for conclusion of an agreement on the above subject to the American Ambassador in Korea
on June 10, 1959 and on October 15 the Acting Foreign Minister
sent another note to the American Charge d'Affaires urging the

0256

U.S. acceptance of our proposal.

Mr. Lane told me that at present the Korean proposal is under active consideration by the authorities of the State and Defense Departments. However, he was not in a position to predict a definite date for reply by the United States Government since the United States decision on the proposed agreement would depend upon its general policy with regard to the conclusion of an over all status forces agreement with Korea. The U.S. Government is of the opinion that it would be inevitable to discuss other agreements concerning several subjects on the status of U.S. forces in Korea after the conclusion of the particular agreement now in question. And to the general policy of the U.S. Government on the conclusion of a status of forces agreement with Korea even excluding the subject of criminal jurisdiction there still exists differences of opinion among responsible officials.

However, the State Department officials are generally sympathetic toward the Korean position and are trying to have a decision on the proposed agreement within a month if possible.

I have cabled to the Foreign Ministry the result of my meeting with Mr. Lane as attached.

0257

(November 7, 1959)

Proposed agreement on the usage of facilities and areas in use by United States forces in Korea

As one of the steps toward a comprehensive agreement on the status of U.S. forces in Korea (firstly proposed in 1955), the Foreign Ministry proposed to the United States on June 10, 1959 to commence negotiation for an agreement on the usage of facilities and areas in use by U.S. forces in Korea.

Pending U.S. reply, the Ministry urged again the U.S. Government on October 15 to expedite the settlement. Efforts were made both in Seoul and Washington through diplomatic channels.

According to a recent report from the Washington Embassy, the State Department is trying to have a decision on the proposed agreement within a month, if possible.

Meanwhile, the Foreign Ministry, in cooperation with various Ministries concerned, is working for this negotiation, collecting necessary data, etc.

0258

駐美大第 9-648 號

檀紀四二九二年 十一月 十二日

大韓民國駐美國大使

政務局류로인서에
□□□□□로재분류
(1962. 2.15)

發接 4292.11.18

外務部長官 귀하

件名 주한 미국군대가 상용하는 토지, 건물
및 시설에 관한 한미간의 협정체결에 관한 건

(대외정조제 二三九호, 단기 四二九二년 一〇월 一五일자)

건명 협정체결에 관하여는 거반 "딜론" 미국
국무차관의 방한 및 조외무부장관과 "허터" 미국
국무장관간의 회담시에 각각 우리정부의 적

(국정인) 태도가 반명되어 현재 미국으로도 상당히

大韓民國駐美國大使館

0253

활발한 검토를 계속주이여 본건 협정체결에

광한 성과가 있을것으로 생각되옵기 이를

보고하나이다.

0260

공　　　　란

공   란

공   란

공　　　란

공   란

공   란

공   란

공 란

공　　　란

공   란

공　　　　란

공   란

공 란

공　　란

공　　　　　　　란

공   란

공　　란

공　　　　　란

공 란

공   란

공 란

공 란

공 란

공   란

공   란

공   란

공   란

공　　　란

공   란

공   란

공   란

공   란

공   란

공   란

공　　　란

공   란

공 란

공   란

공　　란

공   란

공　　　　　　　　란

공　　란

공   란

정/리/보/존/문/서/목/록

기록물종류	문서-일반공문서철	등록번호	906 9579	등록일자	2006-07-27
분류번호	741.12	국가코드	US	주제	
문서철명	한.미국 간의 상호방위조약 제4조에 의한 시설과 구역 및 한국에서의 미국군대의 지위에 관한 협정 (SOFA) 전59권. 1966.7.9 서울에서 서명 : 1967.2.9 발효 (조약 232호) ★원본				
생산과	미주과/조약과	생산년도	1952 - 1967	보존기간	영구
담당과(그룹)	조약	조약		서가번호	--
참조분류					
권차명	V.8 체결 교섭, 1960-61				
내용목차	★ 1961.4.15 제1차 한.미국간 교섭회의 (서울) 　　　 4.25 제2차 한.미국간 교섭회의 (서울) ★ 사진 있음 ★ 일지 : 1953.8.7　　　이승만 대통령-Dulles 미국 국무장관 공동성명 　　　　　　　 - 상호방위조약 발효 후 군대지위협정 교섭 약속 1954.12.2　　　정부, 주한 UN군의 관세업무협정 체결 제의 1955.1월, 5월　미국, 제의 거절 1955.4.28　　　정부, 군대지위협정 제의 (한국측 초안 제시) 1957.9.10　　　Hurter 미국 국무차관 방한 시 각서 수교 (한국측 제의 수락 요구) 1957.11.13, 26 정부, 개별 협정의 단계적 체결 제의 1958.9.18　　　Dawling 주한미국대사, 형사재판관할권 협정 제외 조건으로 행정협정 체결 의사 전달 1960.3.10　　　정부, 토지, 시설협정의 우선적 체결 강력 요구 1961.4.10　　　장면 국무총리-McConaughy 주한미국대사 공동성명으로 교섭 개시 합의 1961.4.15, 4.25 제1, 2차 한.미국 교섭회의 (서울) 1962.3.12　　　정부, 교섭 재개 촉구 공한 송부 1962.5.14　　　Burger 주한미국대사, 최규하 장관 면담 시 형사재판관할권 문제 제기 않는 조건으로 　　　　　　　 교섭 재개 통고 1962.9.6　　　 한.미국 간 공동성명 발표 (9월 중 교섭 재개 합의) 1962.9.20-　　 제1-81차 실무 교섭회의 (서울) 　 1965.6.7 1966.7.8　　　 제82차 실무 교섭회의 (서울) 1966.7.9　　　 서명 1967.2.9　　　 발효 (조약 232호)				

마/이/크/로/필/름/사/항

촬영연도	★롤 번호	화일 번호	후레임 번호	보관함 번호
2006-11-22	I-06-0067	03	1-161	

0001

발신번호:

발신일시:

수신인: AMBASSADOR YANG, KORIC
        WASHINGTON
발신인: FOREIGN MINISTER

ATTENTION: MINISTER HAN

RE JUMIDAI NINE TWO DASH FIVE NINE SEVEN

OCTOBER TWENTY SECOND FIFTYNINE REPORTING STATE

DEPARTMENT WOULD MAKE DECISION ON PROPOSED

AGREEMENT FOR FACILITIES AND AREAS WITHIN ONE

MONTH PD MORE THAN ONE MONTH AFTER THE SAID

REPORT NO REACTION AS YET PD PLEASE REPORT

IMMEDIATELY WHEN AMERICAN SIDE WILL ~~TAKE UP~~

~~THE ISSUE PD~~ GIVE DEFINITE RESPONSE PD

(THE END)

수 신 인: WOIMUBU
발 신 인: KORIC

담당	과장	국장	차관	장관	공
					람

RE PROPOSED AGREEMENT FOR FACILITIES AND AREAS STATE
DEPARTMENT SAID TODAY U.S. EMBASSY IN SEOUL WOULD BE
INSTRUCTED TO START NEGOTIATIONS FOR AGREEMENT VERY
SOON PD STATE DEPARTMENT FURTHER EXPLAINED BEFORE SUCH
INSTRUCTIONS ARE MADE A RECONCILIATION BETWEEN STATE
DEPARTMENT AND DEFENSE DEPARTMENT IS NECESSARY PD
STATE DEPARTMENT EXPRESSED GREAT OPTIMISM FOR EARLY
RECONCILIATION AND STRESSED AGAIN US RESPONSE TO
PROPOSAL IN NEAR FUTURE PD

0003

원 본	
사 본	

외무부수신시간: 9:57 a.m., Jan.14
해독완료시간: 11:55 a.m., Jan.14
암호해독담당: H. 남제

✓ (이전문은 허가없이는 복사하여서는 안된다)

외 무 부 정 무 국

발 신

암 호 전 문

발신번호: MW-0179

발신일시: 23 0930

JANUARY 22, 1960

수 신 인: AMB YANG KORIC

발 신 인: FOREIGN MINISTER

ATTENTION MIN HAN

RE WM ZERO ONE TWO ZERO ON FACILITIES AND AREAS AGREEMENT
PD ACCORDING TO U S A EMBASSY IN SEOUL CM THE EMBASSY
DID NOT YET RECEIVE ANY INSTRUCTION FROM WASHINGTON ON
THE MATTER PD PLEASE PRESS AGAIN WASHINGTON AUTHORITIES
TO START NEGOTIATION WITHOUT DELAY PD REPORT AFTER ACTION

발지 송시		암작 호성		원보 안관	

(이전문은 허가없이는 복사하여서는 안된다)

0004

외 무 부 정 무 국

착 신	암 호 전 문

가 번 호 : WM-0160
암호번호 : MWB-4
발신시간 : 271800

수신인 : WOIMUBU

발신인 : KORIC

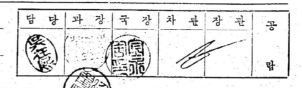

담 당	과 장	국 장	차 관	장 관	공 람

RE CONCLUSION OF AGREEMENT FOR FACILITIES AND AREAS
IN KOREA THE FOLLOWING WAS CONFIRMED YESTERDAY WITH
STATE DEPARTMENT CLN

ONE: STATE DEPARTMENT RECEIVED FROM SEOUL LAST
WEEK PROPOSED U.S. DRAFT FOR NEGOTIATION AND CONCLUSION
OF THE AGREEMENT PREPARED JOINTLY BY AMB MCCONAUGHY,
GENERAL MAGRUDER AND DR MOYER.

TWO: STATE DEPARTMENT IMMEDIATELY PLACED PROPOSED
DRAFT BEFORE ITS LEGAL ADVISORS FOR STUDY. UPON
COMPLETION OF THEIR STUDY, PROPOSED DRAFT WILL BE
TRANSMITTED TO LEGAL ADVISORS OF DEFENSE DEPARTMENT
FOR ANOTHER STUDY.

THREE: IN THIS REGARD STATE DEPARTMENT EXPRESSED
OPTIMISM SAYING THAT MOST OF THE DIFFERENCES BETWEEN
STATE DEPARTMENT AND DEFENSE DEPARTMENT WERE RECONCILED
AND THERE WOULD BE NO DIFFICULTIES IN COMPLETING THE
DRAFT AND INSTRUCTING EMBASSY IN SEOUL TO BEGIN
NEGOTIATIONS SHORTLY.

FOUR: TO OUR INQUIRY REGARDING THE QUESTION OF
TIME, STATE DEPARTMENT REPLIED, IN TWO OR THREE WEEKS.

(THE END)

0005

원 본	E. & A. Section
사 본	Treaty Section

(이전문은 허가없이는 복사하여서는 안된다)

외무부수신시간 : Jan 28, 10:30

해독완료시간 : Jan. 30

암호해독담당 :

COPY
STRICTLY
CONFIDENTIAL

KOREAN EMBASSY
WASHINGTON, D. C.

26 January 1960

MEMORANDUM

TO   : Ambassador You Chan Yang

FROM   : First Secretary Lho

SUBJECT : Proposed Agreement on Facilities and Areas now being
           used by United States Forces in Korea.

        In accordance with Government cable instructions I
visited Mr. Samuel O. Lane at his office in the State
Department at 4 O'clock this afternoon to discuss the above
subject matter.

        I asked Mr. Lane how much progress was being made
by the United States to conclude the Agreement on Facilities
and Areas in Korea. Mr. Lane told me that last week the
State Department had received from Seoul a proposed draft
prepared jointly by Ambassador McConoughy, General Magruder
and Dr. Moyer for the negotiation and conclusion of the
Agreement. The State Department has placed the proposed
draft before its legal advisors for perusal and, he said,
upon completion of their study, it will then be transmitted
to the Defense Department for another study.

        However, Mr. Lane expressed optimism for an early
completion of the draft saying that most of the differences
between the State Department and the Department of Defense
had been reconciled and the Embassy in Seoul would be
instructed to begin negotiations shortly. I then asked Mr.
Lane the duration of the term shortly, and he replied, in
about two or three weeks.

        I explained to Mr. Lane that our Government urgently
needed the completion of the Agreement. Since the hair
shaving incident, I said, the people and the National
Assembly have demanded an early settlement of the Agreement.
To this Mr. Lane optimistically replied that the Embassy in
Seoul would soon be instructed to commence negotiations with
the Korean side.

        Before the close of the meeting, I emphasized once
again our desire and need for the conclusion of the Agreement
as soon as possible.

0006

단기 4293 년 1 월 30 일

1. 좋 택의 입장은, 현재 토지 와 건물 및 시설의 사용에 관해서
아무런 협정이 없는듯이 되어 있는데, 미국측이 마이어 협정 제 3 조
13 항의 규정에 따라 사용해 왔음을 주장하는 경우, 현안 협정을
이 마이어 협정을 미군에 관하여 수정 또는 보충하는 것으로 할
것인가 또는 좋전의 우리 입장을 견지할 것인가,

2. 현안 협정에서 보상방법등을 구체적으로 규정하는 경우, 협정
적용의 시기(始期)를 언제부어 할것인가,

3. 현재까지 사용해온 것에 대한 보상액과 그 청산방법을, 현안
협정에 규정할 것인가 또는, 1958 년의 공의물 용역 청산 협정의 경우
처럼, 별개의 협정으로서 할것인가, 또 청산방법에 있어서 지불
수단 및 지불시기등이 문제임.

4. 작전지대에는 현안협정을 적용하지 않는 다는 경우, 이것을
구체적으로 규정할 것인가 또는 합동위원회를 통하여 추후 별도로
합의할 것인가, 또한 이 경우의 작전지대의 정의를 어떻게
내릴 것인가, (귀농선을 고려할 것임)

5. 다른 조약 예를 보면, 토지의 임대료를 받지 않는 것이
대부분인데, 우리 경우에는 어떻게 할것이 ⓒ (국유재산, 공유재산,
민유재산의 구별)

0007

6. 일론의 경우에는 서한과 구역 내의에 있어서의 쌍방간의 권리행사에 與此 에關聯을 規定다고 있으나 우리나라의 현실 (유엔국의 작전권 보유)에 비추어 이를 現안 協定에다規定할수 없다고 생각됨.

7. 미일간 협정의 경우처럼, 현안 협정에 항공, 항해, 기상관측, 전신, 전짜발사등에 관한 상호협력 및 권한 관계를 규정할 것인가,

8. 미국측은 간단한 각서교환 또는 합의각서의 형식으로 체결할 것을 희망하는 듯한데, 이에 대한 우리측의 입장 여하,

0008

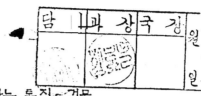

주한 미국 군대가 사용하는 토지, 건물
및 시설에 관한 협정 초안에 대한 검토

1.2 항에 대하여 :

　　현재까지 한국은 미국측에 대하여 각종 재산을 미국측의 사용을 위하여
제공하여 왔는 바, 본 협정은 한미 상호 방위 조약에 따라 미국군대가 한국
내에서 동 조약의 목적을 수행하기 위하여 사용하는 한국의 공, 사유 재산을
규율의 대상으로 삼고 있다. 시안은 그 작성 원칙의 하나로서 지금까지
미군에 제공한 한국 재산은 아무 협약 근거 없이 제공된 것으로 하고 있으나,
현재까지 미국측에 대하여 여러가지 목적을 위하여, 여러가지 근거하에,
또한 여러가지의 한국 재산이 공여되었다는 점에 비추어 본 협정 피 적용
재산에 관한 좀 더 명확한 규제가 있어야 할 것 같다. 특히 미국 군대의
사용을 위하여 제공된 한국 재산이 지금까지 사실 그것이 타당한가 아닌가
여부를 논외로 하고 소위 ‖마이얘‖협정 제3조 제13항에 따라 제공된 것으로
적어도 (형식적으로도) 되어 있는 이상, 미국측은 이러한 사정을 원용(援用)
할 가능성이 있다는데서 다음과 같은 점이 문제된다고 생각된다.

　　(가)　시안 제2항의 arrangement　　에관하여서 구체적으로 그
arrangement 가 어떠한 것을 뜻하는 것인지 즉 재산의 제공 행위에 그치는
것인지 이미 제공된 토지나 건물의 보상 또는 임대료 지불관계를 지칭하는
것인지 전기 두 가지를 전부 포함하는 것인지 의문이 생긴다. 별도의 해명을
하지 않는 한 미국측에서는 이미 미군에 제공된 재산에 관하여 임대료 및
보상의 문제까지 포함하여 arrangement　　가 끝났다고 할 가능성이 없지
않아 있다. 그렇게 되면 이미 제공한 재산 가운데서 arrangement　　가

0009

끝나지 않은 재산은 없게 되며, 제3항에서 이미 제공한 재산에 대한 보상 및 임대료를 미국이 지불한다는 것과 맞지 않게 된다. 이 점에 관한 검토가 필요할 것 같다.

(나) 지금까지 아무 근거 없이 재산을 제공하였다는 것보다 본 협정이 적용할 재산을 "어떠한 협정이나 양해에 의하여 제공되었거나 또는 협정의 근거 없이 제공되었거나를 막론하고 현재 미국 군대가 방위 조약의 목적을 수행하기 위하여 사용하는 모든 한국의 공, 사유 재산"이라고 명시함이 어떠한가? 그렇게 규정하면 현재 미국 군대가 사용하는 모든 재산이 본 협정의 적용 대상이 되어, 종래 예를 들면 한미간 재정 및 재산에 관한 최초 협정에 의하여 제공된 재산 중 적어도 현재 미군이 사용 중인 재산은 본 협정의 규제의 대상이 되도록 길을 열어 두도록 되지 않을까 생각된다. 이것은 다른 나라의 경우와 달리 우리나라가 종래 여러가지 양해하에 이미 많은 재산을 제공하고 있었다는데서 특히 고려가 필요할 것 같다.

시안은 작성 원칙의 하나로서 본 협정의 폐지 또는 종결에 관한 규정을 두지 않기로 한다고 하고 있는데 본 협정이 한미 상호방위 조약에 기초를 두는 이상, 동 조약과 운명을 같이 한다는 규정을 두는 것이 어떠한가?

시안은 또 작성 원칙으로서 작전 지대 내에 있는 재산에 관하여는 보상 대상에서 제외하는 것이 타당하다고 하고 구체적으로 이는 합동위원회에서 결정하도록 함이 가하다고 하고 있는데, 이는 결정 여하에 따라 우리나라에 중대한 이해관계가 있다고 볼 수 있으므로 나중에 합동위원회에서 결정하도록 남겨 두는 것보다 본 협정 교섭과정에 있어서 따로 획일적인 원칙을 상호간 합의하여 둠이 가할 것 같다.

0010

- 3 -

3항에 대하여 :

제制度로서 **arrangement** 를 합동위원회에서 결정된다고 하고 있고 제3항에서 임대료 및 보상에 관한 문제를 또 한 합동위원회에서 결정하기로 되어 있는데 양자의 관계가 완전히 조화되지 않는 것 같다.

4항에 대하여 :

비록 미군의 사용하에 들어갔다고 하더라도 미군이 건물이나 토지 또는 시설을 사용하는데 있어서 한국의 공공의 안전 (public safety)에 배려(配慮)를 가하도록 함이 좋다고 생각되므로 ‖미군이 토지, 건물 및 시설을 사용하는데 있어서 한국의 공공의 안전에 주의를 기우려야 한다‖는 규정을 설치함이 어떠한가?

미일 행정협정 (개정) 제3조의 규정과 같이 미국이 사용 재산에 관하여 가질 수 있는 권리를 명확히 하는 일방 (또한 미일 행정 협정 합의 의사록에서 규정한 것 같이 그러한 권리를 좀 더 명확히 따로 상호 합의하는 것도 좋을 것 같음) 미국측의 권리 행사에 부대되는 의무를 규정하는 것이 좋을 것 같다.

5항에 대하여 :

본 항에 의하면 사용중의 토지, 건물 및 시설의 반환 또는 추가 제공의 필요성 여부를 한미 양 정부가 검토하기로 되어 있는데, 이는 합동위원회를 통하여 검토한다는 뜻의 다른 표현인지? 아니라면 이도 합동위원회를 통하여 검토함이 어떠한가?

6항에 대하여 :

토지, 건물 및 시설의 사용 목적이 소멸하였다고 어디서 결정하는지

0011

명백하지 않은데, 이것도 합동위원회에서 결정한다고 명시함이 어떠한가?

7항에 대하여 :

본 항에 의하면 아국측에서 잠정적으로 사용할 수 있는 미군 사용 중의
재산을 사격장이나 연병장등에 한하는 인상을 주는 점이 없지 않으므로,
차라리 such as target ranges and maneuver ground   는
삭제함이 어떠한가? 물론 시안의 규정으로도 다른 재산을 사용할 수 없는
것은 아니다.

8항에 대하여 :

미군이 사용하다가 반환한 재산이 미군의 사용 후 다시금 사용하기
곤난할만큼 중대한 효용감소가 되면 곤난하므로 (특히 건물이나 시설의 경우에
있어서) 우선 미군에서 사용할 시 사용 재산의 효용을 감소하지 않도록
사용한다는 규정을 두고 중대한 효용 감소가 있을 때 특별 보상을 하도록 함이
좋을 것 같다. 이에는 미군에서 사용재산을 중대하게 변개할 시 한국측의
동의를 얻도록 하는 방법도 생각할 수 있다.

9항에 대하여 :

미국측에서 사용 재산의 원상 회복을 위하여 보상을 하는 반면, 아국측
에서는 부가된 이익에 대한 보상을 안하면 균형이 안 맞는 감이 없지 않으므로
부가 이익에 대한 아국측의 호의적 보상 정도는 규정함이 어떠한가? 이 정도는
사유 재산인 경우에 있어서도 구상할 순 있을 것으로 생각된다.

0012

12항에 대하여 :

협약 규정에 관한 기술적 검토는 물론 합동위원회에서 할 수 있을 것이나 개정의 청의 및 합의들은 외교 경로 재교섭을 통하는 것이 가하지 않을까 생각된다.

협정이 체결되면
일반문서로 재분류

공통문서로 재분류(정정처리순)

0013

구미과 의견

주한 미국군 대가 사용하는 토지, 건물
및 시설에관한 협정 초안에 대한 검토

검토필(1962. 11. 9.)

1. 본 협정의 성격에 관하여.

ㄱ. 본 협정이 규율할 토지, 건물 및 시설은 한미 방위협정에 의하여
미군이 사용하는 토지, 건물 및 시설에 그 범위를 한정하였는데,
다른 근거에 의하여 (마이야 협정, 재정 및 재산에 관한 최초협정,
한미간의 원조협정 및 미 군사고문단 설치에 관한 협정 등) 미국에
제공된 유사 재산에 관하여도 본 협정이 supersede 하게함이
어떠한가 ?

검토필(1965. 6. 30.)

그렇지 않는한, 전기 여러 근거에 의하여 미군에게 제공된 재산을
위하여 다른 하나의 협정이 체결되어야 할것으로 사료됨.

ㄴ. 한미 방위협정에 의한 미군 주둔의 목적이 존속하는한 미군은
무기한으로, 제공된 토지, 건물 및 시설을 사용할수있게 되어있는데,
이렇게되면 예기치 않은 국제 정세의 변경으로 대한민국이 국가
생존을 위하여 필요할때 이들 토지, 건물 및 시설을 복구할 아무런
수단이 없지 않은가 ? 더욱이 대한민국이 미군과 관계없이 독립
하여 국방을 담당할 필요가 있을경우를 예상하더라도, 이러한
특별한 경우를 위한 반환조건이 필요할것으로 사료됨.
다른 방도로서, 특별한 사정이 없는한 계속 제공한다는 조건하에
일정한 기한을 두고 (5년이나 10년) 동 협정을 renew 하는
것도 무방할것임.

ㄷ. 작전지대에 포함되어있는 토지, 건물 및 시설은 임대료 및 보상의
대상에서 제외되며, 합동위원회가 이를 결정짓도록 되어있는데,
작전지대와 비작전지대는 어떠한 성질과 criteria 에 의하여
분류되는가? 이 분류가 우리나라의 이해관계를 크게 지배할것인데

0014

이러한 결정은 그종 대상에 피추어 합목 무원화에서 결정짓는것
보다는 협정 조문속에 그 일반적인 규례를 규정함이 마당하다고
사료되며, 만일 그렇지 않는다면, 극단의 경우를 억측하면,
U.N.C. 하의 주둔군이 사용하는 정부의 토지, 건물 및 시설이
작전지대에 속한다고 미국측이 주장할수도 있을것이다.

2. 조문에서 :

제2항: Arrangements as to specific facilities and
areas for this Agreement, not already reached
by the two Governments until this Agreement
comes into force, shall be agreed upon by the
two Governments through the Joint Committee
provided for in Article___ of this Agreement
에 관하여 :

동 조문에 의하면, 양국 정부에서 이미 합의 제공된 토지,
건물 및 시설을 제외하고, 합의안된 토지, 건물, 시설에
관하여만 합동위원회에서 그 공역 및 조건등에 관하여 합의
하도록 되어있는데, 이미 제공된 토지, 건물 및 시설에 관하여
그 조건등을 규율하지 않는다면, 본 협정의 의의는 거의
없다 할것이다. 즉, 앞으로 미군에게 제공될 토지, 건물
및 시설은 그수가 거의 없을것임으로 이미 공역된 재산에
대한 규율이 중요한것이기 때문이다. 따라서 not already
reached by the two Governments until this
agreement comes into force
의 귀절을 삭제함이 좋을것으로 사료됨.

동 조문은, 다음 제 3항의 임대료 및 보상의 소급지불 요구와
상반되는것으로 사료됨. 물론 본 협정을 소급 적용하지 않는
다면, not already ------- 의 조문이 있어도 무방할것임

0015

제3항 : 임대료와 보상료를 미화로 받는다고 생각할 때, 미군이 사용
하는 재산의 가격은 일차적으로 한화로 산출되므로, 이것을
미화로 환산 (500 弗) 한다면 한국시장 가격에 의하여
산출된 가격 (1000 弗) 위, 500弗 환산되므로 미국측의
채무가 배가하는 결과가 됨을 고려하여야 할것임. 이러한
가격을 합동위원회에서 결정 짓는다고만 규정되어 있는데,
동 가격 산출의 기준을 at reasonable price
consistent with local economic condition within the Republic of Korea

등으로 추가 규정함이 좋을것으로 사료됨. 그것은, 한국
경제의 inflation 경향을 보아서도 유리한것으로 간주됨.
더욱이 이러한 임대료 및 보상료를 소급하여 요구할경우 현재의
한국 경제에 준한 가격에 의한다는 조문이 필요할것임.

4항에서 : 미군이 부설한 물건에 대한 반출 및 처분을 한미간의 협정에
의하여 행할수 있게 되어있는데, 성격상 이것보다 더 종 대한문제
(임대료의 지불여부, 가격의 결정등) 를 합동위원회에 맞기고
있음에 비추어, 동 처분문제도 협정에 의하지 않고, 합동 위원회
에서 결정함이 여하?

5항에서 : 본 조항에서 한국은 미군에게 토지, 건물 및 시설을 추가
제공할수 있도록 규정되어 있으나, 여기서의 추가제공은
실제적으로는 제2항에서 규정한 신규제공 이므로 불 필요한
내용으로 간주됨. 즉 제2항에서 대한민국 정부는 앞으로
미군이 필요로하는 재산을 그들의 사용을 위하여 제공하게되어
있으므로 추가 제공은 언어상 상이할따름 이며, 실은 신규제공
인것임

6항에서: 제공된 재산은 미군이 그 사용목적의 소멸과 함께 반환

하도록 규정되어 있는데, 군계적으로 동 목적의 소멸 여부를

결정 짓는것은 누군가? 비군측? 합동 위원회? 또는 양국

정부의 합의?

현재 미국측이 사용하고 있는 여러 재산 (조선호텔, 내자아파-트

등) 의 반환의 애로를 보아, 좀 더 상세한 반환 시기에 관한

절차를 규정할 필요가 있을것으로 사뢰됨.

8항에 대하여:

ㄱ. 동 조문은 미군의 제공된 재산의 원상복구의무를 완전히 면제

하였는데, 미군이 ~~태규모다~~ 급격한 변조를 초래케할 ~~것의~~

대한민국의 동의를 얻게함이 어떠한가? 가령 조선호텔 건물의

일부를 그들의 주차장을 위하여 파손 한다든지, 또는 댄스홀을

만들기 위하여 내부의 벽을 전부 헐러놓든지 하는경우.

ㄴ. 미군에 제공된 개인소유 재산의 원상복구 의무를 미국측이

endeavor to take appropriate measures as practicable

as possible for the restoration ....

한다는 조건하에 면제 하였는데, 본 조건은 추상적이며, 도의적

의무에 끝이는 것이고, 구체적으로 미군이 개인소유 재산 원상

복구의 의무를 갖지 않는것이다. 그렇다면, 이러한 개인 재산의

원상복구를 우리정부가 부담하여야 할것이다. 원상복구 의무

면제의 원측에는 동의하나, 개인 재산에 대한 동 조건을 일층

구체화 시켜, 일정한 범위를 정하여 그 범위를 초과하여 demolish

된 개인 재산에 대하여는 합동 위원회의 결정에 따라 미국측이

원상복구하여야 할것으로 규정함이 가할것임.

0017

한·미국 간의 상호방위조약 제4조에 의한 시설과 구역 및 한국에서의 미국군대의 지위에 관한 협정(SOFA)
전59권. 1966.7.9 서울에서 서명 : 1967.2.9 발효(조약 232호), V.8 체결 교섭, 1960-61   327

10항에 대하여 :

ㄱ. 동 조항에서 규정된 합동위원회는 그 직무의 중대성에 비추어
그 기능, 구성 및 운영에 대하여 좀더 상세히 규약하여둠이 가할
것으로 사료됨. 그것은 우리측에 어떠한 재산을 제공하는 입장에
서있다면 별문제이나, 이미 제공된 재산에 대하여 미국측으로부터
그 보상을 요구하는 입장에 있으므로 동 위원회에서 미국측이
유리한 지위에 서 있게 됨을보아, 동 위원회에 대하여 비교적
구체적인 조직 및 절차를 동 협정에 규정시킴을 원측으로 하여야
할것으로 사료됨.

ㄴ. 동 조항이 제정하는
Military Organ 과 Administrative Services
의 기능 및 조직에 대하여도 본 협정에서 상세히 규정할 필요는
없으나, 일반적인 기능 및 조직에 대하여 원측을 세워 두는것이
옳을것으로 간주됨.

* 이러한 협정이 체결된다고 가상한다면, 현재 미군에 재산에 대한
상세한 data 의 정리가 시급할것으로 사료됨

/D R A F T/

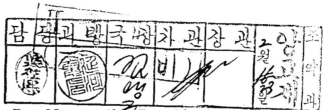

TO   : His Excellency the President

FROM   : Vice Minister of Foreign Affairs

SUBJECT : Recommendation on a Note for an ~~early~~
           settlement of the status of ~~United States~~
           ~~forces in Korea~~

검토필(1962. 12. 17.) 검토필(1966 1 . 30 .)

        It has been a long pending problem for our
government to conclude a comprehensive agreement with
the United States on the status of United States
forces in Korea, which remains unsettled due to the
reluctance on the part of the United States government
to do so.

검토필(1966 12. 30.)

        In its resolution of January 18, 1960 adopted
at the thirty-third plenary meeting of its thirty-
third session, the *Republic of Korea* National Assembly recommended that
the government concludes without delay an agreement
on the status of United States forces in Korea.

        In fact, our government in April 1955 requested
the United States government to settle the problem
with a comprehensive agreement similar to those
entered into between NATO countries or between the
United States government and certain other governments.

        In the meantime, our government came to consider
possibility of solving problem by problem by several
separate agreements on accumulation basis, for
instance, our government in June 1959 proposed the
United States government to commence negotiation for
an agreement on the facilities and areas in use by
its forces, pending the proposal for comprehensive

0019

- 2 -

agreement. ~~However, this did never mean that our government withdrew the original proposal~~ *for a comprehensive agreement.*

~~Under~~ the circumstances it is advisable for our government to press again the United States government not only for commencement of negotiation on the proposed agreement regarding the facilities and areas but also for settlement of certain other questions such as the customs functions, entry and exit of personnel, jurisdiction over the United States military personnel, etc. If this recommendation meets *with* Your Excellency's approval, the Ministry will send to the United States Embassy a note, draft of which is attached hereto.

For your Excellency's reference, A Review on Development for Negotiation and English translation of the aforesaid resolution of the National Assembly are attached hereto as ANNEX A and ANNEX B respectively.

Most respectfully, ~~yours,~~

0020

D R A F T

February __, 1960

Excellency:

I have the honour to refer to long pending problems relating to the status of United States forces in Korea which still remain unsettled between our two governments. I have the further honour to recall that for the purpose of exploring settlement of such problems, my government on numerous occasions brought to the attention of your government its desire to conclude agreements on the subject matter, particularly through the Ministry's communications dated December 2, 1954, April 28, 1955, January 5, 1957, June 29, 1957, November 13, 1957, November 26, 1957, June 10, 1959 and October 15, 1959.

As there is a growing concern of the Korean people seeking early ~~conclusion of an agreement on the status of United States forces~~ *settlement of the problems*, my government is strongly convinced that early ~~settlement of~~ *solution to* the aforesaid problems would serve to keep cordial relations between the Korea people and American military personnel.

In view of the foregoing, I have the further honour to state that my government is ~~most~~ *earnestly* desirous of commencing negotiation for agreements on the status of United States forces, ~~in particular, an agreement on the~~ *giving priority to the settlement of* facilities and areas in use by United States forces.

0021

My government would be ~~most~~ grateful if ~~your~~ *you are good* ~~enough to take necessary steps to government would meet this anxious~~ desire of my government.

Accept, Excellency, ~~the renewed~~ assurances of my highest consideration.

Acting Minister of Foreign Affairs

협정체결시 일반문서로
재분류

보통문서로 재분류(협정체결시)

ANNEXES

A Review on Development for Negotiation

1. <u>General review</u>

The pattern of efforts made by the Korean government for establishing the status of United States forces in Korea may be divided into three categories.

<u>First</u>, the Korean government attempted in 1954 to solve a specific problem of urgency by proposing a provisional agreement regarding customs functions for the purpose of checking smuggling through supply routes of the United Nations armed forces. The United States, however, rejected this proposal.

<u>Secondly</u>, during a period from 1955 to 1957, the Korean government concentrated its efforts on conclusion of a comprehensive agreement covering the overall status of forces which the United States government entered into with certain other governmnts. It was also during this period that it requested the United States government to settle the status of United States forces instead of the entire United Nations armed forces in Korea if it was difficult and time consuming to obtain the prior consent of the allies within the United Nations Command for the proposed negotiation, in view of the fact that United States forces actually constituted preponderant components of the United Nations armed forces. Pressed repeatedly

0024

for negotiation of the proposed agreement, the United States informally suggested late 1957 that a separate agreement on certain particular items instead of the proposed comprehensive agreement be favorable.

Thirdly, after 1957 when no favorable reaction of the United States on the proposed comprehensive agreement was foreseen, the original intention of the Korean government for such agreement was shifted to consideration of several separate agreements covering particular problems, such as taxation and customs duties, entry and exit of personnel, settlement of claims, criminal jurisdiction, on a basis as far as agreeable with the United States. Of these separate agreements presumably undesirable to the United States, it was particularly reluctant to conclude an agreement regarding criminal jurisdiction which would actually change the existing status covered by the agreement of 1950 providing for exclusive jurisdiction of the United States court-martial over members of United States forces. The program of the Korean government for the separate agreements was initiated in June of 1959 with its proposal of an agreement on the facilities and areas in use by United States forces, which is still under consideration by the United States authorities in Washington.

한·미국 간의 상호방위조약 제4조에 의한 시설과 구역 및 한국에서의 미국군대의 지위에 관한 협정(SOFA) 전59권. 1966.7.9 서울에서 서명 : 1967.2.9 발효(조약 232호), V.8 체결 교섭, 1960-61 335

II. Chronological development:

1. <u>December 2, 954,</u> a proposal was made by
the Acting Foreign Minister to the United States
Ambassador to commence negotiation on a provisional
agreement regarding customs functions with respect to
the United Nations armed forces in Korea. A draft
text prepared by the Korean government was forwarded
to the United States side.

2. <u>January 27, 1955,</u> implicating a refusal
to the Korean proposal of December 2, 1957, the United
States Ambassador expressed his opinion that regulations
covering new procedures prepared by the United States
military authorities would meet the requirements of
the Korean government without the necessity of negotiating
a formal agreement.

3. <u>April 28, 1955,</u> the Foreign Minister proposed
to the United States Chargé d'Affaires commencement of
negotiation for a comprehensive administrative agreement
regarding the status of the United Nations armed forces
in Korea. A draft text prepared by the Korean government
was forwarded to the United States side.

4. <u>May 14, 1955,</u> General Taylor, Commander in
Chief of the United Nations Command, informed the
Foreign Minister that he approved a new procedure under
which Korean customs officials would be accorded an
improved and reasonable opportunity to exercise their
responsibilities.

5. <u>June 13, 1955,</u> the Foreign Minister
informed General Lemnitzer, successor of General Taylor,
of the proposal of April 28, 1955 on the comprehensive

0026

administrative agreement under which the customs
functions would be also defined.

6. <u>July 26, 1955</u>, General Lemnitzer informed
the Foreign Minister of the United States Ambassador's
opinion regarding the Korean proposal for the comprehensive status of forces agreement that he did not
like to take up major negotiations before completing
a proposed treaty of friendship, commerce and navigation as well as an agreement guaranteeing investments.
General Lemnitzer also indicated that the task of
obtaining the prior consent of the allies within the
United Nations Command for the proposed agreement would
be difficult and time consuming. On the opinions
contained in the aforementioned Lemnitzer's letter,
comments were made by the Foreign Minister that existing
conditions would not prevent the both sides to start
the proposed negotiation.

7. <u>January 5, 1957</u>, the Foreign Minister urged
the United States Ambassador to accept the proposal of
April 28, 1955, making a comment on the United States
position on such proposal. At the same time, he
proposed that negotiations be started first for defining
the status of United States forces instead of the
entire United Nations armed forces in case the consent
of the allies had not been obtained.

8. June 29, 1957, with the Foreign Minister's
letter addressed to the United States Ambassador, the
Korean proposal made on April 28, 1955 and renewed on
January 5, 1959 was stressed again to be accepted by
the United States government.

0027

9. September 10, 1957, with a memorandum
containing an extensive review by the Korean government on the existing conditions, the Korean proposal
was brought to the attention of then Under Secretary
of State Christain Herter during his visit to Korea.

10. October 10, 1957, the United States
Ambassador at a meeting with the Foreign Minister
made a suggestion that there be room for reaching a
separate agreement on particnear items.

11. November 13, 1957, the Foreign Minister
confirmed that the United States Ambassador's suggestion of October 10, 1957 be acceptable to the Korean
government.

12. November 26, 1957, a memorandum was
forwarded to the United States Ambassador on the
general position of the Korean government in respect
of the suggested separate agreements regarding 1)
procurement, taxation and customs duties, 2) settlement
of claims, 3) facilities and areas, 4) entry and exit
of personnel and 5) criminal jurisdiction.

13. September 18, 1958, the United States
Ambassador at the Foreign Ministry orally revealed
the United States position that his government might
reach agreements with the Korean government on such
problems as of purely administrative nature on
condition that the Korean side would not further propose
negotiation for an agreement on jurisdiction, as next
step, so long as the present circumstances in Korea
continue to prevail. Such position however, was not

0028

approved by His Excellency the President.

14. June 10, 1959, the Foreign Minister
proposed to the United States Ambassador commencement
of negotiation for an agreement on the facilities and
areas in use by United States forces in Korea, one of
those separate agreements described in the Foreign
Ministry's memorandum of November 26, 1957.

15. According to a recent report from Korean
Embassy in Washington, D. C., the State Department
is preparing their own draft for the proposed agreement
on the facilities and areas.

한·미국 간의 상호방위조약 제4조에 의한 시설과 구역 및 한국에서의 미국군대의 지위에 관한 협정(SOFA)
전59권. 1966.7.9 서울에서 서명 : 1967.2.9 발효(조약 232호), V.8 체결 교섭, 1960-61   339

Resolution of the National Assembly

January 18, 1960

(Translation)

RECOMMENDATION ON EARLY CONCLUSION OF
AN ADMINISTRATIVE AGREEMENT BETWEEN
THE REPUBLIC OF KOREA AND THE UNITED
STATES OF AMERICA

TEXT:

It is called that the executive enter without
delay in to an administrative agreement between the
Republic of Korea and the United States of America
concerning the legal status of the armed forces
stationing in Korea.

REASON:

I. Basic factor for essentiality of an administrative
agreement

Whereas an administrative agreement has not
been entered into between the Republic of Korea and
the United States of America regarding the status of
United States forces which have stationed in this country
during these fifteen years as occupation forces after
Korea's liberation and as the United Nations armed forces
since the outbreak of the Korean War:

1) the status of United States forces is such
that as complete extraterritoriality with respect of the
Korean customs functions, consisting of a major factor
causing tremendous loss of the government budget and
instability of national economy;

0030

2) a pending settlement of civil and criminal
jurisdiction over members of United States forces
causes ugly and unfriendly incidents hardly tolerable
to the two countries both;

3) the Republic of Korea is not compensated for
the use by such forces during a period of only nine
years from 1950 to 1958 of the facilities and areas of
national, public, vested or private property, which
amount to $446,000,000 (HW 59,400,000,000) as assessed
by the Reconstruction Bank of Korea; and

4) unilateral procedures for entry into and exit
from Korea by members of United States forces cause
various difficulties of vitality for this country.

On the other hand, the foregoing situation is a
basic subject to be settled at any rate, in view of
the recognition by the United Nations General Assembly
of sovereignty of the Republic of Korea, friendly
relation of the two countries remaining firm allies and
its legal, political, economic and social conditions.

II. International circumstances and U.S.-Japan relation

The United States has already entered into the
aforesaid administrative agreement with certain other
countries all over the world ranging from Western
Europe to Middle and Far East where its forces have
been deployed, thus, guaranteeing the rights and interests
of the other parties. Furthermore, Japan, above and
over its basic problem, actively endeavors to increase
the amounts of compensation for Okinawa under the United

0031

States military administration, and even compels the United States to support its deportation scheme of Korean residents to the northeren part of Korea, taking opportunity of revising the Security Treaty between them.

In view of the above, a proposal on a recommendation to the executive is submitted to conclude without delay the agreement under reference.

0032

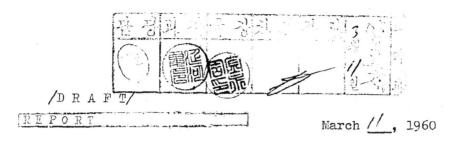

/D R A F T/

March *11*, 1960

TO : Office of the President

FROM : Vice-Minister of Foreign Affairs

SUBJECT: Negotiation for the settlement of the status of United States force in Korea

In ~~accordance~~ *connection* with the Ministry's Recommendation KPO/95 dated February 25, 1960, I invited American Ambassador McConaughy to my office at 6:30 p.m. yesterday and handed a note for an early settlement of the status of United States forces in Korea giving priority to the settlement of the use of the facilities and areas, a copy of which is attached hereto. Ambassador McConaughy said that he would transmit the *said note* ~~proposal of our government~~ to the State Department *and he would do what he could do in this regard.*

Most respectfully,

0033

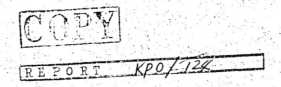

REPORT KPO/124

March 11, 1960

TO   : Office of the President
FROM   : Vice-Minister of Foreign Affairs
SUBJECT: Negotiation for the settlement of the
          status of United States force in Korea

        In connection with the Ministry's

Recommendation KPO/95 dated February 25, 1960,

I invited American Ambassador McConaughy to my

office at 6:30 p.m. yesterday and handed a note

for an early settlement of the status of United

States forces in Korea giving priority to the

settlement of the use of the facilities and areas,

a copy of which is attached hereto. Ambassador

McConaughy said that he would transmit the said note

to the State Department and he would do what he

could do in this regard.

                                Most respectfully,

0034

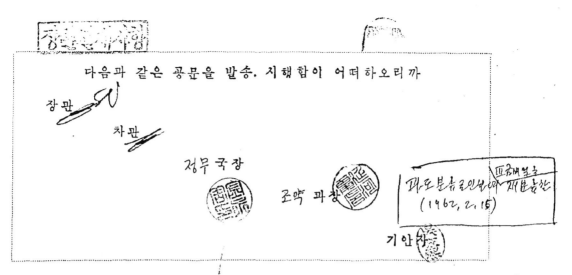

다음과 같은 공문을 발송·시행함이 어떠하오리까

장 관

차 관

정 무 국 장

조 약 과 장

파도분(?)로인(?)마 표(?)유(?)해 볼 노
재(?)한(?)
(1962. 2. 15)

기 안

편찬무별	류	단기 429 3년 3월 1일 기안
보존종별	종	단기 429 년 월 일 결재
기 장 발 송		단기 429 년 월 일 발송·시행

외 정 (조) 제 367 호 단기 429 년 월 일

외 무 부 장 관

주 미 대 사 귀 하

전 명 : 한미간의 군대지위협정 체결에 관한 건

　　　위
　　미의 건, 정부는 별첨과 같은 단기4293년 3월 10 일자의 공한
으로 주한 미국 군대의 지위에 관한 현안의 제문제를 관계조약 체결
로서 조속히 해결할 것을 미국측에 다시 촉구하는 동시에 특히 토지,
건물 및 시설의 사용문제를 우선적으로 해결할 것을 거듭 강조한 바
있아오니 이건에관하여 현지외교교섭을 계속 추진하시고 동 결과를 보고하여주심을
있음을 통보하오니 참고하시과 바라나이다.

　　　　　　　　　　　　　　　　　이 상

별 첨 : 단기4293년 3월10일자 공한 PT-8 사본

0035

March 10, 1960

Excellency:

I have the honour to refer to long pending problems relating to the status of United States forces in Korea which still remain unsettled between our two governments. I have the further honour to recall that for the purpose of exploring the settlement of such problems, my government has on numerous occasions brought to the attention of your government its desire to conclude agreements on the subject matter, particularly through the Ministry's communications dated December 2, 1954, April 28, 1955, January 5, 1957, June 29, 1957, November 13, 1957, November 26, 1957, June 10, 1959 and October 15, 1959.

As there is a growing concern of the Korean people seeking early settlement of the problems, my government is strongly convinced that early solution to the aforesaid problems would serve to maintain cordial relations between the Korean people and American military personnel.

His Excellency
　　Walter P. McConaughy,
　　　　Ambassador of the United States of America,
　　　　Seoul.

0036

In view of the foregoing, I have the honour
to state that my government is earnestly desirous of
commencing negotiation for agreements on the status
of United States forces in Korea giving priority to
the settlement of facilities and areas in use by
United States forces. I should be grateful if you
would be good enough to take the necessary steps to
meet this desire of my government.

Accept, Excellency, the renewed assurances of
my highest consideration.

Acting Minister of Foreign Affairs

협정 체결시 일반문서로
재분류

0037

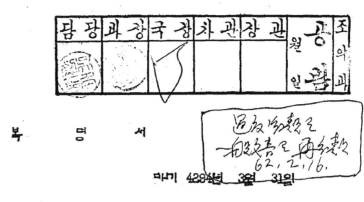

담당	과장	국장	차관	장관	공	조
					월	약
					일	과

복 명 서

단기 4294년 3월 31일

조약과 근무 사무관   박 남균
      〃   〃   오 임렬

외 무 부 장 관   귀 하

　　　지난 3월 18일 부터 10일 간 한미행정협정 준비에
참고 하고저 미군이 사용한바 있고 현제 사용하고 있는 하기
지역의 토지 및 시설에 대한 시찰결과를 다음과 같이 요약
보고 하나이다.

記

1. 부 산:

　　1)　부산지방해무청 관하 부산부두 L.S.T Beach 11번
　　　　베이쇼, 2966평은 미 외항사령부에서 1951년 6월 23일
　　　　부터 증발하여 현제까지 사용하고 있으나 사용료에
　　　　대한 당국간의 결정은 보지 못하고 있음.

　　2)　해무청 부산지방관내 매립지 4160평은 4283년 11월
　　　　1일 부터 88년 5월 5일 까지 미군 제226병기단이 사용
　　　　하였음으로 동사용료에 대한 신청을 재기하고 있으나
　　　　결정을 짓지 못하고 있음.

　　3)　체신부산하 부산시 대연동에 소재하고있는 부산전신
　　　　감시국, 건평 670평은 미항공대사령부가 1950년 8월 부터
　　　　1955년 6월 까지 사용 하였던바, 1952년 3월 에 동청사
　　　　가 전소 하고 이에 대한 배상요구를 재기하였으나
　　　　결정을 짓지 못하고 있음.

　　4)　부산시 아미동 소재 부산체신청 청사,건평 470평은 1950
　　　　년 11월부터 1955년 1월 까지 미적십자구탁부에서 사용

0038

하였는바 1956년 부터 본사용료를 청구하고 있음.

5) 부산지방건설국 청사 대지 1481평 및 건물 622평을
미 제7수송항만사령부에서 4283년 8월 부터 4288년 8월
까지 사용 하였으나 사용료에 대하여는 결정을 보지
못하고 있음.

2. 진 해:

1)   진해시 현동소재 82705평을 미제8군 진해지구 군사고문
단이 사용중이며 사용료에 대한 결정은 없음.

2)   진해시 현동 소재 비행장 82705평을 미제8군 으로부터 68년
2월 한국공군에 이양되었으나 사용료에 대하여 결정된바 없음.

3. 오 산:

청수역에 소재하는 서울국제전신전화국 서울중계소대지
110평 및 건평 26평은 미제8군 장거리통신대대 중대본부
로서 1950년 9월 부터 1959년 10월 까지 사용하여 왔으며
현제 유엔군 에서 사용중인 무장하 (武裝荷)발송회선을
체신부에 반환직시 본시설로부터도 철수를 요망하고 있으나
사용료에 대하여는 결정된바가 없음.

소속 당국의 견해: 가급적이면 미군이 징발사용중인 대지및
시설에 대한 징발을 해재한것 과 사용료 및 보상조치
(파괴된건물 및 시설)를 요망하고 있으며, 하등의 수속도
없이 사용하고 있는 대지 및 시설은 국유재산법에 의한
사용승인의 일괄화 조치를 연하고 있음.

이   상

0039

착 신

암 호 전 문

가 번 호 :

암호번호 : MWB-12

발신시간 :

수 신 인 : WOIMUBU

발 신 인 : AMB YANG

담 당	과 장	국 장	차 관	장 관	공
					람

REUR LETTER THREE SIX SEVEN DATED ELEVENTH MARCH SIXTY
RE NEGOTIATIONS FOR CONCLUSION OF AGREEMENT ON THE STATUS
OF US ARMED FORCES IN KOREA CMA GIVING PRIORITY TO THE
SETTLEMENT OF FACILITIES AND AREAS IN USE BY US FORCES
CMA IT WAS LEARNED FROM STATE DEPT TODAY THAT AMERICAN
EMBASSY IN SEOUL IS CMA AT PRESENT CMA BEING INSTRUCTED
BY STATE DEPT TO COMMENCE NEGOTIATIONS ON THE SAID
AGREEMENT PD STATE DEPT SEEMS CMA HOWEVER CMA TO BE
MOST SERIOUSLY CONCERNED ABOUT THE PROVISION FOR
CRIMINAL JURISDICTION OVER US FORCES IN KOREA AND IS
PARTICULARLY RELUCTANT TO SEE AN EARLY AMENDMENT TO
THE TAEJON AGREEMENT CONCLUDED IN JULY NINETEENFIFTY
BETWEEN THE ROK AND USA PD

(THE END)

원 본	TREATY SECTION
사 본	E & A SECTION

(이 전 문 은 허 가 없 이 는 복 사 하 여 서 는 안 된 다)

외무부수신시간 :

해독완료시간 :

암호해독담당 : I D K

C040

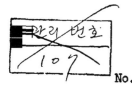

No. 2391

American Embassy,

Seoul, March 30, 1960.

Excellency:

I have the honor to refer to former Foreign Minister Cho's

note of June 10, 1959, and to Your Excellency's note of

October 15, 1959, in which reference was made to a proposal

of the Government of the Republic of Korea for the

negotiation of an agreement on the use of facilities and

areas by United States military forces in Korea.

On behalf of my government I am pleased to accept your

proposal for the initiation of negotiations on a Facilities

and Areas Agreement subject to the following mutual understandings:

(1) that a revision of the arrangements set forth in

the notes exchanged between our two governments at

Taejon on July 12, 1950, will not be proposed by

either side; and (2) that compensation to the owners

or suppliers

His Excellency

Choi Kyu Hah,

Acting Minister for Foreign Affairs,

Seoul.

0041

or suppliers of any real property in Korea which has

been or will be used by the United States Armed Forces

is the responsibility of the Korean Government.

Upon receipt of Your Excellency's acknowledgment that these

understandings are acceptable to the Korean Government, the

United States Government will be pleased to undertake discussions

on the proposed Facilities and Areas Agreement.

Accept, Excellency, the renewed assurances of my highest

consideration.

Walter P. McConaughy

0042

U.S. Note No. 2391 에 대한 검토

조건 (1) 에 관하여 : 미국측은 이것으로, 주한 미국군대의 재판관할권에 관한 현행제도를 그대로 유지 존속시키고저 하는 것인데, 수정제의를 하지 못하는 기간이 하등 설정되어 있지 아니함. 미국은 대건협정의 수정에만 언급하였으므로 쌍방의 합의에 의한 동 협정의 종결이 가능하다고 일단 생각할 수도 있으나, 협정의 종결이 쌍방 당사자의 합의에 의하여서만 가능하다는 점을 고려할 때, 현행제도의 수정을 원하지 아니하는 미국측이 협정의 종결에 동의할 아무런 이유나 근거가 현재로서는 발견되지 아니함. 현재의 한미간의 관계로 미루어 보아, 사정변경을 이유로 하는 협정의 일방적인 폐기 역시 불가능하다고 생각됨.

주한 미국군대지위에 관한 현안 문제중 재판관할권문제 보다 더 긴급한 문제가 있는 경우에는 그것을 우선적으로 해결하도록 하는 것은 당연한 일이며, 따라서, 재판관할권을 장래의 문제로 보류할 수는 있으나, 다른 정치적인 고려를 하지 아니하는 한, 이와같은 해결의 보류는 어디까지나 임시적인 것이어야 하며 미국측의 제안에 일정기한을 추가하여야 할 것임. 검토필 (1965. 6. 30.)

한편 미국측은 일찌기 1958년 9월 18일 당시의 다우링 대사를 통하여 구두로 이와같은 제의를 한바 있으나 한국측은 이를 수락하지 안비취였음.

조건 (2) 에 관하여 : 미국측이 말하는 "보상" (Compensation) 의 내용이 무엇인지 명백하지 아니함. 그런데, 토지, 시설의 소유자 또는 공급자에 대한 보상이라고 한 점으로 보아, 이는 한국정부에 의한 토지, 시설의 징발 또는 수용에 따르는 보상을 의미하는 것

으로 이해되며, 보상은 한국정부의 책임이라고 한 것은 보상에
소요되는 재정적 부담을 한국정부가 진다는 것으로 이해됨. 또한
이러한 보상책임은 기왕에 사용되었거나 현재 사용되는 것 뿐만
아니라, 앞으로 사용될 것에 대해서도 이를 한국정부가 부담한다는
것임.

국유 또는 정부관리 재산의 사용에 대해서는 보상의 문제가
발생할 수 없으므로, 미국측 조건에서는 이러한 재산은 문제삼지
않고 있는 것으로 생각됨.

Rental 또한 미국측 조건에는 보상만을 언급하고, 국유 또는 사유
재산의 사용료(Rental) 에 대해서는 하등 문제삼지 않고 있는데,
이는 미국측이 이러한 사용료 지불에 관하여 한국측과 교섭의 여지
를 남겨두기 위한 것인지 여부를 알아야 하며, 보상 대상으로
"real property " 를 들고 있으므로 그 개념과 합중측이
제의한 " facilities and areas " 의 개념의 일치 여부에
관하여 쌍방의 견해를 또한 조정하여야 할 것임. 단, 한미 쌍방
은 1958 년에 공익물 용역 청구권 청산협정을 체결하여, 유엔군의
공익물(Utilities) 사용에 대한 사용료 청산 문제 및 장래의 사용
조건등에 관하여 일반적 양해에 도달한 바 있으므로 현안 협정의 규정
대상으로 부터 이러한 공익물 사용관계를 제외할 수 있을 것임.

— x. —

1. Criminal jurisdiction
2. Compensation — Rental
3. real property — facilities & areas

일반문어로 재분류
(협정체결후)

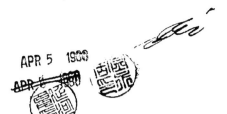

SUMMARY RECORD

Mr. Edwin M. Cronk, Counselor of U.S. Embassy for Economic Affairs, called on Political Affairs Director Kim at the latter's office at 3:30, p.m., April 5, 1960 and referred to the problem of classification of a Note No. 2391 which U.S. Ambassador McConaughy delivered to Vice-Foreign Minister Choi, March 30, 1960, and which is a reply to our proposal for conclusion of an agreement on facilities and areas in use by United States forces. Mr. Cronk said that U.S. Embassy requested the Ministry to deem the said note classified as "confidential" by the sender from the beginning of its issuance though the word "confidential" was not actually put on the said document. He also requested the Ministry to treat the said document by such classification.

Political Affairs Director Kim noted Mr. Cronk's remarks saying that the Ministry cannot but consider the U.S. note in question classified as confidential if the sender wishes to classify it that way. However, he said that the "confidential" classification of the document is one thing and question of publicity about U.S. reply is another. The Ministry is, therefore, in a difficult position on this issue if the U.S. side requests Korean side to say nothing about the problem because our proposal in last June is well known to the public and press.

한·미국 간의 상호방위조약 제4조에 의한 시설과 구역 및 한국에서의 미국군대의 지위에 관한 협정(SOFA)
전59권. 1966.7.9 서울에서 서명 : 1967.2.9 발효(조약 232호), V.8 체결 교섭, 1960-61   355

Political Affairs Director Kim also said that
the Ministry will give due and careful consideration
to the fact that the sender classified as confidential
but is obliged to study a way of making some explanation to the public about recent U.S. reaction to our
proposal. Director Kim added that the Ministry will
treat it in the light of international practice in
which a "confidentral" note is treated.

0046

/D R A F T/

March 31, 1960

REPORT

TO   : His Excellency the President

FROM   : Vice Foreign Minister

SUBJECT : Summary Record of Conversation
            with Ambassador McConaughy
            (Re: KPO-154 of March 31, 1960)

Vice Foreign Minister Kyu Hah Choi had a meeting
with U.S. Ambassador Walter P. McConaughy, at the
latter's request, at Bando Hotel for about an hour
from 3:00 p.m., March 30, 1960. The following is the
gist of conversation which took place at the above
meeting.

I. Ambassador McConaughy handed a note to Vice
Foreign Minister Choi, which is in reply to the
Ministry's letter of June 10, 1959 requesting the U.S.
Government to commence negotiations for conclusion
of an agreement on the facilities and areas now in
use by the U.S. forces in Korea. A copy of the above
U.S. note was submitted to the Office of the President
on March 30, 1960 (KPO-154). The Ministry's observation
and recommendation on the said U.S. reply will be
submitted separately.

II. Ambassador McConaughy turned to the Baguio
Conference of American Diplomats in Asia. According
to Ambassador McConaughy, U.S. diplomats stationed in
Asian countries held a similar conference at Bangkok
in 1950. The Baguio Conference, therefore, was held
to review the overall picture in the area of the past
decade and to study the prospect of the future decade.

Generally speaking, Mr. McConaughy said, the
American diplomats at the Baguio Conference felt that

9-1

0047

to certain extent

crises in Asia were overcome ∨and situation in the
region is better now than it was in 1950. The following
are resumé of views held by conferees as told by
Ambassador McConaughy:

Taiwan: Taiwan is a show-case of economic
stability.

The Philippines: In the Philippines, the Huks
were suppressed and the government is stable and
definitely on the free nations' side.

Burma: Burma, which used to be an ultra-neutral
country, became more cooperative toward the free
nations and situation there is secure.

Thailand: Situation is stable in Thailand.

Indonesia: Indonesia is in lack of stability
both in political and economic fields but her relations
with the United States are better than before.

Vietnam: The Republic of Vietnam registered
more progress than that achieved by Communist Vietminh.

Cambodia: Cambodia turned more toward neutralism
but she is not a Communist country yet.

Laos: Laos is a big question mark, but Communist
efforts in Laos were repelled at least for the time
being.

(Ambassador McConaughy deliberately evaded ~~from~~
~~making~~ any comment on Korea)~~though he referred to the~~
~~situation in Japan.)~~

Ambassador McConaughy stated that the conferees
at the Baguio Conference felt that they should be
gratified to see some progress attained by countries
in the area. They, however, recognized that there is

9-2

0048

no ground for "complacency". In the view of the
U.S. diplomats attending the Baguio Conference,
Communist threat to this area is greater than ever
before. They were particularly disturbed by the
military and economic potentiality of Communist China.
They recognized the need to redouble the U.S. efforts
to meet the danger posed by Communist China.

Some U.S. Congressmen may try to reduce the size
of military and economic aids to this area in next
series of years, but the U.S. diplomats thought that
it was based on "mistaken" assumption. They, therefore,
wrote to Secretary of State, emphasizing the danger
still existing in this area, so that he may use this
point of view when testifying before the Congress.
The following are main points of the said letter (Mr.
McConaughy briefed using a four-page letter):

In Asia which has a population of 800 millions, Japan
is the only major industrial country for free world security.
In this area, situation is generally speaking more
encouraging than a year ago, but U.S. mutual security programs
are still needed as essential means of resisting such
Communist danger by the people in the area and as vital supplement to their own
efforts in the region which is vulnerable to Communist
invasion. Ambassador McConaughy stated that Korea is
listed at the top of the list of such countries.

The American diplomats stressed the necessity
of offering continued economic aid (for defense support),
technical assistance, DLF programs, etc. to the countries
of the region. They believed that their letter would

9-3

한·미국 간의 상호방위조약 제4조에 의한 시설과 구역 및 한국에서의 미국군대의 지위에 관한 협정(SOFA)
전59권. 1966.7.9 서울에서 서명 : 1967.2.9 발효(조약 232호), V.8 체결 교섭, 1960-61 359

be used by Secretary Herter in his explanation to the
Congress when foreign aid question should ~~be~~ undergo
heavy fire of Congressional debate.

The conferees submitted a conclusion and
recommendation, which part is classified as secret.
For confidential information, Ambassador McConaughy
confided to the Vice Foreign Minister the followings:

In general, there was noted a progress in the
Far Eastern countries. The conferees noted that the
nature of the present Communist threat is less dramatic.
Japan constitutes a considerable element of free
nations strength, ~~as she has, in the view of the~~
~~conferees, a remarkable vitality as~~ free nation.
In Indonesia, there exists economic and political
instability and no settlement is in sight at the
present stage. The U.S. diplomats felt relieved
as they noted that the Communist insurgency is
removed. Thailand is considered as a corner stone
of U.S. foreign policy in this area. ~~(Here again,~~
~~Mr. McConaughy refrained from making any comment on~~
~~Korea.)~~ In conclusion, the conferees thought that
the past decade was spent mainly for national survival
to maintain internal security and political integrity.

Communist China's threat to the region is not
only military but also economic. ~~xxxxxxxxxxxxx~~ Except
~~in~~ Japan and ~~Formosa~~ the Republic of China, no great economic progress is
noted in the region. Indonesia made retreat in the
field of economy. The conferees anticipated that the
population of Asia in next decade will increase up
to 2-billions. They expressed fear that Communist China
might become leading power in Asia in the field of
technology. As witnessed in Tibetan and Indian border

9-4

incidents, there is an increasing threat from Communist China. *Peking* ~~Peking~~ seems to have no interest at all even ~~to reach~~ conclud*ing* a <u>modus</u> <u>vivendi</u> with the United States. They agreed that the so-called two-China policy is not acceptable. This point was well enunciated in the speech of Assistant Secretary of State Parsons at Wisconsin on February 19, 1960, in which he reemphasized the firm stand against Red China. The United States conducted talks with Red China at Panmoonjum, Geneva and Warsaw, but this is distinctly separated from the question of recognizing Red China. Ambassador McConaughy said that the U.S. *will continue its* policy ~~is~~ to recognize Free China (Republic of China) and to reject Communist China. The Sino-Russian relations are more cohesive than diversive and it would be a serious mistake if one assumes that there *is* ~~are~~ any *significant* cleavage in Sino-Russian relations. The American diplomats reaffirmed the necessity for the U.S. to maintain close relations with the Republic of China and also the necessity of keeping *a* big standing army in Formosa.

~~America~~ Urgent problems which Indonesia is *confronted* ~~faced~~ with now are how to obtain technical and monetary aids. Generally speaking, the U.S. is better understood by countries in the Far East than a decade ago, but the U.S. should be consistent in meeting the aggression to this area. Mr. McConaughy stated that *Nationalism* ~~, the U.S. diplomats concluded,~~ is growing in this area, which is a good tendency because Nationalism is opposed by Communism.

The American diplomats admitted that the Soviet success in the field of space science resulted in an increased prestige for Soviet Russia among the Asians

9-5

0051

and in this respect, the U.S. suffered a setback.
The conferees recognized the necessity for the U.S.
to be prepared for the possibility of limited war
and the necessity of keeping U.S. ground forces at
the present level. They also felt the necessity of
keeping economic and military aids to the countries
of the region at the present level. In meeting
Asian demand for better life, the U.S. must encourage
free institutions and free enterprises. The conferees
recognized the important role of European countries
in the economic development of Far Eastern countries
and felt it necessary that European countries should
cooperate with the U.S. in this project. They also
recognized the responsibility of Japan in participating
in this economic development program.

As for Okinawa, the American diplomats agreed that
the island should be placed under exclusive U.S.
administration for the time being. They saw no state
of democracy is deeply rooted in Asian countries, while
admitting that the democratic institution in this area
does not necessarily have to be a Western-styled one in view
of its own environment. They recognized, however,
that democracy does not survive in the state of insecurity
or backwardness. There is no distinct tendency of
"regionalism" in the Far East except the case of SEATO.
Economic regionalism has many difficulties and it is felt
necessary that efforts through ECAFE and cooperation by the
United States be sought to attain economic stability
in the region. In this regard, the conferees found it advisable
that exchange programs of Fulbright type or Leaders
Grant-type be continued. Ambassador McConaughy
pointed out that no Fulbright program is operated in Korea.

7-6

0052

In the U.S. foreign policies, a chance to be seized . .

The U.S. future security and wellbeing is heavily dependent upon this area, and the U.S. should dmonstrate that they are acting on firm conviction. Survival is an elementary question ~~which was~~ but this was the major problem in Asia of the last decade.

III.   Ambassador McConaughy then touched upon the Korea-Japan problems. On his way back to Seoul from Baguio, he said he dropped in Tokyo. He talked with Ambassador MacArthur in Tokyo and they were both heartened to see that ~~the~~ mutual exchange of detainees was effected between ~~the two Governments.~~ Korea & Japan. He said that he was told that the Japanese side was watching attentively the attitude of the Korean Government as to whether or not it would repatriate to Japan those Japanese fishermen who ~~are~~ shall have served out their sentences as of April 9, 1960, and later on.

~~He asked whether such Japanese fishermen would be repatriated to Japan as soon as they are released from prisons.~~

Vice Foreign Minister Choi stated that we are carefully watching, ~~carefully~~ too, how far Japan would go on with the detainees issue. He said that the discussion on March 19, 1960 was on those Japanese fishermen who had served out their sentences as of that date and that future development depends on Japanese sincerity on Japan's part.

Ambassador McConaughy said that he knew very well of the Korean feeling on the detainees issue and the seriousness of the effect in case the so-called Calcutta Agreement should be extended. He deplored the fact that the

9-7

한·미국 간의 상호방위조약 제4조에 의한 시설과 구역 및 한국에서의 미국군대의 지위에 관한 협정(SOFA)
전59권. 1966.7.9 서울에서 서명 : 1967.2.9 발효(조약 232호), V.8 체결 교섭, 1960-61   363

active propaganda and brain-washing activities by the ~~KOREAN~~ Communist (_CHORYUN_) ~~CHOSOREN~~ are quite effective.

    Vice Foreign Minister Choi stated that the Free World _including the United State_ should be awakened to the serieousness of Japan's continuance of deportation scheme and urged that the something should be done to stop this scheme by the United States.

            Most respectfully,

9 - 8

/D R.A F T/

March ___, 1960

TO   : His Excellency the President

FROM   : Vice-Minister of Foreign Affairs

SUBJECT: Proposed agreement on the facilities and
           areas in use by United States forces in Korea
           (Re: KPO/154)*dated march 31, 1960*)

검토필 (196 . 12.30.)   판리 60
                                                                      번호 59

        In reply to a proposal made by our Government on

June 10, 1959 for commencement of negotiations to con-

clude an agreement on the facilities and areas in use

by United States forces in Korea, U.S. Ambassador

McConaughy handed a note to Vice-Foreign Minister Choi,

according to which the United States would accept our

proposal on the following "understandings":

        1) that a revision of the arrangements set forth
            in the notes exchanged between our two govern-
            ments at Taejon on July 12, 1950, will not be
            proposed by either side; and

        2) that compensation to the owners or suppliers
            of any real property in Korea which has been
            or will be used by the United States Armed
            Forces is the responsibility of the Korean
            Government.   검토필 (   )

        In the view of the Ministry:

        1) The U.S. position on item 1 of the above

understandings is a similar one which then-American

Ambassador Dowling under instructions from Washington

informally
suggested on September 18, 1958 to the former Vice-

Foreign Minister. (KPO 101 dated September 18, 1958)

According to Ambassador Dowling at that time, the

United States would enter negotiation for status of

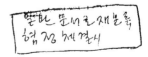

0055

forces agreement of "purely administrative nature", unless it touches upon the problem of criminal jurisdiction. This suggestion was hardly acceptable to us. Significance of the latest U.S. proposal is that the previous *U.S.* view which ~~was informally~~ *had been* delivered was set forth in a formal note; and

2) With regard to the problem of compensation to be paid to owners or suppliers of any real property, if this U.S. condition be accepted, any agreement which may be reached on that basis would bear only a token of significance on our part.

Under the circumstances, the settlement of problems on the basis of the U.S. proposed conditions would achieve some*thing* but would result in concluding the long-pending question concerning criminal jurisdiction against our favor. This will not convince our people.

/REVISE/

외 무 부

년 월 일

It is recommended, therefore, ~~for Your Excellency's approval~~ that the Ministry ~~will~~ continue to contact with U.S. side for obtaining its reconsideration on the "understandings" set forth in the U.S. note under reference, because *it is difficult for our side to* ~~our Government feels it difficult to~~ accept such "understandings" *as they are now*.

사본 1
관리번호 108

COPY

RECOMMENDATION *KPO/160*

April 2, 1960

TO   : His Excellency the President

FROM   : Vice-Minister of Foreign Affairs

SUBJECT: Proposed agreement on the facilities and
          areas in use by United States forces in Korea
          (Re: KPO/154 dated March 31, 1960)

In reply to a proposal made by our Government on
June 10, 1959 for commencement of negotiations to conclude an agreement on the facilities and areas in use
by United States forces in Korea, U.S. Ambassador
McConaughy handed a note to Vice-Foreign Minister Choi,
according to which the United States would accept our
proposal on the following "understandings":

1)   that a revision of the arrangements set forth
     in the notes exchanged between our two govern-
     ments at Taejon on July 12, 1950, will not be
     proposed by either side; and

2)   that compensation to the owners or suppliers
     of any real property in Korea which has been
     or will be used by the United States Armed
     Forces is the responsibility of the Korean
     Government.

In the view of the Ministry:

1)   The U.S. position on item 1 of the above
understandings is a similar one which then-American
Ambassador Dowling under instructions from Washington
informally suggested on September 18, 1958 to the
former Vice-Foreign Minister. (KPO 161 dated September
18, 1958) According to Ambassador Dowling at that time,
the United States would enter negotiation for status of

0057

forces agreement of "purely administrative nature,"
unless it touches upon the problem of criminal
jurisdiction. This suggestion was hardly acceptable
to us. Significance of the latest U.S. proposal is
that the previous U.S. view which had been informally
delivered was set forth in a fromal note; and

2) With regard to the problem of compensation
to be paid to owners or suppliers of any real property,
if this U.S. condition be accepted, any agreement which
may be reached on that basis would bear only a token
of significance on our part.

Under the circumstances, the settlement of
problems on the basis of the U.S. proposed conditions
would achieve something but would result in concluding
the long-pending question concerning criminal jurisdiction
against our favor. This will not convince our people.

It is recommended, therefore, that the Ministry
continue to contact with the U.S. side for obtaining its
reconsideration on the "understandings" set forth in the
U.S. note under reference, because it is difficult for
our side to accept such "understandings" as they are now.

Most respectfully,

0058

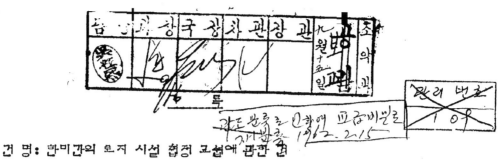

건 명: 한미간의 토지 시설 협정 교섭에 관한 건

　　단기4293년 3월 30일자 미국대사 각서와 관련하여, 토지 시설 협정의

교섭 및 기타 군대지위 문제 해결에 관한 의견교환을 위하여, 아래와 같이

미국대사관 실무자를 초청하고 토의하는 동시에, 군대지위 문제 해결을 위한

절차에 관하여 하나의 비공식 제안을 하였음.

1. 일　　시: 단기4293년 9월 15일 오후 2시— 3시

2. 장　　소: 정무국장실

3. 참석자: 정무국장, 조약과장, 요 사무관

　　　　　Albert E. Pappano,　Robert W. Tucker
　　　　　（ 참사관 ）　　　　　（ 一등서기관 ）

4. 토의내용:

　　국장: (군대 지위 문제의 성격 및 토지 시설 협정 교섭 제의와 한국 내의

여론등에 언급한 후) 토지 시설 협정 교섭 개시의 표견을 제의한 지난 3월30

일자 미국측 각서에 관련된 미국측의 의도와 의미를 알고저 함.

　　파파노: (전문가의 입장에서가 아니라 그냥 알고 있는 사실을 이야기하

겠다고 전제한 다음) 군대 지위 협정은 그 내용이 복잡하고 다양하므로 먼저

토지 시설 문제부터 해결할 용의는 있으되, 교섭 개시전에 미리 원칙을 세워

둘 필요가 있다고 생각되어 두 가지 표건을 제의한 것이며, 미국측은 해결하

기 쉬운 문제부터 한가지식 처리해 나가기를 바람 (이때 덕커가, 토지 시설

협정은 한국측이 먼저 우선적으로 제의한 것이라고 확인함)

　　국장: 문제를 한가지식 해결해 나가는데는 동의함. 그러나 한국측은

토지 시설협정이 체결된 후에도 어느 특정 문제에 대한 토의를 하지않겠다는

보장을 미리부터 줄 수는 없는 것임. 문제를 전부 동시에 해결할 수는 없을지

라도, 그 해결에 착수는 합의할 것임 (한문제의해결때문에 다른문제의해결을 막아버릴수는 없는것임)

　　파파노: 전기 각서 내용 이외의 것은 무엇이라 말 할수 없으나, 미국측

0059

의 견해는 아직 변경 없을 뿐만 아니라 앞으로 변경될 가망성은 거의 없을 것임. 한국측은 전기 보장이 영구적인 것으로 이해하는 듯 하나, 어느 정부 든지 어떠한 문제에 대하여 영원히 보장을 줄 수는 없을 것임.

국장: 어느 문제를 토의 대상으로 부여 제의하지 않는다는 양해하에서 이 일면의 원지 해결에 착수할 수는 있은, 절차상 문제해결의 순서를 정하도록 하여야 할 르건이좋은 것임. 장래에 가능한 교섭에 대하여 미리 문호를 폐쇄할 수는 없는 것임.

파파노: 두가지 조건하에서만 교섭하도록 훈령 받고 있기 때문에, 그것 이 끝난 다음에 즉시로 어떤 문제를 토의할 것인가는 말 할수 없음.

국장: 해결할 문제의 순서를 미리 정하도록 할 것을 비공식으로 제의하는 바이며, 미국측의 회답을 기대함.

파파노: 비공식 제안이므로 비공식으로 회답하겠음. 외무부는 그 회답을 기다리지 않고 전기 미국 각서에 대한 회답을 줄 것인가? 또는 그 후에 할 것인가?

국장: 그 전에 회답한다면, 한국측은 미국측 조건을 거부할 수 밖에 도리가 없을 것이고, 그렇게 되면 교섭을 진행할 수 없게 될 것이므로 그것 은 원하지 않는 바임. 따라서 한국측은 미리 쌍방의 의도가 합쳐진 후에 공식회답 을 하고 장차후 교섭을 진행한후 바라는 것임.

파파노: 전술한 비공식 제안이란, 어느 문제의 토의를 완료하기 전에 다음의 문제 외교섭에여 대하여 합의한다는 것인가?

국장: 토의할 문제의 순서를 잠정적으로 결정하자는 것임.

워커: (갑작이 보상 문제에 언급하여) 보도된 한국정부의 보상 요구는 비 현실적이고 가망이 거의 없을 뿐만 아니라, 미국 내의 국민 여론이나 의회의 감정도 한국측에 불리한 것임. 많은 한국 사람들이 이것을 기대하고 있는 듯 하나, 미국 국민 감정을 신중히 고려하기 바람.

파파노: (워커의 말에 동감이라고 하면서) 한국 여론의 여하를 막론하고 강경한 미국측의 입장을 외무부에서 잘 이해해 주기 바람. 미국 의회의 반응이 좋지 않을 것임.

— 3 —

국장: 그것은 잘 알고 있으며, ~~한국 정부의 관리의 신중한 태도~~. 한국정부는 법상 국민에게 보상할 의무가 있는데 그것을 재정적 관점으로 도저히 하지 못 하고 ~~있다는 처량한 입장에~~ 있음.

럽커: 미국측이 사용하고 있는 것은 대부분이 귀속 재산이며 ~~사유~~에 속하는 것은 얼마 되지 아니함.

국장: 한국정부는 법적 의무를 이행하여야 함. 와싱톤 당국에 그냥 보고만 할 것이 아니라, ~~해결될~~ 모든 문제의 ~~순서~~ 조속 해결을 건의하여 주기 바람.

럽커: 미국정부의 융통성을 ~~너무~~ 과대 평가하고 있는 듯 함.

파파노: 와싱톤에 보고하도록 하겠음.

협정 체결서
일반문서로 재분류

한·미국 간의 상호방위조약 제4조에 의한 시설과 구역 및 한국에서의 미국군대의 지위에 관한 협정(SOFA)
전59권. 1966.7.9 서울에서 서명 : 1967.2.9 발효(조약 232호), V.8 체결 교섭, 1960-61 371

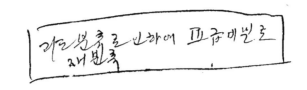

각급본측로 인하여 표준미법로
재법측

건 명 : 한미간의 군대지위협정 체결에 관한 건

(1) 제 관

검토필(196? . ???)

주한 미국군대의 지위에 관한 한미협정에 대해서는 이미 한미 상호방위조약 체결 교섭 당시에 약속된바 있었으며, 그 후 한국정부는 단기 4287 년 시급을 요한 주한 유엔군 관세업무협정 체결을 제의 하였으나 미국측이 이를 거부하였고, 단기 4288 년 부터 단기 4290 년 까지 한국정부는 주한 유엔군 또는 미군의 지위에 관한 포괄적 협정 (소위 "행정협정") 체결을 위하여 노력하였으나 역시 여의치 못하였 으므로, 단기 4290 년 말 이래로는 군대 지위중 상호 합의할 수 있는 문제부터 우선적으로 해결하기로 결정하여 단기 4292년에 미국군대가 사용하는 토지, 시설의 사용조건과 보상에 관한 협정 체결을 제의하기 에 이름.

검토필(196? 6. 20)

검토필(196? . 12. 30)

(2) 교섭 경위

1. 단기 4286 년 8 월 7 일, 한미상호방위조약안 가조인시의 이승만 대통령과 덜레스 국무장관간의 공동성명에서 한미 양 정부는 상호방위조약 발효 후 즉시로 군대지위협정을 교섭하기로 약속함.

2. 단기 4287 년 12 월 2 일, 미국정부는 주한 유엔군의 관세 업무협정 체결을 정식으로 제의하고 한국측의 협정초안을 함께 제시함. 그러나 미국측은, 단기 4288 년 1 월 과 5 월의 양처에 걸쳐, 미군의 독자적인 합리적 통관절차로써 한국측의 요구에 응할 수 있다는 이유로 상기 제의를 거절함.

3. 단기 4288 년 4 월 28 일, 미국정부는 주한 유엔군의 지위 를 포괄적으로 규정하는 군대지위협정(소위 "행정협정") 체결을

0062

정식으로 제의하고, 한국측 협정초안을 하게 채서함.

4. 단기 4290년 1월 5일과 동년 6월 29일의 2차에 걸쳐 한국정부는 전기 군대지위협정 체결을 거듭 미국측에 촉구함. 한국정부는 최초에는 유엔군의 법적지위를 규정하고저 하였으나, 미국측으로 부터 유엔군 파견국 정부간의 의견조정에 시간을 요한다는 시사가 있었으므로, 이대부어는 미국군대 만이라도 위선 그 법적지위를 규정하도록 할 것을 주장하게됨.

5. 단기 4290년 9월 10일, 당시의 허터 국무차관의 내한을 계기로 한국정부는 장문의 구서를 허터 차관에게 수교하여 전기 한국측 제의를 수락하도록 강력히 요구함.

6. 단기 4290년 10월 10일, 당시의 "다우링" 미국대사는 조정환 외무부장관에게, 미국군대의 지위를 부분적으로 해결할 가능성이 있음을 구두로 전달함.

7. 단기 4290년 11월 13일과 동월 26일, 한국정부는 전기 "다우링" 대사의 제안을 확인하고, 군대의 지위를 다섯가지 항목 즉, (1) 과세 및 관세업무, (2) 청구권 청산, (3) 토지 및 시설, (4) 출입국 및 (5) 형사재판관할권등으로 분할하여 각 항목별로 개별 협정을 체결함으로써 문제를 단계적으로 해결할 것을 제의함.

8. 단기 4291년 9월 18일, "다우링" 대사는, 현재의 사정이 존속하는 한 한국정부가 형사재판관할권 협정을 제의하지 아니한다는 조건으로, 순수히 행정적인 사항에 관하여 한국측과 협정할 수 있음을 구두로 전달하여 옴. 그러나 한국정부는 당시의 사정으로 보아 이러한 미국측 제의를 수락할 수 없는 것으로 결정함.

9. 단기 4292년 6월 10일, 한국정부는 전기 "다우링" 대사가 제의한 형사재판관할권 현상유지 여부에 아무런 언급을 아니한 채,

한·미국 간의 상호방위조약 제4조에 의한 시설과 구역 및 한국에서의 미국군대의 지위에 관한 협정(SOFA) 전59권. 1966.7.9 서울에서 서명 : 1967.2.9 발효(조약 232호), V.8 체결 교섭, 1960-61 373

주한 미군부대가 사용하는 토지, 시설에 관한 협정 체결을 정식으로 제의하고 동년 10 월 15 일 동 제안의 수락을 미국측에 다시 촉구함.

10. 단기 4293 년 3 월 10 일, 한국정부는 미국측에 대하여 과거 수년간에 걸친 군대지위협정 체결 노력과 한국민의 희망을 상기 시키면서 토지, 시설 협정의 우선적 체결을 강력히 요구함.

11. 단기 4293 년 3 월 30 일, 미국정부는 (1) 형사재판관할권에 관한 현상을 유지하고, (2) 토지, 시설의 사용에 대한 보상은 한국정부가 그 책임을 진다는 양해아래서 전기 토지, 시설 협정 교섭에 응할 용의가 있음을 통고하여옴. 그러나 이러한 두가지 양해사항은 한국정부로서는 불리한 것이기 때문에 이 점에 관하여 미국측과 다시 접촉할 것을 대통령에게 품의하고 그 결정을 기다리던 중 4. 19 사태로 진전을 보지 못하고 현재에 이름.

일반문서로 재분류
협정 체결시

한미 간의 군대지위 협정 교섭 경과 및 앞으로의 타결책

1. 1953 년 8 월 한미 방위 조약 가조인시의 이승만 · 덜레스 공동 성명 에서 한미양정부는 상호 방위 목적 ...... 군대지위 협정을 교섭하기로 약속함 (주 ...... 조약 은 1954 년 8 월에 발효됨)

2. 1954 년 12 월 정부는 주한 유엔군의 관세 업무에 관한 협정 체결을 제의하고 그 협정안을 제시 하였으나 미국측은 이를 거절 함.

3. 1955 년 4 월 정부는 주한유엔군의 지위를 포괄적으로 규정하는 군대지위 협정 (소위 "행정 협정") 체결을 제의 하고 협정안 을 동시에 제시 하였으며, 그후 1957 년 1 월, 3 월, 및 9 월에 교섭 개시를 촉구함.

4. 1957 년 10 월 미국측은 군대지위 문제를 다변적으로 한미간에 합의할수있는 한도 까지 하나 하나 해결해 나갈것을 제의하여 왔으므로, 정부는 이에 응하여 동년 11 월 미국측에 대하여 (1) 관세 및 관세 업무, (2) 청구권 청산, (3) 토지 및 시설, (4) 출입국 및 (5) 형사재판 관할권 등으로 나누어 각 항목 별로 개별 협정을 체결 할것을 제의 하였던바, 1958 년 9 월 미국측은 한국측이 재판 관할권에 관한 협정을 제의하지 아니할 것으로 보장하는 경우에는 기타의 행정적인 문제 해결에 응 하겠다고 제의하여 왔으나, 정부는 이를 승낙하지 아니함.

검토필 (196 . 12 .)

6. 1968 년 8 월 정부는 ...... 계결남 ...... 에서 주한 미국 군대가 사용 하는 토지 및 시설에 관한 ...... 협의을 제의하고 동년 10 월, 1969 년 3 협의 8 차에 걸쳐 미국 측의 소속을 촉구하였던바, 1969 년 3 월 ...... 미국 측은 (1) 형사 재판 관할권에 관한 협상을 ...... 하고 (2) 토지, 시설 사용에 대한 보상은 한국 정부가 그 ...... 진다는 두가지 ...... 에서 전기 ...... 교섭에 응할것이라고 ...... 나여 옴.

나. 앞으로의 ...... 책

상기 ...... 보고에서 알수있는 바와 같이 가능한 한 ...... 미 협정 ...... 을 ...... 하자는 아국측의 노력에 ...... 오심이로 ...... 하고 미국측은 한국의 ...... 토 ...... 상태에 있다는 이유로 ...... 의 협정의 ...... 을 ...... 여 왔으며, 이 협정 상태의 ...... 로서 ...... 별로 개별적 협정을 ...... 하려는 우 ...... 제안마저도 미국측이 (1) 형사 재판관할권에 관하여 협상을 유지않것와 (2) 토지, 시설사용에 대한 보상을 한국측이 부담같것등 두가지 ...... 을 제시하였기 때문에 아무런 진전을 보지못하고있음. 지금 신정부의 ...... 과 ...... 어 이 문제를 다시 ...... 것이며 그럼 기술상 ...... 있는 태도로 ...... 하는것이 필요함.

이 상

한미군의 교육원제협정 (행정협정) 체결문제
161 2 5

가. 체결교섭 경위　검토필(1966.12.17.)462　판리번호 46

1. 1953 년 8 월 7 일 한미방위조약 가조인시의 이승만, 덜레스 공동성명에서 한미양국 정부는 상호방위조약 발효후 즉시 군대지위협정을 교섭하기로 약속함. (주기; 한미상호방위 조약은 1954 년 2 월에 발효함)　검토필(196

2. 1954 년 12 월 정부는 그 내용상 행정협정의 일부가 될 주한 우언군의 과세업무에 관한 협정 체결을 제의하였으나 미국측은 이를 거부함.　검토필(1966.30)

3. 1955 년 4 월 정부는 주한 우언군의 지위를 포괄적으로 규정 하는 군대지위협정의 체결을 제의하고 동시에 협정안을 제시 하였으며 그후 1957 년 1 월, 6 월, 및 9 월에 다시 교섭의 개시를 촉구함.

4. 1957 년 10 월 미국측은 군대지위협정 문제를 부분적으로 합의 가능한 한도내에서 하나 하나 해결해 나갈것을 제의하여 왔으므로 정부는 이에 응하여 동년 11 월 미국측에 대하여 이 문제를 1) 과세 및 과세업무, 2) 청구권결산, 3) 요지 및 시설, 4) 출입국, 5) 형사재판관할권 등으로 분활하여 각항목별로 개별협정을 체결할것을 제의하였던바, 1958 년 8 월 미국측은 한국정부가 재판관할권에 관한 협정을 제의 하지 않는다는 조건하에 기타의 행정적인 문제의 해결에 응하 겠다고 회답하여 왔으며, 정부는 이를 소락하지 아니함.

5. 1959 년 6 월 정부는 군대지위협정 문제를 개별적으로 해결 할 방침하에 우선 그 첫단계로서 주한 미군이 사용하는 요지 및 시설에 관한 협정체결을 제의하고 동년 10 월과 1960 년

한·미국 간의 상호방위조약 제4조에 의한 시설과 구역 및 한국에서의 미국군대의 지위에 관한 협정(SOFA)
전59권. 1966.7.9 서울에서 서명 : 1967.2.9 발효(조약 232호), V.8 체결 교섭, 1960-61　377

3 월의 2 차에 걸처 미국축의 수락을 축구하였던바,

1960 년 3 월말 미국축은 1) 형사재판관할권에 관한

현상을 유지하고 2) 요지 및 시설에 관한 보상은 한국정부

가 그 책임을 진다는 두 가지 조건하에 전기 협정체결 교섭에

응할것이라고 회답하여 왔고 우 미정부는 이를 받아드릴수

없어 그후 교섭이 정돈상태에 있음.

6. 단기 4294 년 2 월 28 일 한미간에 새로운 경제기술원조

협정이 체결되고 또한 국회는 행정협정의 조속한 체결을

축구하는 결의안을 채택하였으므로 정부는 다시 이 협정의

체결을 위한 적극적인 준비를 진행중에 있음.

나. 협정안의 내용

1. 진술한 고섭경과에서 말한바와 같이 한국측이 누차에 걸처

체결교섭을 서둘러 온 소위 군대지위협정은 그 규정대상이

상당히 광범위하며, 그중에는 주한 미군의 형사재판관할권,

주한 미군이 사용하는 요지 및 시설, 관세 및 과세업무, 미국

군인, 군속, 및 그 가족의 출입국문제, 미군의 구매사무, 각종

과 청구권의 청산문제 등 등 여러가지 복잡한 문제를 내포하고

있는바, 정부는 처음에는 이를 모든 상황을 포괄하여 타입

협정으로 체결코져 하였으나, 미국측은 오이려 이것을 몇개의

개별협정으로 분할 체결할것을 제의하여 왔고 정부도 이에

찬성하여 우선 미군이 사용하는 요지 및 시설에 관한 협정의

체결을 제의하였던 것임.

2. 이에 대하여 미국측은 1) 형사재판관할권 문제에 관하여는

어디까지나 현상을 유지하고 (즉 팬권협정의 존속을 의미

합) 2) 요지 및 시설사용에 대한 보상은 한국정부가 책임진

0069

마는 두 가지 조건하에서만 교섭에 응하겠다는 태도로
나왔고 따라서 현재 교착상태에 빠져있는바, 첫 째,
형사재판관활권 문제에 관하여는 1950 년 7 월 12 일
인곡동,한시 대전에서 체결한 소위 대전협정에서 미국군인에
대한 재판관활권을 전적으로 미국측에게만 부여한 불합리한
조항을 규정하고 있으므로 이 결함을 수정하여 국제법상의
관례에 따라 주둔군이 공무집행중에 범한것에 한하여 미국
군 자체의 재판권을 인정하도록 하자는 것이 우리측의 주장이며
둘 째, 미군이 사용하는 요지 및 시설에 대한 보상문제 역시
우리나라 현경제상태를 고력할때 미국측이 주장하는대로
우리정부단이 일방적으로 책임지기는 곤난한 사정하에 있어
미국측이 어느정도 까지는 보상책임을 지도록 규정하자는 것이
우리의 입장임.

127

1. 중요 협정의 내용

   (1) 한미간의 군사고문단 설치 협정 개정 협정

      단기 4288 년 1 월. 26일에 체결된 한미간의 군사고문단
      설치에 관한 협정 제 1 조를 개정한 것인데 그 내용은
      전 협정에서는 군사고문단을 구성하는 미국 장성 관하수를
      육법 합의가 없는 한 500 명으로 한정하고 있었으나 한국동란
      발발로 국군의 규모 가 확대됨으로 인한 것인 규정을
      삭제하고 양국 정부가 합의하는 수도 구성한다는 것임.

   (2) 한미간의 보험소포 우편 협정

      이 협정 체결로서 미국과 보험소포의 교환업무를 개설하게
      되는 바, 이 협정의 주 내용은 보험소포의 관리 및 반송 이후
      발송시 까지 감심하는 손해를 배상하여 주는 것으로 이 협정은
      미국이 다국우편연합 소포우편문에 관한 약정에 가입하고 있지
      않기 때문에 체결 필요성이 있는 것임.

   (3) 한미 경제기술원조 협정

      이 협정은 종래 미국이 우리나라에 대한 원조관계 협정인
      1948 년의 한미간의 원조협정, 1952 년의 한미간의 미경제조정
      에 관한 협정 과 이에 부첨된 교환각서 및 의사록 그리고
      1953 년의 미경제재건과 재정안정계획을 위한 합동경제위원회
      의 협약을 단일화 하기 위한 협정인데 이 협정은 미국의
      대의 원조관계의 모법인 MSA 법의 개정에 의거하여
      체결된 것임.

   (4) 한비 무역 협정

      한비간의 최적적인 통상관계의 증진을 위하여 체결된 이 협정에
      의거하여 한비 양국은 ICA 자금에 의한 도입물자를 제외
      하고 년간 미불 1400 만을어닮는 상품의 교역을 약속하는 것임.

3. 체결단계에 있는 조약

      위에서 조약 외에 현재 교섭이 완료 되었거나 체결을 위한
      국내절차를 취 하고 있는 조약이 8 개에 달하는 바, 그 중

한·미국 간의 상호방위조약 제4조에 의한 시설과 구역 및 한국에서의 미국군대의 지위에 관한 협정(SOFA)
전59권. 1966.7.9 서울에서 서명 : 1967.2.9 발효(조약 232호), V.8 체결 교섭, 1960-61 383

— 4 —

양자조약이 4개, 그리고 다자조약이 4개인데 그 건명은

아래와 같다.

(1) ~~국제군인채육의 규약 및 기구 가입의 건~~

(2) 국제노동기구 가입과 가입의 건

(3) 국제개발협회 협증ㆍ가입의 건

(4) 대한민국 정부와 국제연합 특별기금간의 국제연합

특별기금 원조에 관한 협정

(5) 제2 국제 석 협정 가입의 건 ―

(6) 한독간의 기술원조 협정

✓ (7) 한이간의 상표ㆍ상호 등록에 관한 협정 (3/7일 조인)

(8) ~~한중 무역 협정~~ 조인됨

 검토 중인 조약

이 이외에 현재 검토 중인 협정도 상당수에 달하는 바 그 중

중요한 협정을 열거하면 아래와 같다.

1. 양자 조약

(1) 한미 영사협정

(2) 한독간의 사증수수료 면제에 관한 협정

(3) 한독 우호통상 항해 조약

(4) 한태 무역 협정

(5) 한월 무역 협정

2. 다자 조약

(1) 국제원자력 기구의 특권 및 면제에 관한 협약

(2) 아세아 태평 우편 연합 협약

(3) 정부간 해사자문기구 협약

(4) 국제전기 통신 협약

(5) 1960 년 해상에 있어서의 인명 안전에 관한 협약

0074

별첨   (주)

No. 2391

From: American Embassy, Seoul, Korea

To: His Excellency Choi Kyu Hah, Acting
       Minister for Foreign Affairs, Seoul.

Date: March, 30, 1960.

(1) that a revision of the arrangements set

forth in the notes exchanged between our two

governments at Taejon on July 12, 1950, will

not be proposed by either side; and (2) that

compensation to the owners or suppliers of

any real property in Korea which has been or

will be used by the United States Armed Forces

is the responsibility of the Korean Government.

본문의 번역문

(1) 1950 년 7 월 12일 대전에서 교환된 양국 정부간의 구서에서

구범된 협정의 개정은 어느 측에서도 이를 제외다지 않을 것이며,

(2) 또한 미국 군대에 의하여 사용되고 있으며 또 장차 사용될

한국에 있는 부동산의 소유자 또는 그 공급자에 대한 보상은 한국

정부가 그 책임을 진다.

0075

민첩

군대 지역 협정 (행정협정)에 포함될 중요한 문제는 아래와 같다.

(1) 토지 및 시설에 관한 문제

한국에 주둔하는 미국군대가 사용하는 토지, 시설 및 건물의

사용 조건, 반환조건 및 이의 사용에 대한 보상문제 등을 포함.

(2) 재판관할권 문제 (○표 참조)

한국에 주둔하는 미국군대, 군속 및 그들의 가족에 대한 형사

및 민사 재판관할권의 관계 등을 포함.

(3) 출입국 문제

미국군대, 군속 및 그 가족등의 한국에의 출입에 수반하는 제

문제를 포함.

(4) 과세 및 관세 문제

미국군대, 군속 및 그 가족등의 임용료 기타 사용 물품에 대한

과세 및 관세문제를 포함.

(5) 손익물 청구권 문제 및 미국군대의 잉여재산 처분문제

손익물 청구권 문제에 관하여서는 1958 년 12 월 18 일에 체결

된 손익물 청구권 청산 협정에 규율하고 있으며, 미국군대의 잉여

재산의 처분에 관하여서는 1959 년 10 월 1 일자의 한미간에 체결

미국잉여재산처분에 관한 협정에 의하여 규율되고 있다.

0076

주한 미국 군대 구성원에 대한 재판 관할권에 관하여는

1950 년 7 월 12 일 체결된 "대전 협정"이 있는 바, 이는

미군 당국에 군대 구성원에 대한 배타적인 관할권을 인정한

것이므로, 앞으로 교섭 체결되어야 할 협정에 의하여 우리

측이 관할권을 행사할 수 있도록 수정되어야 하는 것임.

Ⅲ 급 비밀로 재분류 (1962. 2. 9)

일반문서로 재분류 (별첨 33 체결시)

駐屯軍의 法的地位에 關한 協定의 內容 및 問題点

용원···는 국민의 세금으로써 구입된 것이다 1962. 2.15

一, 協定案의 內容

우리나라에 駐屯하는 外國軍隊 即 美國 軍隊를 包含하는 國際聯合軍隊의 地位에 關한 協定(所謂 行政協定)은 一九五三年 八月에 締結한 韓美相互防衛條約 發效以來 政府

0078

한·미국 간의 상호방위조약 제4조에 의한 시설과 구역 및 한국에서의 미국군대의 지위에 관한 협정(SOFA)
전59권. 1966.7.9 서울에서 서명 : 1967.2.9 발효(조약 232호), V.8 체결 교섭, 1960-61

389

이 용지는 국민의 세금으로써 구입된 것이다

기 그 繼續을 爲하여 꾸준히 努力하여 왔고

이에 對해서는 駐屯軍 全體의 地位를

問題삼았으나 軍隊派遣國政府들間의 見解

新聞에 相當한 時間을 要할 것이라는 觀點에

그에 駐屯軍의 大部分을 占한 米國

軍隊의 法的地位를 優先規定하도록 하고

그後 이를 다른 派遣國軍隊에 適用하도록

하는 方針下에서 交涉에 臨하여 온 것임.

0080

마문PO-3

0081

용지는 국민의 세금으로써 구입된 것이다

軍隊地位協定은 그 規定對象이 相當히 廣,

範圍하여, 그中에는 刑事裁判管轄權,

請求權淸算, 土地 및 施設, 關稅業務, 出

國之購買等 여러가지 問題를 包含하고

있으며, 改廉는 처음에그 이들 모든 事項을

包括하여 單一協定으로 이를 締結코저하

으써, 그 內容도 一九五一年에 美國이 北大

西洋條約會員諸國과 締結한 行政協定 및

외 무 부

0082

0083

이 용지는 국민의 세금으로써 구입된 것이다

一九五二年에 日本과 締結한 同種協定과 類似하게 作成하였던 것임.

그런데, 行政協定을 早速히 締結하자는 韓國側의 屢次에 걸친 提案에 對하여 美國側은 軍隊地位의 問題를 兩側이 合意할수있는 限度內에서 項目別로 個別的인 協定을 締結하므로써 하나하나 解決해나갈것을 提議하여 왔으므로 政府도 이에

0081

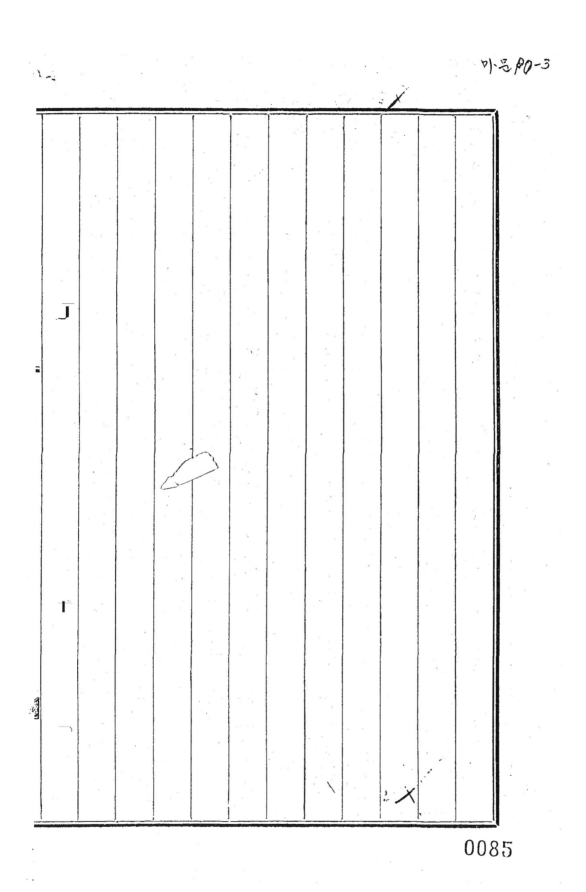

이 용지는 국민의 세금으로써 구입된 것이다

應하여 (一) 課稅 및 關稅業務, (二) 請求權

責等 (三) 土地 및 施設 (四) 出入國 (五) 刑事

裁判管轄權으로 난호아 交涉할 것을

提議하엿던 것이며, 이에 對하여 美國側은

韓國例이 刑事裁判管轄權에 關한 協定을

提議하지안을 것을 保證하는 境遇에는 其他

項目의 協定締結에 應하겠다고 回答하여왔음

政府는 이를 受諾하지안엇던 것임.

0086

0087

이 용지는 국민의 세금으로써 구입된 것이다

그後前記 行政協定의 一部分이될 用役請求

諸淸算問題와 剩餘財産處分問題等은

美國側과 圓滿한 合意에 到達하여 이에

一九五八年十二月 十合協定을 締結하였고

그外에 比較的 解決이 容易하다고 생각되는

「土地및施設에關한協定」을 締結할것을

提議하였으나, 이것 또한 (一)刑事裁判權等管轄

權에関한 現狀을 維持할 (二)土地,施設

0088

0089

이 용지는 국민의 세금으로써 구입된 것이다

使用에 對한 補償은 韓國政府가 責任진다는

麼까지 條件下에 交涉에 應하겠다는 美國側

의 主張으로 現在까지 아무런 進展을 보지

못하고 있음.

二, 問題點

(가) 刑事裁判管轄權問題

美國側이 軍隊地位協定 締結 交涉 不應의

가장 重要한 理由로 내고 있는 駐韓美國

한·미국 간의 상호방위조약 제4조에 의한 시설과 구역 및 한국에서의 미국군대의 지위에 관한 협정(SOFA)
전59권. 1966.7.9 서울에서 서명 : 1967.2.9 발효(조약 232호), V.8 체결 교섭, 1960-61 401

이 용지는 국민의 세금으로써 구입된 것이다

軍人의 刑事裁判管轄問題는 一九五〇年 七月 十二日 大田에서 締結한 在韓美國軍隊의 管轄權에 關한 韓美協定(所謂 大田協定)에서 規定한 바 있으나 同協定은 美國軍에 對한 裁判管轄權을 全的으로 美國側에게 賦與한 不合理한 協定이므로 새로이 協定을 締結하여 美國軍人이 公務執行中에 犯한 犯罪에 限하여 美國軍法會議의 管

한·미국 간의 상호방위조약 제4조에 의한 시설과 구역 및 한국에서의 미국군대의 지위에 관한 협정(SOFA)
전59권. 1966.7.9 서울에서 서명 : 1967.2.9 발효(조약 232호), V.8 체결 교섭, 1960-61   403

이 용지는 국민의 세금으로써 구입된 것이다.

韓權을 認定한 끝한 美國軍人이 犯한 犯罪에 對하여는 韓美共同搜査를 하게

하므로써 不合理한 大田協定의 缺陷을 懸心하자는 것이 우리政府의 方針임.

이러한 政府의 立場은 非便 우리民이

主張하는 것이 아니며 따라가가 締結한

軍隊地位協定도 外國軍人이 駐屯國에서

罪를 犯한 境遇에는 大體로 駐屯國의

0094

0095

裁判管轄權을 認定한 公務執行中에

犯한 것에 限하여 國軍人所屬國家의

裁判權을 認定하는 것이 普通으로 되어 있음

에게 이는 一般的으로 認定된 國際法上의

慣例임.

(나) 土地 및 施設에 對한 補償問題

土地 및 施設에 關한 協定締結의 한 條件中

으(로)서 美國(例)이 要求하는 美國(例)의

0096

한·미국 간의 상호방위조약 제4조에 의한 시설과 구역 및 한국에서의 미국군대의 지위에 관한 협정(SOFA)
전59권. 1966.7.9 서울에서 서명 : 1967.2.9 발효(조약 232호), V.8 체결 교섭, 1960-61   407

이 용지는 국민의 세금으로써 구입된 것이다

使用하는 土地 및 施設에 對한 補償은

韓國政府가 그 責任을 지도록 한다는

기인바 이 條件하에 우리나라의 現

經濟狀態를 考慮할때 받아드리기어려

운 것임.

협정체결시 일반 문제
로 채분류

0098

0039

駐韓美軍이 使用하는 土地와 施設에 對한
補償請求問題

1. 目的

［마프분류로 인가에 Ⅲ 등에 비밀
대분류 1982. 2. 15.］

　駐韓美軍이 使用하는 土地와 施設에 對한 補償金을
美國에 對하여 請求하고저

검토필(196.Ⅹ.12. 30.)

편비
비공 65

2. 現況

　北韓傀儡의 南侵을 擊退하기 爲한 유엔決議에 依하여
韓國에 派遣된 美軍이 그 동안 使用한 土地와 施設
및 建物等에 對하여 全혀 補償을 行치고 있지
않으며 이 土地 施設에 對한 補償問題는 兩
國間의 條約이나 協定에서 言及된 바 없음 이를 爲
한 政府의 交涉도 兩國의 見解差異로 말미아마
結果를 보지 못하였음.

　討論 :

검토필(196. ─ 6. 30.)

　美國政府에 對하여 우리 政府가 提起할 수
있는 可能한 補償要請方法으로서는 아래와 같이
여러가지로 區分할수 있음

　가. 時期的으로 區分하여

　　(1) 6.25 動亂 以後 美軍이 使用한 財産全般에
　　　　對한 補償

0100

(2) 休戰 成立 以後 美軍이 使用한 財産全般에 對한 補償

(3) 앞으로 締結될 韓美行政協定 締結 以後 美軍 이 使用하는 財産全般에 對한 補償

나. 方法 論的으로 區分하여

(1) 美軍의 使用에 供與하기 爲하여 財産取得에 所要된 金額에 對한 補償

(2) 美軍이 使用한 財産에 對한 使用料 請求

다. 財産의 性質에 따라 區分하여

(1) 国有, 私有 財産을 區別하지 않고 美軍이 使用 하는 財産 全般에 對하여 補償을 要求

(2) 私有財産에 對하여서만 補償을 要求

라. 財産의 位置에 따라 區分하여

(1) 所謂 作戰地帶와 非作戰地帶를 區別하여 補償 을 要求하는 方法

(2) 作戰地帶와 非作戰地帶를 區別하지 않고 一括 的으로 補償을 要求하는 方法

政府는 北韓傀儡의 不法 武力 侵略을 擊退하고 韓国 의 自由와 独立을 安護하기 爲한 美軍의 駐韓 目的을 勘案하여 오로지 美軍의 使用에 供與하기 爲한 財産의 徵發로 因하여 政府가 負擔하게된 債務에 對하여만 美国政府의 補償義務를 局限하려는 것이며, 이는 政府의

財政的 窮乏으로 因하여 不得己한 것으로, 美國 政府의 補償으로써 財政的 利得을 얻고저 하는 것은 아님. 따라서 이러한 觀点에서 다음과 같은 結論을 내려야 할것임.

4. 結論

위에서 列擧한 諸方法中에서 現實的으로 合理的이며 上述한 補償要求에 있어서의 原則에 符合하는 方法으로서는:

가. 時期的區分에 있어서는 休戰成立以前 戰斗期에 있어서의 美軍이 使用한 財産에 對한 補償要求는 補償의 産出의 困難性과 기타 政治 道義的인 見地에서 不合理한 点이 있다고 生覺됨으로 이를 除外하고 休戰 成立 以後 美軍이 使用한 土地, 施設 部分에 對한 補償만을 要求한다.

나. 方法論的 區分에 있어서 前記한 原則에 依하여 使用料가 아니라 美軍의 使用에 供與하기 爲하여 政府가 財産을 取得하는데 所要된 金額에 對한 補償만을 要求한다.

다. 財産의 性質에 따른 區分에 있어서는 國有財産에 對한 補償要求는 前述한 補償要求 原則에 合致하지 않으므로 私有財産에 對하여서만 補償을 要求한다

~3~

0102

라. 財産 位置에 依한 區分에 있어서는 이를 우리 側에서 먼저 提示할 必要는 없으나 美國側이 이 点을 强調하는 境遇에는 作戰地帶와 非作戰地帶를 區分하여 作戰地帶內에 있는 財産에 對한 補償은 이를 免除하도록 한다. 이 境遇 作戰地帶와 非作戰地帶의 槪念에 關하여서는 韓美兩國間에 合理的인 基準下에서 合意하여야 할 것이며

5. 建 議 :

休戰成立 以後에 美單이 使用하는 土地. 施設. 建物 中 國有 財産과 作戰地帶內에 있는 土地, 建物 및 施設을 除外한 其他 土地. 建物및 施設에 關하여 美單의 使用에 供與하기 爲하여 政府가 이를 取得하는데 所要된 金額만을 美國側에 要求함. 早速한 行政協定締結로서 本問題를 解決함.

~4~

한·미국 간의 상호방위조약 제4조에 의한 시설과 구역 및 한국에서의 미국군대의 지위에 관한 협정(SOFA)
전59권. 1966.7.9 서울에서 서명 : 1967.2.9 발효(조약 232호), V.8 체결 교섭, 1960-61

美軍이 使用한 土地, 施設에 關한 補償要求額數

가. 土地에 關한 補償額數: (休戰以後—4291年度 까지)

　約 18.845百萬圜 (約 188億4千5百萬圜)

나. 建物에 關한 補償額數: (休戰以後 4291年度 까지)

　約 4.498百萬圜 (約 44億9千8百萬圜)

관리
번호 47

다. 總計

　約 23.343 百万圜 (約 233億4千3百萬圜)

라. 補償要求額數의 正確性

검토필 (196. . 12-30.)

　國防部가 作成한 徵發補償要明細書는 國防部가

發付한 徵發台帳에 依據하여 推算한 것으로

　나 算出基準등 여러가지로 그 正確性이 稀薄

한것임　특히 이 額數는 유엔군 使用財産全

般에 對한 補償要求 額數를 算出한 것이기

때문에 그 中에 美軍이 使用한 財産部分이

어느 程度인지에 對하여서도 疑問視됨

따라서 協定이 正式으로 締結되면 이에 關한

綜合的 調査가 必要한것임

일반문서로 재분류
(협정 체결시)

~5~

0104

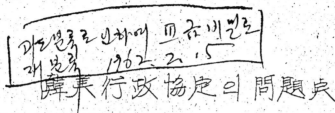

韓美行政協定의 問題点

1. 總 論

韓美行政協定의 內容과 精神에 있어서는 ~~特~~

(1) 韓國이 戰敗國으로서 被占領 地域이된바가 없는, 新生 独立國이라는 点에서 后進國 主权이 터한層 鞏固化 되도록 可能한限 相互同等 互惠原則下에서 다루어 저야 한다는点

(2) 韓國의 國家利益과 目... 民主的한 統一國家 形成 및 経済的 政治的 民主自立의 成就에 있는만큼 이에 이바지 할수있도록 다루워저야 한다는点

(3) 美軍의 韓國의 駐屯이 他國의 例와같은 單純한 單專基 地의 設定維持를 爲한것이 아니고 韓國의 直接的 防衛 任務를 爲하여 UN決政에 따라 行허지고 있으며 그러한 駐屯事実은 우리나라 國土防衛의 絶対的인 要素가 되고 있다는 点

(4) 6·25 動亂을 通하여 韓美両軍이 共同戰線으로 싸웠고 또한 継續하여 韓國軍이 美軍의 作戰指揮下에 놓여 있으며 나 가서는 韓國의 莫大한 ~~援助가~~ 앞으로 도 継續必要하다는 点等을 參酌하여

첫째

  協定은 國際慣例에 따라 最少限의 特典을 美駐屯軍에게
附與하고 韓國法令의 適用을 最大限으로 擴張하는 方向으
로 이루워 지므로서 우리나라 主權을 더욱 對內外에 宣
揚하게하며

둘째

  駐屯 美軍의 防衛作戰 任務가 보다 忠實하고 健全하게
遂行될수 있도록 그들에게 可能한限 最大의 處遇를 베푸
러 주므로서 國家主權의 安全을 더욱 保障하며

셋째

  美軍의 駐屯이 韓國経済自立에 惡影響을 주지 않을뿐더러
나아가서 도음이 되도록 各種 経済事項에 있어서 國民経
済의 實情이 衆載하게 反映되도록 한다

以上 세가지 精神은 一見二律背反的이나 實인즉 相互通하는
것이다 卽 駐屯美軍의 防衛態勢의 强化維持는 곧 우리나라
主權과 領土의 保安에 経済的으로 寄與되는만큼 己를犧牲한○○
의 成就도 어려운 것이다

2. 以上見地에서 協定에있어서 外務部案을中心으로 特히 問題
點이 되는것을 살펴 본다면 다음과 같다

~ 2 ~

0106

第1 一線作戰地区 (field combat zone 를 区劃하여 其他
地域과 달리 取扱한다

第2 一線作戰地区內에서는 軍人 軍屬에 限하여 軍保安上
必要時는 身分証明書의 所持를 要치 않는다.

√ 第3 施設과 地域의 使用

(1) 協定發劾当時 既使用之分은 相互合意된것으로 看做한다

(2) field combat zone 內에서의 施設및 地域使用에 있어
    서는 厚하게 取扱한다 (例 外郭地帶路線及 民間人交通
    破壞에 対한 訴請)

(3) 韓美合同使用之分은 韓國軍이 使用하는것으로 看做한다
    (但 用役과 維持에 있어서는 除外)

(4) 返還時 美軍은 軍援에 依한 代價淸算을 못한다

√ 第4 文 通

軍事的 室中交通統制 (及統制는 作戰指揮权者의 決定에 따
른다

韓國軍保安上 出入制限区域 (事前通告)

第5 運載免許

  KATUSA의 運載免許

第6 服 裝

· 不必要하다

~3~

0107

第7. 武器鑑帯

私用의 軍人 軍屬과 家族에 限하여 制限하고 特히 獵銃은
韓國法令에 따르도록 한다

第8 Custom 其他課稅

私有車輛과 附屬品의 輸入은 自由로히 한다

mail은 公用에 限하여 No inspection 命令에 依하
여 移動하는 部隊나 車輛은 No inspection

第9 現地購買

美軍이 購買하는 物品 用役은 國貨로 早速히 請算토록 한다

第10 PX等

PX物品의 市中流出防止策

營外 service 營利行爲는 韓國法令適用

第11 APO

不法使用防止策의 講究

第12 刑事管轄權

美軍家族의 犯罪도 軍人에 準하여 取扱한다

一線作戰地区內의 犯罪는 一切 美軍에 一任

KATUSA에 限해서는 MP의 搜査权 認定

韓國人에 対해서는 一切不許

~4~

0108

韓美 合同使用 勤務하는 地域施設에 있어서는 S.P 의

搜査權認定

第13 訴請

KATUSA의 公務中 犯한 搜査는 美軍이 責任진다

第14 M.P.C

必히 規定 特히 不法去來者의 団束策

~~第15 此地設中 使用料~~

~~装備料는 ~~~~現在에도 ~~~~問題 ~~~~되었는 ~~~~것이~~~~라 ~~~~除外~~

~~問題~~

~~線~~

~~美~~~~外에 ~~~~使用料~~

~~束~~~~하여 ~~~~以外) 使用合~~

~~利用~~

~~美國~~~~~~ ~~~~使用~~~~은 ~~~~利~~

第16 K.M.A.G 団員도 本協定에 依한다

第17 美8軍의 作戰指揮權을 尊重한다

美8軍意下 (第4호表明)

일반문17로 재녹음
협정 체결시

~5~

0109

한미행정 협정의 내용과 그 추진　　　　　　　[1961.3]

(상단 필기) 아래 별족으로 비치어 교구 바끰？ 체범호 965도 2.15

1. 한미행정협정의 내용

일반적으로 행정협정이라고 불리우고 있는 "주한미군의 지위에 관한 협정"은 1953년 8월 한미상호방위조약 가조인이때 한국측에 의하여 그 교섭 및 그 체결이 추진되어 왔지만 미국측의 불응으로 아직 체결을 보지못하고 있다. 무릇 일국의 군대가 타국에 주둔하는 경우에는 그 것이 임시적방문이든 군사점령과 같은 장기적인 것이든 간에 그 외국군대에 대하여 특수한 지위가 인정되는것이 국제법상의 관례이며, 특히 2 차 대전 이후 집단안전보장체제의 형성발전과 함께 이와 같은 외국군대의 지위는 관계국간의 협정에 의하여 규율하는 경향이 많아지고 있고, 그 대표적인 예가 미국과 북대서양기구 가맹 제국간에 체결한 행정협정, 미일행정협정등이다.

현재, 우리정부가 교섭을 추진하고 있는 한미간의 "행정협정" 도 이와 같은 국제선례에 따라 우리나라에 주둔하고 있는 미국군대의 지위를 규제하자는 것인바, 그렇게 함으로서 "비군주둔"이라는 사실도 반영하야 야기될 가능성이 있는 양국간의 분쟁으로 미연에 오해를 피하고 한미간의 우호관계를 더욱 증진시키는 한편 주권국가로서의 우리나라의 권위를 일층 보호할 것이기 때문이다. 이와 같이 "행정협정"의 규정 대상은 문자그대로 주둔군의 지위전반에 걸치는 광범위한 것이며, 그 중요내용을 항목별로 구분하면 다음과 같다.

　1. 주한 미군의 형사재판관할권

　2. 주한미군이 사용하는 토지 및 시설

　3. 미국군인, 군속 및 그 가족의 출입국 사항

　4. 관세업무 및 과세문제

0110

(우측 도장) 판리 번호 67

(우측 세로 도장) 정리 (1965. 12. 30)

　　　5. 각종 청구권 문제

　　　6. 미군의 구매사무, 노무관계사무, 용역제공 등

2. 행정협정의 초점

　　상기단바와 같은 행정협정이 규정되어야 할 여러가지 항목중 미국정부와의 사이에 가장 곤난이 예상되는 항목은 가) 주둔미군의 형사재판관할권과 나) 미군이 사용하는 토지 및 시설에 관한 것으로서 실제로 이두문제는 현재까지 이협정의 체결 자체를 오래 끌어온 결정 중요한 이유이며, 기타의 제문제는 비교적 교섭이 용이 할것으로 예상하고 있다.

가) 주둔미군의 형사재판관할권 문제

　　형사재판권관할 문제에 관하여는 1950 년 7 월 12 일자로 대전에서 한미양국정부간에 체결된 "재한미국군대의 관할권에 관한 협정"이 있으며, 이협정에서는 미국군인의 모든 재판관할권을 전적으로 미국측에게만 부여하므로서 우리나라의 법권이 전여 미치지 못하게 되어 있는데, 이는 6.25 동란 발발 즉후의 전시상태하에서 부득이한 일이 었으므로, 이를 수정하여 국제법상의 관례에 따라 주둔군인이 공무집행중에 범한것에 한하여 미국군자체의 재판권을 인정하도록 하자는것이 우리측의 주장이며, 이에 대하여 미국측은 여전히 현상 유지로 고집하고 있다.

나) 미군이 사용하는 토지 및 시설문제

　　현재 주둔 미군이 사용하는 토지 및 시설은 모두 무상으로 사용하고 있으며, 그 대가를 금액으로 환산하면 실로 거액에 달하고 있으므로 우리나라 강제실정을 고려할 때 미군이 사용하는 토지 및 시설에 대한 보상금을 어느정도 까지는 미국측이 부담 ━━━━

한·미국 간의 상호방위조약 제4조에 의한 시설과 구역 및 한국에서의 미국군대의 지위에 관한 협정(SOFA) 전59권. 1966.7.9 서울에서 서명 : 1967.2.9 발효(조약 232호), V.8 체결 교섭, 1960-61　421

됐자는 것이 우리측의 주장이나, 미국측은 이 보상책임은 한국 정부가 진다는 조건 하에 이 협정 체결교섭에 응하겠다는 태도를 취하고 있다.

한미 행정협정
체결교섭 경위

가) 1953년 8월 7일 한미방위조약 조인시의 이승만, 덜레스 공동성명에서 한미양국정부는 상호방위조약 발효후 즉시 군대지위 협정을 교섭하기로 약속함.

나) 1954년 12월 정부는 그 내용상 병정협정의 일부가 된 주한 유엔군의 관세면류에 관한 협정 체결을 제의하였으나 미국측은 이를 거부함.

다) 1956년 4월 정부는 주한 유엔군의 지위를 포괄적으로 규정 하는 군대지위협정의 체결을 제의하고 동시에 협정안을 제시하였으며 그후 1957년 1월, 6월 및 9월에 다시 교섭의 개시를 촉구함.

라) 1957년 10월 미국측은 군대지위협정 문제를 부분적으로 합의 가능한 한도 내에서 하나 하나 해결해 나갈것을 제의하여 왔으므로 정부는 이에 응하여 동년 11월 미국측에 대하여 이 문제를 1) 과세 및 관세업무, 2) 청구권정산, 3) 우기 및 시산, 4) 출입국, 5) 형사재판관할권 등으로 분환하여 각항목별로 개별협정을 체결 할것을 제의하였던바, 1958년 9월 미국측은 한국정부가 재판관할권 에 관한 협정을 제의 하지않는다는 조건 하에 기타의 협정적인 문제의 해결에 응하겠다고 회답하여왔으며, 정부는 이를 수락하지 아니함.

마) 1958년 6월 정부는 군대지위협정 문제를 개별적으로 해결할 방침하에 우선 그 첫단계로서 주한 미군이 사용하는 운지 만 석저하

관한 협정 체결을 제의하고 동년 10 월과 1960 년 3 월에

2 차에 걸쳐 미국측의 수락을 촉구하였던바, 1960 년 3 월 말

미국측은 1) 형사재판관할권에 관한 현상을 유지하고 2) 토지

및 시설에 관한 보상은 한국정부가 그 책임을 부담토록 동의

요건하에 전기 협정 체결 교섭에 응할것이라고 회답하여 왔고

우리정부는 이를 받아드릴수없어 그후 교섭이 정돈상태에있음.

바) 단기 4292 년 2 월 28 일 한미간에 새로운 경제기술원조협정이

체결되고 또한 국회는 행정협정의 조속한 체결을 촉구하는 건의안을

채택하였으므로 정부는 다시 이 협정의 체결을 위한 적극적인 준비를

진행중에 있음.

일반 문서로 재분류

<u>한미 공동 발표 문</u>　[4.10, 1961]

"월터.피.매카나기" 주한미국 대사는 "매그루머" 장군과 같이 장면 국무총리를 방문하고 미국은 주둔군의 법적지위에 관한 협정을 체결하기 위한 준비가 되었다고 말하였다. 이 자리에는 현 국방장관, 김외무차관 "그린" 공사도 참석하였다.

장국무총리는 이에 대하여 이 협정 문제가 이와 같이 진전된 것을 환영한다고 말하였다. 쌍방은 내주에 이 협정 체결을 위한 교섭을 시작하기로 합의하였다. 이 협정에는 상당히 복잡한 문제가 포함되어 있기 때문에 상당한 시일이 걸릴것이라는 점을 쌍방은 시인하였다.

외 무 부 정 무 국

발 신

암 호 전 문

발신번호 :

발신일시 :

수신인 : 주미대사

발신인 : 장 관

관리번호 ___112___

건명 : 한미행정협정 체결의 건

1. 주한 미대사관 당국자에 의하면 현지미대사관은 미국정부가 표기협정을 체결할 의사가 있다는 통고를 국무성으로부터 받았을 뿐이고 교섭개시에 관하여는 훈명 받은바 없다하오니 조속히 본건 교섭을 진행시킬수 있도록 미국무성 당국과 절충 하시고 그결과를 보고 하시기 바람. 검토필(1966 6. 30)

2. 과거 미국정부는 미군이 사용하고있는 시설 및 구역에 대한 보상금의 지불을 반대하여 왔음. 본건 협정체결 교섭개시에 합의한 지난 4월 10일자 장면. 매카나기 공동성명에는 이문제 에 관한 구체적인 언급이 없으나, 동성명으로 미국의 동문제에 대한 종래의 태도를 변경한 것으로 간주되는데, 이에 관하여 미국 당국의 의사를 은밀히 타진하여 보고하시기 바람. 시고 만일 미국의 태도가 종전과 다름이 없다면, 이는 한미 행정 협정 체결의 근본 취지와 목적 에 위배 어긋나는것이니 아측 견해대로 보상금 관계도 협정 기포함시켜야 하다는 점을 강조 납득 하도록 노력 하시옵고 그 결과를 보고 하시압

(이전문은 허가없이는 복사하여서는 안된다)   0115

한·미국 간의 상호방위조약 제4조에 의한 시설과 구역 및 한국에서의 미국군대의 지위에 관한 협정(SOFA)
전59권. 1966.7.9 서울에서 서명 : 1967.2.9 발효(조약 232호), V.8 체결 교섭, 1960-61   **425**

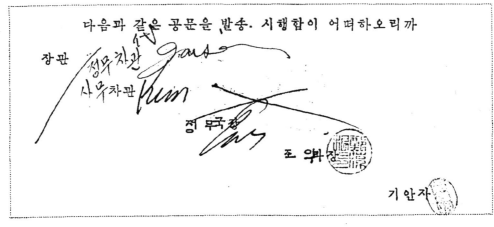

다음과 같은 공문을 발송·시행함이 어떠하오리까

장관

정무차관

사무차관

정무국장

조약과장

기안자

편찬류별	류	단기 4294 년 4 월 14 일 기안
보존종별	종	단기 429 년 월 일 결재
기 장 발송		단기 429 년 월 일 발송·시행

외 ( ) 제   호   단기 429 년   월   일

외 무 부

귀 하

전 명 : 한미 행정협정 체결 교섭대표단 임명의 건

(품 의)

위의 건, 한미 행정협정 체결을 위한 아국측 교섭대표단을

하기와 같이 임명함이 어떠하오리까

기

외 무 부   정무국장   윤 석 헌

조약과장   정 순 근

영사과장   와 합 기

영사   리 법 석

영서기관   신 카 흠

사무관   권 동 만

국 방 부 대일 총무국장   준장

0116

재 무 부   ~~시세국장~~
          세관국장

법 무 부   법무국장

  기타부 소관사항이 토의될 때에는 해당부처의 관계국장을
포함시킴.
                    이 상

일반문서로 재분규

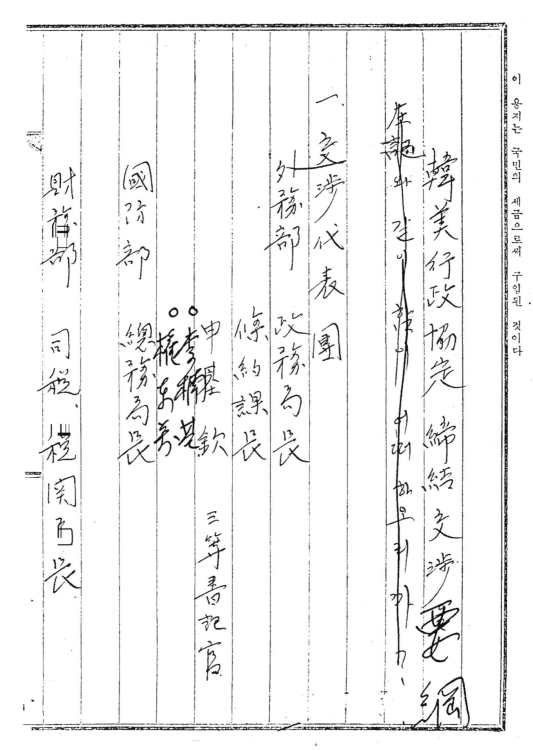

韓美行政協定 締結交涉

一. 交涉代表團

外務部 政務局長
　　　條約課長

申[申喆欽]　三等書記官

國防部
　　總務局長

李[李○柄○?]

財務部
　　司能、　稅關局長

이 용지는 국민의 세금으로써 구입된 것이다

0118

이 용지는 국민의 세금으로써 구입된 것이다

法務部. 法務局長

및

其他 部 所管事項이 討議될때에는 該當 部處의 關係局長을 包含시킴,

二, 交涉會議는 四月十七日부터 始作하여 每週 平均 一,二回 程度로 갖기로함,

三, 會議場所는 外務部 政務局長室로함.

三, 交涉要綱은 合同問題에 對한 基本的

0119

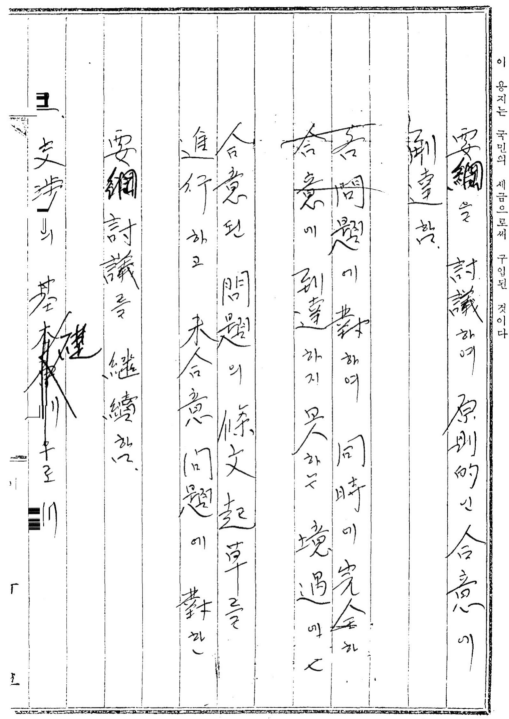

要綱을 討議하여 原則的인 合意에
到達함.

合意에 到達하지 못하는 境遇에는
合意問題에 對하여 同時에 完全히

合意된 問題의 條文起草를
進行하고 未合意問題에 對한

要綱討議를 繼續함.

이 용지는 국민의 세금으로써 구입된 것이다

美國이 北大西洋條約 機構 및
日本과 締結한 同種의 協定을
模型으로 함.

일반문서로 재분류

이 용지는 국민의 세금으로써 구입된 것이다

0121

과도분류로 비서에
일반호서로 해운로
1962. 외.18

용지는 국민의 세금으로써 구입된 것이다

韓美行政協定 討議進行要領

前番 會談時 我國側이 提出한 討議

題目分類에 關한 美國側이 回答을

要求함.

二. 美國側이 이를 受諾겐다면 實際的인

題目의 分類는 本會談에서 할 것이

아니라. 앞으로 있을 實務者會談에서

하며 또한 同實務者會談에서

0122

이 용지는 국민의 세금으로써 구입된 것이다

(1) 別 問題를 取扱하는 途中에 어려운 問題가

나오면 ~~앞으로 돌리고~~ 于先 쉬운 問題부터

合意하여 條文을 檢討草案하며

~~일~~일로 돌린 어려운 問題에 對하여는

兩側이 主張을 調整하기 爲하여

臨時 協議함

三. 萬若 美國側이 問題目分類를 反對할

時는 美國側의 會議進行方法이

무엇인가를 問議함

0123

이 용지는 국민의 세금으로써 구입된 것이다

四. 會議進行의 具体的 方法으로서 討議의
基礎가 될 草案이 必要하므로 我國側이
不遠 草案을 作成完了하여 提出함

다음

議題는 美日 行政協定 및 十도 協定과
規定된 거이므로 草型과 其他 物定에 我國의
特殊한 問題들을 含함.

(KATUSA)

特殊한 問題 또는 카츄사의 身分 問題

PX 連營 택시 問題 및 軍契約者에

關한 問題 等이라 말함

0124

이 용지는 국민의 세금으로써 구입된 것이다

六. 個別問題에 對한 討議는 앞으로 實務
者間에 이루어지도록 合意할 것으로

七. 앞으로의 交涉方法은 委員會를
必要코 我國草案을 基礎로 (權威로)
贈予間을 合意하여 갈 것임

八. 準備的인 會談은 今次로써 끝이고
다음부터는 實務的인 討議로 들어
가되 日時는 追後 實務者를 通
하여 決定토록 할것임 (約二週向)

0125

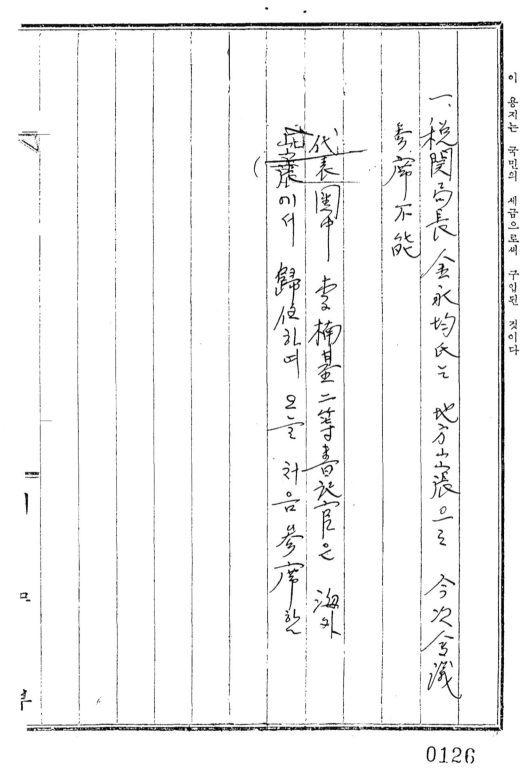

一、稅關局長 金永均氏은 地方出張으로 今次 会議
參席不能

代表團 李楠基 二等書記官은 海外
出張이서 歸任하며 오늘 처음 參席한

(

이 용지는 국민의 세금으로써 구입된 것이다

0126

United States Group for Negotiating an
Agreement Covering the Status of the
United States Forces Stationed in the
Republic of Korea

Minister Marshall Green, Charge d'Affaires ad interim,
     American Embassy, Seoul

Brigadier General Charles Billingslea, Deputy Chief of Staff,
     Eighth United States Army

Donald L. Ranard, Chief, Political Section, American Embassy,
     Seoul

Robert W. Tucker, Deputy Chief, Economic Section, American
     Embassy, Seoul

Colonel Cornelius deW. W. Lang, Deputy Chief of Staff,
     United States Forces, Korea

Elmer Hulen, Deputy Chief, Political Section, American
     Embassy, Seoul

Charles T. Mayfield, Chief, Consular Section, American Embassy,
     Seoul

Lieutenant Colonel John W. Price, J-5 Division, United States
     Forces, Korea

     Rapporteur: Robert G. Rich, Jr., Political Section,
          American Embassy, Seoul

     Press Officer: Thomas R. Kruse, United States
          Information Service, American Embassy, Seoul

0127

REPUBLIC OF KOREA

MINISTRY OF FOREIGN AFFAIRS

Negotiation team for Korean side

√	Mr. Suk Heun YUN,	Director, Political Bureau, Ministry of Foreign Affairs
√	Mr. Young Keun KIM,	Director, Customs Bureau, Ministry of Finance
√	Mr. Kyung Ho LEE,	Director, Legal Affairs Bureau, Ministry of Justice
√	Mr. Gie Hyung REE,	Brig. General, Ministry of National Defense
	Mr. Soon Kun CHUNG,	Chief, Treaty Section, Ministry of Foreign Affairs
	Mr. Nam Kee LEE,	Second Secretary, Ministry of Foreign Affairs
	Mr. Bum Suk LEE,	Consul, Ministry of Foreign Affairs

0128

Definitions (定義：軍人·軍屬 및 家族에 對한)

Entry and Exit (出入國 地)

o Facilities and Areas (土地 및 施設)

o Criminal Jurisdiction (刑事裁判權)

o Claims and Civil Jurisdiction (請求 및 民事裁判權)

△ Procurement and Labor (現地 購買 및 勞動)

△ Taxation (課稅)

△ Customs Duties (關稅)

△ Non-Appropriated Funds Organizations (P.X. Club, 新聞 等)

△ Contract (特殊 契約)

△ Foreign Exchange control (外換管理)

△ Military Payment Certificate (軍票)

△ Military Post Office   (軍事郵便)

Driving Permit or License   (運轉免許)

Uniform and Markings   (制服 等)

Carrying of Arms   (武器携帶)

Training   (訓練)

Meteorology   (氣象)

Sanitary _____   (保健 衛生)

Provision for period of active (戰時의 境遇)

Joint Committee   (合同委員會)

*
o most important

△ of secondary importance

일반용어로 재분류

0129

국장전결사항

다음과 같은 공문을 발송·시행함이 어떠하오리까

장관

차관

(정무국장)

조약과장

기안자

편찬류별	류	단기 429 년 월 일 기안
보존종별	종	단기 429 년 월 일 결재
기장 발송		단기 429ㅌ년 4월 15일 발송·시행

의조(조) 제 2072 호   단기 429ㅌ 년 4 월 15일

외 무 부 정 무 국 장

방 교 국 장 귀하

건 명 : 보도 의뢰에 관한 건

머외의 건에 관하여, 한미행정협정 교섭회의가 오는 17 일

오후 3 시 외무부장관실에서 개최되는바, 이에 관한 하기

발표문을 금일 (15 일) 오후 3 시에 발표하여 주시기를 바라오며

또한 동회의를 위하여 뉴스 촬영반 및 보도반을 주선하여 주시기를

바라나이다.

일반문서로 재분류

— 기 —

발 표 문

주한 미군의 지위에 관한 제 1 차 한미행정협정 해결을위한 교섭회의가

4 월 17 일 하오 3 시부터 한국측을 대표하여 외무부 김용식

사무차관, 미국측을 대표하여 그린에 대사대리 와 양국관계

실무자의 참석하에 외무부장관실에서 개최될 예정임.

0130

외정 (교) 제2072호

정 무 국 장

방 교 국 장 귀 하

건 명 : 보도의뢰에 관한 건

머리의 건에 관하여, 한미행정협정 교섭회의가 오는 17 일
오후 3 시 외무부장관실에서 개최되는바, 이에 관한 다기 발표문은
금일(15 일) 오후 3 시에 발표하여 주시기를 바라오며 또한 동회의를
위하여 누-스촬영반 및 보도반을 주선하여 주시기를 바라나이다。

— 기 —

발 표 문

한미행정협정 체결을 위한 교섭회의가 4 월 17 일 다오 3시부터
외무부장관실에서 한국측을 대표하여 외무부 김용식 사무차관,
미국측을 대표하여 버그 미인 대사대리와 양국관계 실무자의 참석하에
개최될 예정임。

0131

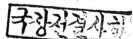

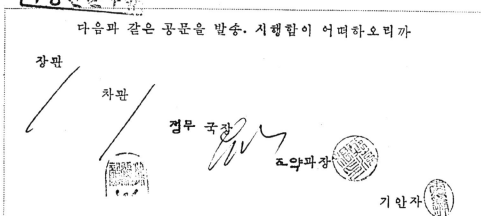

다음과 같은 공문을 발송. 시행함이 어떠하오리까

장관

차관

정무 국장

조약과장

기안자

편찬류별	류	단기 4294년 4월 15일	기안
보존종별	종	단기 429 년 월 일	결재
기장 발송		단기 4294년 6월 15일	발송. 시행

의정 (조) 제 2071 호   단기 4294년 4월 15일

외 무 부 장 관

국 무 총 리 귀하

건 명: 한미행정협정 체결 교섭의 건

위의 건, 4월 17일 하오 3시부터 외무부장관실에서 동회의에서는
한미 행정 협정 체결을 위한 최초회담을 개최하오며, 당일 아울에는
양국 대표 김용식 외무부 사무차관과 "그린" 대사대리와 회담 간의
개최인사 교환과 앞으로의 계속 교섭을 위한 교섭절차에 관하여
토의하기로 되었아오며, 동협정체결을 위한 아국측 대표단을
하기와 같음을 보고하나이다.
이하생략

─ 기 ─

외무부   정무국장   윤 석 헌

조약과장   정 순 근

2등서기관   이 남 기

영 사   이 범 석   0132

국방부 대표 준장 <del>표현</del> 지헌 준장

재무부 대표 세관국장 김영근(KIM YOUNG KEUN)

법무부 대표 법무국장 이경호

기타부 소관사항이 토의될 때에는 해당부처의 관계국장을 포합시킴.

이 상

일반문서로 재분류

0133

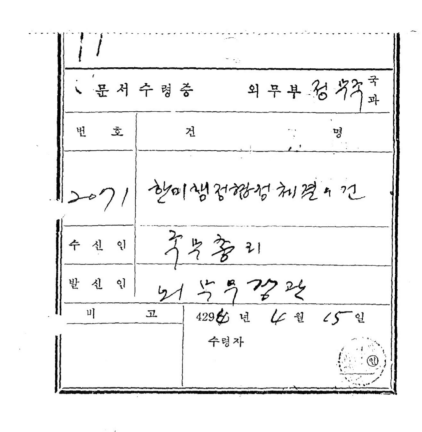

문서수령증		외무부 정무국과
번 호	건	명
2071	한미행정협정 체결의 건	
수 신 인	국무총리	
발 신 인	외무부장관	
비 고	4298년 4월 15일 수령자	㉑

0134

외정 (조) 제 2077 호

단기 4294 년 4월 15일

의 무 부 장 관

국 무 총 리 귀하

건명: 한미행정협정 체결 교섭의 건

위의 건, 4월 17일 하오 3시부터 의무부 장관실에서
한미행정협정 체결을 위한 최초회담을 개최하오며, 동회의에서는
양국을 대표하여 김용식 외무부 사무차관과 버그대인 대사대미간의
인사 교섭과 앞으로의 교섭을 위한 절차에 관하여 토의하기로
되었아오며, 동협정체결을 위한 아국측 대표단은 다기와 같이
구성하였음을 보고 하나이다.

― 기 ―

의 무 부 정부국장 윤 석 헌
         조약과장 정 순 근
         통상서기관 이 남 기
         영   서 이 범 석

0135

국방부   이기편 ㅤ준장
재무부   세관 국장
법무부   법무국장   이경호

기타부 소관사항이 로의됨 때에는 해당부처의 관계국장을 포함시킴.

                          이   상

일반문서로 재분류

0136

외 무 부 발 표

4 월 17 일

한미행정협정 체결을 위한 제1차 고섭회의가 금일
하오 3시부터 외무부장관실에서 한국측을 대표하여
외무부 김용식 사무차관, 미국측을 대표하여 "그리인"
대사대리와 양국관계 실무자의 참석하에 개최되는바
동 한미실무자의 명단은 다음과 같다.

한국측 참석자

윤 석 헌	외무부 정무국장
김 영 준	재무부 세관국장
이 경 호	법무부 법무국장
이 지 형	국방부 준장
전 순 근	외무부 조약과장
이 남 기	외무부 2등서기관
이 범 석	외무부 영사

미국측 참석자

마샬 그리인	주한 미국대리대사
샬스 빌링그스리	미제8군 참모차장
도날드 L. 레이날드	미 대사관 정치과장
로버트 W. 탁커	미 대사관 경제과차장
코르넬리우스 랑 대령	주한 미군 참모차장
엘머 훌렌	미대사관 정치과 차장
샬스 T. 메이필드	미 대사관 영사부장
죤 W. 프라이스중령	주한 미군 5과장
로버트 G. 리이치2세	미 대사관 정치과 기록관
토마스 R. 쿠루즈	주한 미국대사관 공보언 공보관

0137

Negotiation Team for Korean Side

1. Mr. Suk Heun YUN,   Director, Political Bureau, Ministry of Foreign Affairs

2. Mr. Young Keun KIM,   Director, Customs Bureau, Ministry of Finance

3. Mr. Kyung Ho LEE,   Director, Legal Affairs Bureau, Ministry of Justice

4. Mr. Gie Hyung REE,   Brig. General, Ministry of National Defense

5. Mr. Soo Kun CHUNG,   Chief, Treaty Section, Ministry of Foreign Affairs

6. Mr. Nam Kee LEE,   Second Secretary, Ministry of Foreign Affairs

7. Mr. Bum Suk LEE,   Consul, Ministry of Foreign Affairs

United States Group for Negotiating an Agreement Covering the Status of the United States Forces Stationed in the Republic of Korea

1. Minister Marshall Green,   Charge d'Affaires ad interim, American Embassy, Seoul

2. Brigadier General Charles Billingslea,   Deputy Chief of Staff Eighth United States Army

3. Donald L. Ranard, Chief,   Political Section, American Embassy, Seoul

4. Robert W. Tucker,   Deputy Chief, Economic Section, American Embassy, Seoul

5. Colonel Cornelius deW. W. Lang,   Deputy Chief of Staff, United States Forces, Korea

6. Elmer Hulen,   Deputy Chief, Political Section, American Embassy Seoul

7. Charles T. Mayfield,   Chief, Consular Section, American Embassy, Seoul

8. Lieutenant Colonel John W. Price,   J-5 Division, United States Forces, Korea

Rapporteur: Robert G. Rich, Jr., Political Section, American Embassy, Seoul

Press Officer: Thomas R. Kruse, United States Information Service, American Embassy, Seoul

0138

MINUTES
OF
STATUS OF FORCES NEGOTIATIONS BETWEEN THE GOVERNMENTS
OF THE REPUBLIC OF KOREA AND THE UNITED STATES

OPENING SESSION

(April 17, 1961)

1. Time and Place: From 3:00 to 3:40 p.m. on April 17, 1961
at the Ministry of Foreign Affairs

2. Conferees:

ROK Side :	Mr. Yong Shik Kim	Administrative Vice Minister, Ministry of Foreign Affairs
	Mr. Suk Heun Yun	Director, Political Bureau, Ministry of Foreign Affairs
	Mr. Young Keun Kim	Director, Customs Bureau, Ministry of Finance
	Mr. Kyung Ho Lee	Director, Legal Affairs Bureau, Ministry of Justice
	Brig. Gen. Gie Yung Ree	Ministry of National Defense
	Mr. Choon Hee Kang	Director, Economic Bureau, Ministry of Foreign Affairs
	Mr. Moon Yong Rhie	Chief, Europe & America Section, Ministry of Foreign Affairs
	Mr. Soon Kun Chung	Chief, Treaty Section, Ministry of Foreign Affairs
Press Officer :	Mr. Bum Suk Lee, Consul, Ministry of Foreign Affairs	
Rapporteur :	Mr. Sang Yong Park, Ministry of Foreign Affairs	
US Side :	Mr Marshall Green	Minister and Charge d'Affaires ad interim, American Embassy, Seoul

61-5-1

0139

0140

Brig. Gen. Charles Billingslea	Deputy Chief of Staff, Eighth United States Army
Mr. ~~Donald~~ L. Fanard	Chief, Political Section, American Embassy, Seoul
Mr. Robert W. Tucker	Deputy Chief, Economic Section, American Embassy, Seoul
Col. Cornelius deW. W. Lang	Deputy Chief of Staff, United States Forces, Korea
Mr. Elmer Hulen	Deputy Chief, Political Section, American Embassy, Seoul
Mr. Charles T. Mayfield	Chief, Consular Section, American Embassy, Seoul
Lt. Col. John W. Price	J-5 Division, United States Forces, Korea
Press Officer:	Mr. Thomas R. Kruse, United States Information Service, American Embassy, Seoul
Rapporteur :	Mr. Robert G. Rich, Jr., Political Section, American Embassy, Seoul

3. Opening Addresses:

    Vice Minister Kim for the ROK side:

        No. 1
      (as attached)

    Minister Green for the US side:

        No. 2
      (as attached)

4. Introduction: Vice Minister introduced the Negotiation Team for the ROK side; Minister Green introduced the US Group for the negotiation.

61-5-2

0141

0142

5. Gist of talks:

Vice Minister Kim: First of all, ~~the~~ agenda must be agreed upon. Records of our meetings should be kept. Would you ~~ike to make any~~ comments on these procedural matters?

Minister Green: I suggest that ~~the contents of~~ the Agreed Minutes be confined to ~~substance of talks~~ agreed upon and ~~that~~ the contents to be released to the press should be agreed upon ~~in advance~~. Both sides should be alert on press leaks and in case of leaks clarification must be made ~~from~~ the responsible party ~~to the other, if asked~~. by

Vice Minister Kim: I agree. Do you have any idea on the procedure of the talks?

Minister Green: English will be ~~spoken~~ used during the meetings, with interpreters when necessary. Where and how often will the meetings be held?

Vice Minister Kim: As often as possible at the Ministry—at least once a week. The date of next meeting will be agreed upon at the end of each session.

Minister Green: I agree generally. In my absence Mr. Ranard will head the US side. Items for discussion are many and complex: Entry and exit of military personnel, privileges and immunities, areas and facilities, criminal jurisdiction, and miscellaneous issues. Among these subjects, privileges and immunites will include a number of important matters such as customs duty, tax, contractor, driving license and carrying arms, etc. Before going into the discussion of each item, whole picture of status of forces agreement should be presented and general principles of each issue have to be discussed first.

Vice Minister Kim: ~~Overall picture must be examined. Facts should first be examined to facilitate negotiations.~~ Just for the convenience of our negotiation I would like to suggest that the items be divided into ~~two~~ groups: comparatively easy matters and matters considered to require some negotiation before going into the stage of drafting. For the

- 3 -

0143 61-5-3

- 2 -

0144

first category we can exchange drafts and immediately work on them. What's your opinion on this suggestion?

Minister Green: We didn't expect the ~~discussion~~ ~~talks~~ would proceed this far. I ~~personally agree with~~ you, but ~~we have~~ our view ~~some staffing problem, I will answer your~~ ~~suggestion~~ at the next ~~meeting.~~ will be given

Vice Minister Kim: I suggest the ~~coming~~ Monday, April 24, for the next meeting.

Minister Green: The coming Tuesday, April 25 is preferred.

Vice Minister Kim: No objection.

6.   Press Release

(Minister Green read his draft of the joint statement for press release. No objection was raised by Vice Minister Kim.) The agreed joint statement is as attached(No.3).

Ⅱ급비밀로 재분류

- 4 -

61-5-4

0145

0146

Opening Statement by Vice Foreign Minister Yong Shik Kim at
Negotiations on US-ROK Status of Forces Agreement

April 17, 1961

Minister Green, Friends and Colleagues:

We are here today to start negotiations for an agreement
which will bear a special significance in the annals of the United
States-Republic of Korea cooperation.

We have long been endeavoring to have a status of forces
agreement with the United States Government whereby not only will
the status of the United States forces in this country be regulated
on a more formal basis, but also the cooperation between the two
countries will be facilitated. I am happy that the United States
Government has come to share the view of the Republic of Korea
Government that such an agreement would be both necessary and
mutually beneficial.

The Republic of Korea is fully aware of the fact that the United
States forces are present in Korea at its invitation on a mission to
defend this country from the Communist aggression and that their
presence is vital to the security not only of the Republic of Korea
but of the entire free world. At the same time I know the United
States will look upon the problems we have, sympathetically.

I do not under-estimate the complexity of the problem or
difficulties which we might encounter in the course of our negotiations.
However, I am convinced that there are no problems too difficult to
surmount, when we negotiate in a spirit of our traditional friendship
and understanding. I am hopeful that we will reach an agreement,
mutually satisfactory, within a reasonably short period of time.

I thank you.

0147

For the expeditious conclusion of Status of
Forces Agreement, I would like to suggest a few
principles for our coming negotiation.

1. The United States concluded similar agreements
   with a number of countries, such as Japan,
   NATO and others. I suggest that we should
   follow the pattern of such precedents, particularly those of Japan and NATO.

2. In view of the friendly relations existing
   between our two Governments and the clamor
   of the Korean people for the agreement, I
   wish that the both sides try the best for
   the speedy negotiation. If I suggest, both
   sides should meet at least once or twice a
   week.

3. There are two groups of the subjects to be
   included in the agreement: first, those
   regarded as comparatively easy to reach an
   agreement; second, those regarded as complex
   and requiring some negotiations. And for the
   first group, we could exchange drafts and
   immediately work on them before going into
   the stage of drafting. We commence the
   negotiation for the second group after
   settling the first group. If I roughly
   divide the subjects; Entry and Exit, Military
   Post Office, Driving Permit and License,
   Non-Appropriated Funds Organizations (PX,
   Club, Newspapers, etc.), Military Payment
   Certificate, Uniform and Markings, Carrying
   Arms, and Ban on Political Activities belong
   to the first group; and Facilities and Areas,
   Criminal Jurisdiction, Claims and Civil Jurisdiction, Taxation and Customs Duties, and
   others belong to the second.

0148

UNITED STATES INFORMATION SERVICE

SEOUL KOREA

No. 2

No. 61-218
April 17, 1961

Press Release

STATEMENT BY MINISTER MARSHALL GREEN,
CHARGE d'AFFAIRES, AMERICAN EMBASSY,
AT THE OPENING OF STATUS OF FORCES
NEGOTIATIONS BETWEEN THE GOVERNMENTS
OF THE REPUBLIC OF KOREA AND THE
UNITED STATES, SEOUL, KOREA
APRIL 17, 1961

We are met here today to enter into negotiations covering the status of United States military forces stationed in the Republic of Korea for our mutual defense and for the protection of independence and human freedoms which are most dear to both our nations. At this moment it seems appropriate to recall the sacrifices and great efforts that have marked almost eleven years since the fateful June of 1950 when, in response to the call of the United Nations, American soldiers, sailors and airmen joined their comrades from Korea and other free nations to repulse the forces of international Communism.

It is well to remember that those aggressive forces, though beaten back, still stand ready and perilously near at hand. We cannot foresee the future, nor do we know when or in what manner this menace will be removed from our lives. What we do know is that we stand united and that united we will stand. In our unity lies ultimate victory over the forces of tyranny, paving the way for establishment of a stable, peaceful world order.

The exacting tasks upon which we are embarking today are undertaken in the spirit of that same unity of purpose and resolve upon which our common security rests. The negotiation of any Status of Forces Agreement is necessarily time-consuming because so many complicated issues are involved. Yet we are resolved to move ahead with steadiness and promptness and with all due regard to our common interests.

I also speak today on behalf of General Magruder, Commander of the United States Forces in Korea, whose representatives are part of our negotiating team. He joins me in extending best wishes to all those many dedicated Korean and American officials who will be involved directly or less directly in these negotiations. We know that success will crown our labors.

***   ***   ***

-end-

0149

0150

MINISTRY OF FOREIGN AFFAIRS
PRESS RELEASE

외 무 부 발 표

NO. 3

Joint ROK-US Statement on First Meeting
for Negotiations of ROK-US SOFA

April 17, 1961

At today's meeting Vice Minister of Foreign Affairs Yong Shik
Kim speaking for the Republic of Korea and Minister Marshall Green
for the United States, exchanged addresses welcoming the opening
of negotiations for a Republic of Korea and United States Status of
Forces Agreement. The Korean negotiating group comprised
representatives of the Ministry of Foreign Affairs, Ministry of
National Defense, Ministry of Justice and Ministry of Finance.
The American negotiating group was composed of representatives
of both the American Embassy and of United States Forces in
Korea.

Vice Foreign Minister Kim and Minister Green then introduced
the Korean and American officials who will assist them in the
conduct of negotiations.

The initial discussions dealt with the place at which future
meetings should be held, the frequency of meetings, and various
preliminary administrative matters. It was also agreed that the
two sides would from time to time issue joint press statements
in order to keep the public informed of the progress of negotiations.

Today's meeting successfully laid the foundations for the
efficient and harmonious conduct of substantive negotiations
at future meetings, the next of which has been set, by common
agreement, for April 25.

61-5-8

0151

한미 주둔 군지위 협정 교섭 제 1 차
회의에 관한 한미 공동 발표

오늘 회의에서 대한민국 측을 대표한 외무부 김용식 사무
차관과 미국측을 대표한 마 삽 그린 공사는 한미간 주둔군지위
협정에 관한 교섭의 시작을 환영하는 인사를 교환하였다.
한국측 교섭단은 외무부, 국방부, 법무부 및 재무부의 각부 대표
로서 구성되고 미국측 교섭단은 주한 미대사관과 주한미군 당국의
대표들로서 구성되었다.

외무부 김사무 차관과 그린 공사는 교섭에 있어서 그들을
보좌할 양측의 실무자들을 소개하였다. 회의는 먼저 점차 개최할
회의의 장소와 회수 및 여러가지 예비적 행정사항을 취급하였다.
양측은 교섭의 진전상황을 일반 국민에게 주지시키기 위하여 때때로
공동 발표를 하는데 합의하였다.

오늘 회의에서는 앞으로 효과적이고 우호적으로 실질적 교섭을
진행하기위한 기초를 성공리에 닦아 놓았다.

다음 회의는 4월 25일에 개최하기로 합의하였다.

bi-t-P (E)

0153

0154

한·미국 간의 상호방위조약 제4조에 의한 시설과 구역 및 한국에서의 미국군대의 지위에 관한 협정(SOFA)
전59권. 1966.7.9 서울에서 서명 : 1967.2.9 발효(조약 232호), V.8 체결 교섭, 1960-61   465

First meeting of negotiations on ROK-US Status of Forces Agreement held at the Foreign Ministry on April 17, 1961.

For the Korean side: from left to right they are;

Mr. Moon Yong Rhie, Chief, Europe & America Section, wholly hiden, Mr. Kyung Ho Lee, Director, Legal Affairs Bureau, Ministry of Justice, partially hiden, Mr. Suk Heun Yun, Director, Political Bureau, Vice Minister Yong Shik Kim, standing, Brig. General Gis Hyung Ree, Mr. Young Keun Kim, Director, Customs Bureau, Ministry of Finance, Mr. Choon Hee Kang, Director, Economic Bureau, Mr. Soon Kun Chung, Chief, Treaty Sec on of the F eign Ministry.

0156

MINISTRY OF FOREIGN AFFAIRS
PRESS RELEASE

외 무 부 발 표

한미 주둔군 지위협정 교섭
제 2 차 회의

4월 25일

오늘 회의에서 [감용주] 사무 차관을 수반으로 한 한국측 대표단과 "그린" 공사을 수반으로 한 미국측 대표단은 미국과 한국 간의 주둔군 지위협정에 포함될 광범위한 문제에 관하여 토의하였다。 양측은 앞으로 교섭을 촉진하는데 가장 좋은 회의 진행 방법에 관하여 합의하였고 또한 특별히 실무자들에 의한 고력가 요망되는 항목에 대하여 의견을 교환하였다。

다음 회의는 5월 2일 하오 3시에 개최될것이다。

일반문서로 재분류

0157

MINUTES OF
STATUS OF FORCES NEGOTIATIONS BETWEEN THE GOVERNMENTS
OF THE REPUBLIC OF KOREA AND THE UNITED STATES

SECOND PLENARY SESSION

(April 25, 1961)

1. Time and Place: From 3:00 to 3:55 p.m. on April 25, 1961
   at the Ministry of Foreign Affairs

2. Conferees:

ROK Side:

Mr. Yong Shik Kim	Administrative Vice Minister, Ministry of Foreign Affairs
Mr. Suk Heun Yun	Director, Political Bureau, Ministry of Foreign Affairs
~~Mr. Young Keun Kim~~	~~Director, Customs Bureau, Ministry of Finance~~
Mr. Kyung Ho Lee	Director, Legal Affairs Bureau, Ministry of Justice
Brig. Gen. Gie Yung Ree	Ministry of National Defense
Mr. Soon Kun Chung	Chief, Treaty Section, Ministry of Foreign Affairs
Mr. Nam Ki Lee	Treaty Section, Ministry of Foreign Affairs
Press Officer:	Mr. Bum Suk Lee, Consul, Ministry of Foreign Affairs
Rapporteur :	Mr. Sang Yong Park, Ministry of Foreign Affairs

US Side:

Mr. Marshall Green	Minister and Charge d'Affaires ad interim, American Embassy, Seoul
Brig. Gen. Charles Billingslea	Deputy Chief of Staff, Eighth United States Army

0158

Mr. Donald L. Ranard	Chief, Political Section, American Embassy, Seoul
Mr. Robert W. Tucker	Deputy Chief, Economic Section, American Embassy, Seoul
Col. Cornelius deW. W. Lang	Deputy Chief of Staff, United States Forces, Korea
Mr. Elmer Hulen	Deputy Chief, Political Section, American Embassy, Seoul
Mr. Charles T. May-field	Chief, Consular Section, American Embassy, Seoul
Lt. Col. John W. Price	J-5 Division, United States Forces, Korea
Press Officer:	Mr. Thomas R. Kruse, United States Information Service, American Embassy, Seoul
Rapporteur:	Mr. Robert G. Rich, Jr., Political Section, American Embassy, Seoul

3. Gist of Talks

Vice Minister Kim: At the last meeting we discussed about how to proceed the negotiations and our side suggested as a matter of procedure to divide items into two categories— one that needs negotiations in some length and the other that can be discussed by exchanging drafts. Have you thought about it?

Minister Green: Yes, we have thought about it in some length. We feel that Criminal Jurisdiction is rather a separate item—a distinctive issue which may involve high level talks. Other items may be broken down into four main components: Facilities and Areas, Entry and Exit, Privileges and Immunites, and the Miscellaneous— smaller items. We would hope to have drafts for the first four items.

Facilities and Areas involves, among other things, definitions of military personnel, dependents, civilian components and contractors; the way they are operated; access to, and restoration of, Facilities and Areas.

0159

As for Entry and Exit I'd like to ask Mr. Mayfield to present our view.

Mr. Mayfield:
I assume that Entry and Exit is the most simple section of the talks. This item involves, first of all, the definition of who is going to be covered. In our mind, persons to be covered are three categories: armed forces servicemen, civilian components and contractors, and their dependents. Since we foresee no problems we expect that issues could be settled along the same line as we have now. About 2,000 civilians which number we will cover may be an additional burden, but I see no real problem there. I would be glad to discuss on this matter with anyone your side would appoint. One thing I want to point out is that Exit Permit is a special thing to be considered in Korea.

Minister Green:
As for Privileges and Immunities Mr. Tucker will present our view.

Mr. Tucker:
The main areas of discussion for this item are: the question of vehicles which involves such questions as driver lisence and car markings, etc.; customs procedure in which mutual realization of customs matters are important and in which area of cooperation is broad; local procurement which relates to such questions as the facilities the ROK government provides for the central supply system of the US armed forces, the functions of Korean firms engaged in the procurement services, tax exemption, contractors for and under the US armed forces, inappropriated funds organizations such as post exchanges, clubs, etc.; and finally the question of carrying fire arms which we take for granted.

In addition to these, there are other important matters: use of PX by commercial representatives, control of Military Payment Certificate System, operation of the US Reserve System as inherent privileges and the right to train for that purpose American civilians in Korea.

I might add more items for discussion later on.

Minister Green:
In the Miscellaneous may be included such items as Labor Relations (requirement), Foreign Exchange Control, Ratification, Duration of the Agreement, and Amendment.

0160

Vice Minister Kim:	As I suggested before, Criminal Jurisdiction and Areas and Facilities may be included in the first category with the rest of items be in the second category. As regards the first category I see no difficult problems because there are the precedents. As regards the first category, however, we need some procedure to be agreed upon for speeding negotiations.
Minister Green:	We differ on that suggestion. Question of Facilities and Areas may be an easy item, but does include basic definitions. I am willing to discuss about this further, but I recommend separation of the two items, that is, to isolate Facilities and Areas from Criminal Jurisdiction.
Vice Minister Kim:	We suggested Criminal Jurisdiction and Facilities and Areas for the special category for the sake of convenience—not for the nature of the problems itself. It seems to me that certain problem such as Criminal Jurisdiction needs an intensive study, but this need not be separated in the Agreement. What is your opinion?
Minister Green:	As to what is involved in our discussion, let's hear what General Billinslea has to say.
General Billingslea:	What is important in our negotiations is to have a philosophy without which none of the agreement is rightly understood. Hence, we should look upon an agreement as a living document—as a continuing process. Therefore, the essence of the negotiations is that we should look upon this continuing process thoughtfully and carefully—looking at the whole problem, not the detailed pieces of it.
Minister Green:	The point is that an agreement such as we pursue does not break down evenly or exactly. What we should do is to pin down where the problem is. Pinning down of definitions is extremely important, because without which we cannot tackle the problems.
Vice Minister Kim:	Shall we agree for the sake of convenience that we put Criminal Jurisdiction into the first category and all other items except Facilities and Areas into the second category? Let's study at the next meeting whether to include or separate Facilities and Areas into or from Criminal Jurisdiction.

0161

-5-

Minister Green:	Could I ask you that you would be able to break down items for Subcommittees? Is this your idea?
Vice Minister Kim:	The way to proceed our negotiations is that we talk about issues before exchanging drafts. I see no difficulties in this method. But as regards Criminal Jurisdiction we should have an intensive study before we exchange drafts. This is our idea.
General Ree:	Korean people have long since desired for the conclusion of this Agreement and they now want our negotiations to proceed in a prompt manner. I think, therefore, separation of items and discussion of easy items first may bring about such impression that the US side is dragging—postponing negotiations.
Minister Green:	We do want to go ahead as rapidly as possible. We do (as stated in our opening address) not want to go into any beaurocratic maze. Please understand, general, that our suggestion is not in the least related with beaurocratic handling. Please do not misunderstand our position.
Vice Minister Kim:	I want to make it clear that we suggested to classify Criminal Jurisdiction into the first group and the rest of the items except the question of Facilities and Areas into the second group, for the sake of convenience. I suggested before that we give consideration to classification of Facilities and Areas at the next meeting.

As for the Subcommittees Mr. Yun, Director of Political Bureau of this Ministry will be discussing on the question of Criminal Jurisdiction, and Mr. Chung will take care of all other items.

Plenary meetings will be held as often as possible, and I am prepared to personally talk with you, Minister Green, any time. |
Minister Green:	We are not prepared to break down our staff into Subcommittees. Minister, would you want me to meet you right after this meeting or some other time?
Vice Minister Kim:	After this meeting, if you wish.
Minister Green:	Is this all you want to bring up today? What's about the press release?

0162

Vice Minister Kim:	Contents of the press release should be to the effect that at today's meeting there was no discussion in substance.
Minister Green:	I'll read aloud our draft ~ the joint press release for today's meeting. (The Joint press release, as attached, was adopted.)
Vice Minister Kim:	In the case of the Status of Forces Agreement with Japan, how long did it take to get down to the business?
Lt. Col. Price:	It took eight months before they actually got to working.
Colonel Lang:	In the case of China, negotiations started back in 1952 and not yet completed.
Vice Minister Kim:	How about the NATO countries?
Colonel Lang:	Average eight months.
Vice Minister Kim:	Well, then, let's have ours in eight weeks. When will we have the next meeting?
Minister Green:	For PR purpose let's say we'll meet at the same time next week.
Vice Minister Kim:	Next Tuesday---that is agreed upon. Now, shall we adjourn?

(The meeting adjourned.)

Ⅲ급비밀로 재분류

0163

<u>DRAFT JOINT PRESS RELEASE</u>

<u>Status of Forces Agreement Negotiations</u>

At today's meeting the Republic of Korea negotiating group

headed by Vice Minister of Foreign Affairs Yong Shik Kim and

the United States negotiating group headed by Minister Marshall

Green discussed the broad range of subjects to be included in

a full status of forces agreement between the Republic of Korea

and the United States.

In exchanging views, the two sides agreed to the procedures

best suited for expeditiously carrying out the negotiations and

gave consideration to those issues which may require special

attention by working groups.

(The next meeting will be held at the same time next week)

0164

31. 二

MINUTES OF

STATUS OF FORCES NEGOTIATIONS BETWEEN THE GOVERNMENTS
OF THE REPUBLIC OF KOREA AND THE UNITED STATES

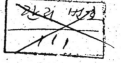

SECOND PLENARY SESSION

(April 25, 1961)

1. Time and Place: From 3:00 to 5:5t p.m. on April 25, 1961
   at the Ministry of Foreign Affairs

2. Conferees:

ROK Side:

Mr. Yong Shik Kim	Administrative Vice Minister, Ministry of Foreign Affairs	
Mr. Suk Heun Yun	Director, Political Bureau, Ministry of Foreign Affairs	
~~Mr. Young Keun Kim~~	~~Director, Customs Bureau, Ministry of Finance~~	
Mr. Kyung Ho Lee	Director, Legal Affairs Bureau, Ministry of Justice	
Brig. Gen. Gie Yung Ree	Ministry of National Defense	
Mr. Soon Kun Chung	Chief, Treaty Section, Ministry of Foreign Affairs	
Mr. Nam Ki Lee	Treaty Section, Ministry of Foreign Affairs	
Press Officer:	Mr. Bum Suk Lee, Consul, Ministry of Foreign Affairs	
Rapporteur :	Mr. Sang Yong Park, Ministry of Foreign Affairs	

US Side:

Mr. Marshall Green	Minister and Charge d'Affaires ad interim, American Embassy, Seoul
Brig. Gen. Charles Billingslea	Deputy Chief of Staff, Eighth United States Army

0165

Mr. Donald L. Ranard   Chief, Political Section,
American Embassy, Seoul

Mr. Robert W. Tucker   Deputy Chief, Economic Section,
American Embassy, Seoul

Col. Cornelius deW.
W. Lang   Deputy Chief of Staff, United
States Forces, Korea

Mr. Elmer Hulen   Deputy Chief, Political Section,
American Embassy, Seoul

Mr. Charles T. May-
field   Chief, Consular Section,
American Embassy, Seoul

Lt. Col. John W. Price   J-5 Division, United States
Forces, Korea

Press Officer: Mr. Thomas R. Kruse, United
States Information Service,
American Embassy, Seoul

Rapporteur: Mr. Robert G. Rich, Jr.,
Political Section, American
Embassy, Seoul

3. **Gist of Talks**

Vice Minister Kim: At the last meeting we discussed about how to proceed the negotiations and our side suggested as a matter of procedure to divide items into two categories— one that needs negotiations in some length and the other that can be discussed by exchanging drafts. Have you thought about it?

Minister Green: Yes, we have thought about it ~~in some length~~. We feel that Criminal Jurisdiction is rather a separate item—a distinctive issue which may involve high level talks. Other items may be broken down into four main components: Facilities and Areas, Entry and Exit, Privileges and Immunites, and the Miscellaneous— smaller items. We would hope to have drafts for the first four items.

Facilities and Areas involves, among other things, definitions of military personnel, dependents, civilian components and contractors; the way they are operated; access to, and restoration of, Facilities and Areas.

0166

As for Entry and Exit I'd like to ask Mr. Mayfield ~~to present our view.~~

Mr. Mayfield: ~~I assume that~~ Entry and Exit is the most simple ~~section of the talks.~~ This item involves, first of all, the definition of who's going to be covered. In our view, persons to be covered are ~~three~~ categories: armed forces servicemen, civilian components, ~~and~~ contractors, and their dependents. ~~Since we foresee no problems we~~ expect that issues could be settled along the same line as we have now. ~~About 8,000 civilians which number we will cover may be an additional burden, but I see no real problem there.~~ I would be glad to discuss on this matter with anyone your side would appoint. One thing I want to point out is that Exit Permit is a special thing to be considered in Korea.

Minister Green: As for Privileges and Immunities Mr. Tucker will present Our View.

Mr. Tucker: The main areas of discussion for this item are: the question of vehicles which involve such questions as driver's lisence and car markings, etc.; customs procedure in which mutual realization of customs matters are important and in which area of cooperation is broad; local procurement which relates to such questions as the facilities the ROK government provides for the central supply system for the US armed forces, the functions of Korean firms engaged in the procurement services, tax exemption, contractors for and under the US armed forces, inappropriated funds organizations such as post exchanges, clubs, etc.; and finally the question of carrying fire arms which we take for granted.

In addition to these, there are other important matters: use of PX by commercial representatives, control of Military Payment Certificate ~~System~~, operation of the US Reserve System as inherent privileges and the right to train for that purpose American civilians in Korea.

I might add more items for discussion later on.

Minister Green: In the Miscellaneous may be included such items as Labor ~~Relations~~ requirements, Foreign Exchange Control, Ratification, Duration of the Agreement, and Amendment.

0167

Vice Minister Kim: As I suggested before, Criminal Jurisdiction and
                      Areas and Facilities may be included in the first
                      category with the rest of items be in the second
                      category. As regards the second category I see no
                      difficult problem because there are the precedents.
                      As regards the first category, however, we need
                      some procedure to be agreed upon for speeding
                      negotiations.

Minister Green: We differ on that suggestion. Question of Facilities
                      and Areas may be an easy item, but does include
                      basic definitions. I am willing to discuss about
                      this further, but I recommend separation of the
                      two items, that is, to isolate Facilities and Areas
                      from Criminal Jurisdiction.

Vice Minister Kim: We suggested Criminal Jurisdiction and Facilities
                      and Areas for the special category for the sake of
                      convenience--not for the nature of the problems.
                      itself. It seems to me that certain problem such
                      as Criminal Jurisdiction needs an intensive study,
                      but this need not be separated in the Agreement.
                      What is your opinion?

Minister Green: As to what is involved in our discussion, let's
                      hear what General Billinslea has to say.

General Billingslea: What is important in our negotiations is to have
                      a philosophy without which none of the agreement
                      is rightly understood. Hence, we should look upon
                      an agreement as a living document--as a continuing
                      process. Therefore, the essence of the negotiations
                      is that we should look upon this continuing
                      process thoughtfully and carefully--looking at the
                      whole problem, not the detailed pieces of it.

Minister Green: The point is that an agreement such as we pursue
                      does not break down evenly or exactly. What we
                      should do is to pin down where the problem is.
                      Pinning down of definitions is extremely important,
                      because without which we cannot tackle the problems.

Vice Minister Kim: Shall we agree for the sake of convenience that we
                      put Criminal Jurisdiction into the first category
                      and all other items except Facilities and Areas
                      into the second category? Let's study at the next
                      meeting whether to include or separate Facilities
                      and Areas into or from Criminal Jurisdiction.
                              in the first category.

0168

Minister Green:	Could I ask you that you would be able to break down items for Subcommittees? Is this your idea?
Vice Minister Kim:	The way to proceed our negotiations is that we talk about issues before exchanging drafts. I see no difficulties in this method. But as regards Criminal Jurisdiction we should have an intensive study before we exchange drafts. This is our idea.
General Ree:	Korean people have long since desired for the conclusion of this Agreement and they now want our negotiations to proceed in a prompt manner. I think, therefore, separation of items and discussion of easy items first may bring about such impression that the US side is dragging--postponing negotiations.
Minister Green:	We do want to go ahead as rapidly as possible. We do as stated in our opening address not want to go into any beaurocratic maze. Please understand, General, that our suggestion is not in the least related with beaurocratic handling. Please do not misunderstand our position.
Vice Minister Kim:	I want to make it clear that we suggested to classify Criminal Jurisdiction into the first group and the rest of the items except the question of Facilities and Areas into the second group, for the sake of convenience. I suggested before that we give consideration to classification of Facilities and Areas at the next meeting.
	As for the Subcommittees Mr. Yun, Director of Political Bureau of this Ministry will be discussing on the question of Criminal Jurisdiction, and Mr. Chung will take care of all other items.
	Plenary meetings will be held as often as possible, and I am prepared to personally talk with you, Minister Green, any time.
Minister Green:	We are not prepared to break down our staff into Subcommittees. Minister, would you want me to meet you right after this meeting or some other time?
Vice Minister Kim:	After this meeting, if you wish.
Minister Green:	Is this all you want to bring up today? What's about the press release?

0169

–6–

Why shouldn't we give an optimistic view to the press?

Vice Minister Kim: ~~Contents of the press release should be to the effect that at today's meeting there was no discussion in substance.~~

Minister Green: I'll read aloud our draft of the joint press release for today's meeting.
(The joint press release, as attached, was adopted.)

Vice Minister Kim: In the case of the Status of Forces Agreement with Japan, how long did it take to ~~get down to the business?~~ *conclude the negotiating?*

Lt. Col. Price: It took eight months before they actually got to working.

Colonel Lang: In the case of China, negotiations started back in 1952 and not yet completed.

Vice Minister Kim: How about the NATO countries?

Colonel Lang: Average eight months.

Vice Minister Kim: Well, then, let's have ours in eight weeks.

When will we have the next meeting?

Minister Green: For PR purpose let's say we'll meet at the same time next week.

Vice Minister Kim: Next Tuesday—that is agreed upon. Now, shall we adjourn?

(The meeting adjourned)

0170

DRAFT JOINT PRESS RELEASE

Status of Forces Agreement Negotiations

At today's meeting the Republic of Korea negotiating group

headed by Vice Minister of Foreign Affairs Yong Shik Kim and

the United States negotiating group headed by Minister Marshall

Green discussed the broad range of subjects to be included in

a full status of forces agreement between the Republic of Korea

and the United States.

In exchanging views, the two sides agreed to the procedures

best suited for expeditiously carrying out the negotiations and

gave consideration to those issues which may require special

attention by working groups.

(The next meeting will be held at the same time next week)

일반운서로 재분류

일반문서로 재분류
(협정 체결시)

0171

주한 미국 군대 지위 협정 체결 문제 (협정 협정)

61. 5.

1. 개 요   검토필(196? 12. 7.)

기
문건 번호

미국 군대가 한국에 주둔한지 이미 10 년이 넘는 오늘까지 이들의
지위에 관한 협정을 체결하지 못하고 있는데 군제적 협정 관념에 입각한
이러한 합리적인 협정의 결여는 정부가 이 이상 묵과할 수 없는 팽배한
국민 여론을 조성하고 있다. 정부는 미균이 사용하고 있는 토지와
시설에 대한 보상 책임을 감당할 수 없으며, 또한 구 시대적인 주둔군의
그 구성원에 대한 배타적 재판 관할권을 계속해서 인정할 수 없다.
출입국 관리 및 관세 문제도 규제하여 밀수입등을 억제하여야 한다.

검토필(1965. 12. 30.)

2. 협정이 시급히 체결되어야 할 근거   검토필(1965 6. 30.)

(1) 외국 군대의 법적 지위는 전시 점령과 같은 특수한 경우를
제외하고는 조약에 의하여 규제함이 국제법상 확립된 원칙임.

(2) 미균이 사용하고 있는 토지 및 시설에 대한 보상은 국가의
재정 형편상 정부가 감당하기는 불가능한 것임.

(3) "대전 협정"에 의하여 정부가 미균 당국에 인정한 그
구성원에 대한 배타적 재판 관할권은 우리 나라 주권의 중대한 제약일
뿐이며, 한국민에 대한 가해 사건을 위오하여 한국민의 대미 감정이
악화할 우려가 있음.

(4) 출입국 및 관세 문제를 규제하여 미균인을 통한 밀수입을
억제하여야 함.

(5) "한국이 전시하에 있다"라는 미국측의 구실은 합미 경제
협정의 체결로써 더 인정할 수 없는 것임.

(6) 잠면 정권과는 협정 교섭에 응한 미국측이 혁명 정부에
대하여 회피적 태도를 취한다면 한국민은 미국의 일관성없는 책략적
태도에 불만을 가질 것임.

(7) 미국측이 계속해서 협정 체결을 지연시킨다면 감대국이
약소국을 부당하게 대우하며 심지어 한국을 강점하고 있다는 인상을
주어 북한 괴뢰의 선전 자료가 될 것임.

0172

마.목90-12(2)

0173

3. 협정 체결에 관한 현재까지의 교섭 경위

(1) 1953 년 8 월 7 일 이승만—"덜레스" 공동 성명에서 협정 체결 교섭을 개시할 것을 약속함.

(2) 1953 년 12 월 정부는 유.엔군의 관세 업무 협정 체결을 제의하였으나 미국측은 이를 거부함.

(3) 1955 년 4 월, 1957 년 1 월, 6 월 및 9 월 정부는 협정 체결을 제의하고 동 협정안을 제시.

(4) 1957 년 10 월 미국측은 협정 체결 문제를 부분적으로 해결할 것을 제의하였으며, 정부는 이에 응함.

(5) 1958 년 9 월 미국측은 재판 관할권을 제외할 것을 조건으로 기타 문제의 해결에 응할 것을 희망. 정부는 이를 수락하지 않음.

(6) 1959 년 정부는 토지 시설에 관한 개별 협정 체결을 제의하고 그후 2 차에 걸쳐 수락을 촉구함.

(7) 1960 년 3 월 미국측은 형사 관할권과 토지 시설에 관한 보상 문제를 현상대로 할 조건으로 교섭에 응할 뜻을 회보하였으며, 정부는 이를 수락하지 않음.

(8) 1961 년 4 월 10 일 장 면—"매카나기" 공동 성명으로 교섭 개시 합의함.

(9) 1961 년 4 월 17 일 제 1 차 한미 회의.

(10) 1961 년 4 월 25 일 제 2 차 한미 회의에서 광범위한 문제를 토의함.

(11) 1961 년 4 월 26 일 정일형—"러스크" 공동 성명으로 협정 체결을 위한 교섭에 노력할 것에 합의.

(12) 제 3 차 회의는 미국측의 요청으로 현재까지 지연됨.

0174

한미간의 미국군대 지위협정 체결 문제

1. 협정체결에 관한 지금 까지의 과섭 경위

   (1) 1953 년 8 월 7 일 이승만—덜레스 공동성명에서 협정 체결 교섭을
       개시할 것을 약속 함.

   (2) 1953 년 12 월 정부는 유엔군의 관세업무협정 체결을 제의하였으나
       미국측은 이를 거부 함.

   (3) 1955 년 4 월 정부는 협정 체결을 제의하고 유엔군의 지위에 관한
       우리측의 협정초안을 제시함.

   (4) 1957 년 10 월 미국측은 협정체결문제를 부분적으로 해결할 것을
       제의하여 왔으므로 정부는 이에 응함.

   (5) 1957 년 11 월 정부는 본 협정을 5 개부분으로 나누어 개별적으로
       해결할 것을 제의하였음.

   (6) 1958 년 9 월 미국측은 재판관할권문제를 제외할 것을 조건으로
       기타 문제 해결에 응할 것을 희망하여 왔음. 정부는 이를 수락하지 않음.

   (7) 1959 년 정부는 토지, 시설에 관한 개별협정 체결을 제의하고 그 후
       2 차에 걸쳐 교섭개시를 촉구 함.

   (8) 1960 년 3 월 미국측은 재판관할권과 토지,시설에 관한 문제를 현상대로
       둘것을 조건으로 교섭에 응할 뜻을 희보하여 왔으나, 정부는 이를 거부함.

   (9) 1961 년 4 월 10 일 한미 양국정부 공동성명(장면—매카나기)에서
       협정 체결 교섭 개시에 합의함.

   (10) 1961 년 4 월 17 일 협정체결을 위한 제 1 차 한미 회의 개최

   (11)   "   4 월 25 일 제 2 차 회의에서 대체적인 토의가 있었음.

   (12) 1961 년 4 월 26 일 정일형—러스크 공동성명에서 협정체결을 위한
        교섭에 노력할 것을 합의 함.

   (13) 1961 년 5 월 2 일 개최예정이던 제 3 차 회의는 미국측 요청으로
        무기연기 됨에 현재에 이르렀음.

2. 협정체결에 관한 조약과의 준비상황

   (1) 협정체결을 위한 한미간의 교섭과 병행하여 우리측의 제 1 차 초안을

0176

작성하고 이에 대한 관계부처의 의견을 종합하였음.

(2) 앞으로의 교섭재개에 대비하여 조약과에서는 전기한 초안 등을 중심으로 오는 2 월 28 일 까지 전반적인 문제에 걸쳐 재검토를 가하고 앞으로 재개될 교섭에 대비하여 필요한 관계자료를 총정리할 예정 임.

일반문서로 재분류 (협정체결시)

0177

주한 미국 군대 지위 협정 체결 문제 (행정 협정)

1. 개 요

검토필(1962.12.)

미국 군대가 한국에 주둔한지 10 년이 넘는 오늘 까지 주둔군 지위에

대한 협정을 체결하지 못하고 있는 데 정부는 이여

합의은 이 이상 간과할 수 없으며 이는 또한 미국에 대한 한국 국민의

신뢰도를 저해할 우려가 많은 뿐만 아니라 현재 미군이 서울 하고 있는

호지 및 시설에 대하여 빈곤한 현재의 경제 상태하에서 우리 정부가

그 책임을 부담하는 것은 입에 가운 일이며 아니 할 수 없다. 한미 행정

협정 체결이 없음으로 바미아마 야기되는 문제는 이에 한정되는 것이

아니 다 주둔군에 대한 형사 관할권의 문제는 위시하여 주권국의 권위

및 관세에 대한 규 제문 등으로 만 문제가 많다. 언이나, 본 주둔군 지위

협정 체결은 검수 미군의 한국에 있어서의 모든 활동을 제안하려는 것은

아니며 한국 군민의 미국에 대한 신뢰섬과 유대를 강화하고저 하는데에

있는 것임나

검토필(196 6.30)

2. 협정이 시급이 체결되어야 할 근거

(1) 국제법상 주권 국가에 외국 군대가 주둔하기 위하여서는

군대 주둔에 관한 조약상의 근거를 필요로 할 뿐만 아니라 전시 점령과

같은 특수한 경우를 제외하고는 외국 군대의 주둔국에서의 지위 및 주둔에 수반하는 여러가지 법적 절차를 규율하는 명문 규정을 구비하는 것이 국제법상 관례임 동시에 주둔국의 주권과 독립성을 존중하는 의미에서도 이에 관한 협정이 마땅히 구비되여야 하는 것임니다.

(2) 현지의 정부의 재정 사정으로서는 미군이 사용하고 있는 막대한 지역의 토지 및 시설에 대한 우리 정부의 보상 책임 부담이 불가능한 입편에 있으므로 이에 대한 미국측의 적절한 표시가 시급히 요청되는 바임니다.

(3) 현재 주둔군의 형사 관할권에 관한 협정이 없으며 1950 년 한국 동란이 발발한 직후 당시의 시급한 특수 사정에 의거하여 체결된 소위 대전 협정은 미국 군대의 구성원에 대한 배타적 관할권은 미국군 에게 만 인정하였으므로 한국인에 대한 미국군의 가해행위에 대하여 우리 관할권이 없으므로 한국국민과 주둔군과의 마찰을 미연에 방지하고 이에 대한 배려책이 없어 한국 국민의 미국에 대한 우호 감정에 영향을 미침 우려가 답원.

(4) 미국 군대 구성원에 대한 출입국 및 관세등을 규제하는 적절한 협정이 없으므로 의외 상품의 불법 반입의 우려가 있어 미약한 우리 경제에 저해가 있어서는 안된 것임니다.

0179

(5) 미국 정부는 지금 그가지 한국이 전시하에 있다 는 것을
프면상의 이유로 한미군대 지위 협정 체결은 거부 또는 지연시켜
왔으나 금년 2 월에 체결된 한미 경제 협정으로 한국이 전시에서
평시로 복귀하였음을 인정하였으므로 이 이상 협정 체결 교섭은 더
지연시킬 이의 명분이 없는 것입니다.

(6) 금년 4 월의 장 면— "메카나기" 공동 성명에서 미국 정부는
장면 정권과 협정의 체결을 위한 교섭 개시에 정식으로 합의하였고
실제로 2 차에 검처 교섭한바 있는 데 만약 미국이 혁신 정부와
협정 체결 교섭에 응하지 않는다면 위에서 말한 장면— "메카나기"
공동 성명이 그 당시 국민 여론의 지환을 받고 있던 장면 정권을
지원함으로써 약화될 국민 여론을 무시키며는 미국 정부의 임시적임
방면에 지나게 많았다는 인상을 국민에게 줌으로써 미국에 대한 한국
국민의 신의토를 저해할 우려가 있음.

(7) 이미 아세아 아프리카의 옛 식민지 국가들이 독립하였고
또한 자유 평등의 국제 조류가 전세계에 풍미하고 있는 현재 만약
미국이 군대 지위 협정을 이 이상 지연시킬 경우에는 강대국이 약소국
을 정당하고 평등하게 대우하고 있지 않다는 인상을 세계에 줄뿐만
아니라 미국이 한국을 강점하고 있다는 북한 괴뢰의 선전 자료의

0180

하나가 될 우려가 있음.

3. 협정 체결에 관한 지금까지의 교섭 경위

(1) 1953년 8월 7일 한미 상호 방위 조약 가조인 시 더 승 만—

덜레스 공동 성명에서 한미 양국 정부는 상호 방위 밖으 직시 한미간의

군대 지위 협정 체결을 교섭하기로 약속하였다.

(2) 1954년 12월 정부는 그 내용이 행정 협정의 일부가 될 주한

유엔 군의 군세 인부에 관한 협정 체결을 제의하였으나 미국측은 이를

거부하였다.

(3) 1955년 4월 정부는 주한 유엔군의 지위를 포괄적으로 규정

하는 군대 지위 협정의 체결을 제의하고 동시에 동 협정안을 제시하였으며

그후 1957년 1월, 6월 및 9월에 다시 교섭 개시를 촉구하였다.

(4) 1957년 10월 미국측은 군대 지위 협정 체결 문제를 부분적

으로 합의 가능한 한도 내에서 개별적으로 해결해 나갈 것을 제의하여

왔으므로 정부는 이에 응하여 동 년 11월 미국측에 대하여 이 문제를

1) 과세 및 관세 면부, 2) 청구권 청산, 3) 토지 및 시설,

4) 출입국, 5) 형사 관할권 등으로 분할하여 각 당목별로 개별

협정을 체결할 것을 제의하였던 바, 1958년 9월 미국측은 한국 정부가

재판 관할권에 관한 면접을 제의하지 않는 다는 조건하에 기타의 행정적인

한·미국 간의 상호방위조약 제4조에 의한 시설과 구역 및 한국에서의 미국군대의 지위에 관한 협정(SOFA) 전59권. 1966.7.9 서울에서 서명 : 1967.2.9 발효(조약 232호), V.8 체결 교섭, 1960-61

문제 미전에 응하겠다고 매답하여 왔으며 정부는 이를 수락하지 아니하였다.

(5) 1959 년 정부는 군대 지위 협정 문제를 기번적으로 해결할 방침아에 그 첫 단계로서 주한 미군이 사용하는 요지 및 시설에 관한 협정 체결을 제의하고 동 년 10 월과 1960 년 3 월 2 차에 걸쳐 미국측에 수락을 요구하였음.

(6) 1960 년 3 월 미국측은 1) 형사 재판 관할권에 관한 협상을 유지하고, 2) 요지 및 시설에 대한 보상은 한국 정부가 그 책임을 진다는 2 가지 조건아에 전기 협정 체결 교섭에 응할 것이라고 회답하여 왔고 정부는 이를 수락할수 없어 그 후 교섭은 검토 상태에 빠졌다.(별첨 ⑦ 참조)

(7) 1961 년 2 월 28 일 한미간의 새로운 경제 협정이 체결됨에 따라 정부는 다시 협정 체결을 위한 적극적인 준비를 추진하여 오던 중 동년 4 월 10 일자 장 면—ㅣㅣ메카나기ㅣㅣ 공동 성명에서 형사 재판 관할권에 관한 문제를 포함한 협정 체결을 위한 한미 간의 교섭 개시에 합의하였음.

(8) 1961 년 4 월 17 일 협정 체결을 위한 제 1 차 한미 회의가 외무부에서 개최되었는 바 동 회의에서는 양 대표의 인사와 양측 대표단 의 소개가 있은 다음 실질적인 문제의 논의없이 4 월 26 일에 제 2 차

0182

회의를 갖기로 하고 산회하였다.

(9) 1966년 4월 25일에 개최된 제 2 차 회의에서는 동 협정에

포함된 골자에 관 문제에 관한 토의가 있었으며 실질적인 문제에 관한

구체적인 토의는 6월 2일에 개최될 제 3 차 회의에서 토의하기로

합의하였으나 제 3 차 회의는 미국측의 요청으로 지금까지 지연되고

있음.

(10) 1966년 4월 26일 정 외무부장관 및 "딘·러스크" 미국무

장관은 공동성명을 발표하고 "한국과 미국은 교섭을 통하여 행정협정

을 적당한 시기에 체결하도록 모든 노력을 다할것에 합의를 보았다"고

고한바있다.

한·미국 간의 상호방위조약 제4조에 의한 시설과 구역 및 한국에서의 미국군대의 지위에 관한 협정(SOFA)
전59권. 1966.7.9 서울에서 서명 : 1967.2.9 발효(조약 232호), V.8 체결 교섭, 1960-61

건 명: 한미행정 협정 체결 교섭에 관한 건

　　　최 정무국장은 한미 행정 협정의 체결을 위한 교섭 재개를
위하여, 작 7월 5일 오후 5시 미국 대사관 메나아드 참사관을 외무부로
초치하고, 약 30분간 다음과 같은 담화를 교환하였음.

　　　　　　　　　　　― 검토필 (196 . . .)

　　　최 국장은 동 교섭을 위하여 조속한 시일 내에 회담을
가질 것을 촉구하는 한편, 교섭 진행 방법 (1. 먼저 초안
교환, 2. 초안에 대한 상호 검토, 3. 의견 차이점에 대해서만 교섭함)에
대하여 설명하였음. 이에 대하여 동참사관은 비공식으로는 동의하였음

　　　메나아드 참사관은 지난 6월 17일 본국 정부로 부터 미국이
동 교섭에 응할 의사가 있음을 훈령하여왔고, 이것에 관하여는 7월 3일
그린 공사가 외무 차관에 전달한 바 있다고 말 하였음. 또한 그는 전기
훈령이 교섭을 재개하라는 훈령이 아니므로, 다시 본국 정부에 교섭
재개를 위한 훈령을 요구할 것이다고 말 하였음 검토필 (1966. 6. 30.)

　　　　　　　　　　　　　　　　이 　상

0184

외교문서 비밀해제: 주한미군지위협정(SOFA) 2
주한미군지위협정(SOFA) 서명 및 발효 2

초판인쇄 2024년 03월 15일
초판발행 2024년 03월 15일

지은이 한국학술정보(주)
펴낸이 채종준
펴낸곳 한국학술정보(주)
주 소 경기도 파주시 회동길 230(문발동)
전 화 031-908-3181(대표)
팩 스 031-908-3189
홈페이지 http://ebook.kstudy.com
E-mail 출판사업부 publish@kstudy.com
등 록 제일산-115호(2000. 6. 19)

ISBN 979-11-7217-013-4 94340
      979-11-7217-011-0 94340 (set)

이 책은 한국학술정보(주)와 저작자의 지적 재산으로서 무단 전재와 복제를 금합니다.
책에 대한 더 나은 생각, 끊임없는 고민, 독자를 생각하는 마음으로 보다 좋은 책을 만들어갑니다.